306(evo)

THE EVOLUTION OF CULTURE

THE EVOLUTION OF CULTURE

AN INTERDISCIPLINARY VIEW

Edited by

Robin Dunbar, Chris Knight

and

Camilla Power

Edinburgh University Press

© Editorial matter and organisation
Robin Dunbar, Chris Knight and
Camilla Power, 1999

Edinburgh University Press
22 George Square, Edinburgh

Typeset in Garamond
by Norman Tilley Graphics, Northampton, and
printed and bound in Great Britain
by MPG Books Ltd, Bodmin

A CIP record for this book is available
from the British Library

ISBN 0 7486 1075 8 (hardback)
ISBN 0 7486 1076 6 (paperback)

CONTENTS

THE CONTRIBUTORS

Leslie C. Aiello is Professor of Biological Anthropology and Head of the Department of Anthropology at University College London. She is also co-editor of the *Journal of Human Evolution*. Born in 1946, she was educated at the University of California, Los Angeles (BA 1967; MA 1970) and the University of London (PhD 1981). Her research interests centre on the evolution of human adaptation. Research into postcranial anatomy of the fossil hominins led to the publication (with M. C. Dean) of *An Introduction to Human Evolutionary Anatomy* (1990) and to an ongoing major research project (with B. A. Wood, George Washington University, USA) into postcranial evolution and diversity in Plio-Pleistocene hominins. Her broader interests in the general field of human palaeobiology, and specifically in the relationship between dietary change and brain evolution and in the evolution of language and cognition, have led to a number of publications including an edited volume (with N. Jablonski) on *The Origin and Diversification of Language* (1998).

Alan Barnard is Reader in Social Anthropology at the University of Edinburgh. Since the early 1970s he has conducted extensive research among hunter-gatherers and former hunter-gatherers in Botswana and Namibia. He is author of *Research Practices in the Study of Kinship* (with Anthony Good, 1984), *A Nharo Wordlist with Notes on Grammar* (1985), *Hunters and Herders of Southern Africa: A Comparative Ethnography of the Khoisan Peoples* (1992), *Kalahari Bushmen* (a children's book, 1993) and many articles. He is also co-editor of the *Encyclopedia of Social and Cultural Anthropology* (with Jonathan Spencer, 1996).

Philip G. Chase received a Doctorate in Anthropology from the University of Arizona in 1983 and has been at the University of Pennsylvania Museum of Archaeology and Anthropology since 1987. He has studied the Middle Paeleolithic and the transition from Middle to Upper Paeleolithic from two perspectives, as a zooarchaeologist and as a researcher into the archaeological evidence for the evolution of symbolism and of human intelligence. He has analyzed the faunal collections from Combe Grenal and La Quina and from his own excavations at Cagny-lÉpinette and Fontéchevade.

Robin Dunbar studied Psychology and Philosophy at Oxford University before undertaking a PhD in Psychology at Bristol University. He is now Professor of Evolutionary Ecology in the School of Biological Sciences, University of Liverpool, where he leads a large research group studying the behavioural ecology and evolutionary psychology of human and non-human primates. He was previously Professor of Anthropology at University College London and Professor of Psychology at Liverpool University.

James R. Hurford is Professor of Linguistics at Edinburgh University. He has a broad interest in reconciling various traditions in linguistics which have tended to conflict. In particular, he has worked on articulating a framework in which formal representation of grammars in individual minds interacts with statistical properties of language as used in communities. The framework emphasizes the interaction of evolution, learning and communication. He is perhaps best known for his computer simulations of various aspects of the evolution of language.

Catherine A. Key is currently a lecturer in the Department of Anthropology at University College London. She teaches courses on Human Evolution and the Evolution of Cognition, reflecting her research interests in the evolution of cognition and behaviour. Prior to this she was a research assistant in the same department, using comparative analyses of human and non-human primates to investigate postcranial adaptations in the early hominids. She is currently completing her PhD thesis on Co-operation, Paternal Care and the Evolution of Hominid Social Structure.

Chris Knight received an MPhil degree in Russian literature from the University of Sussex in 1977 and a Doctorate in Anthropology from the University of London in 1987. He is now Reader in Anthropology at the University of East London. In addition to many journal articles on human origins, he is author of *Blood Relations: Menstruation and the Origins of Culture* (1991) and co-editor (with Jim Hurford and Michael Studdert-Kennedy) of *Approaches to the Evolution of Language: Social and Cognitive Bases* (1998).

Geoffrey F. Miller earned a BA in Biological Psychology from Columbia University, New York, in 1987, and a PhD in Cognitive Psychology from Stanford University, California, in 1993. He moved to England with an

NSF-NATO post-doctoral research fellowship, working at the University of Sussex. He worked as a research scientist at the Max Planck Institute for Psychological Research in Munich, and is now a senior research fellow at University College London. He has published about thirty-five academic papers and presented over fifty conference talks and colloquia, ranging across the areas of visual perception, cognition, learning, robotics, neural networks, genetic algorithms, human mate choice, evolutionary game theory and the origins of language, music, culture, intelligence, ideology and consciousness. His main research area is evolutionary psychology, and he is currently writing a trade book about the role of mate choice in human mental evolution.

Steven Mithen is Reader in Early Prehistory at the University of Reading. He studied at Sheffield, York and Cambridge Universities and has research interests in human evolution and early prehistory, with specific regard to cognition and the use of computer simulation. As an active field archaeologist he has conducted excavations on hunter-gatherer settlements in Western Scotland and is currently co-director of the Dana-Ghuywer-Faynan Early Prehistory Project involving the excavation of terminal Pleistocene settlements in southern Jordan.

Daniel Nettle received his PhD in Anthropology from University College London. He is currently a fellow of Merton College, Oxford, where he studies the evolution of linguistic and cultural diversity, both at a theoretical level and through field studies in West Africa.

Camilla Power has degrees in Mathematics from Oxford University and in Social Anthropology from London University, and is presently PhD candidate in the Department of Anthropology, University College London. She has authored a number of articles on sex, gender, cosmetics and the evolutionary origins of ritual.

Ian Watts was awarded his PhD in 1998. His doctoral research, carried out at the Department of Anthropology, University College London, is primarily concerned with the ochre record from the Upper Pleistocene Middle Stone Age of Southern Africa.

PREFACE

The original impetus for this book was a conference on 'Ritual and the Origins of Culture' organized by Chris Knight at the School of Oriental and African Studies, University of London, in March 1994 under the auspices of the Human Evolution Interdisciplinary Research Group. The theme of 'ritual' behaviour, both animal and human, had been chosen to promote contact between biological and social anthropologists. The conference built on a successful series of annual meetings organized by the Royal Anthropological Institute with much the same aim in mind.

The success of the 1994 event led naturally to the idea of a book; the present volume is the result. The long gestation period inevitably resulted in shifts in emphasis and changed priorities. During the editing process, we have tried to produce a coherent volume focused on the evolutionary emergence of culture. The inclusion of language as an essential element in that evolutionary story seemed a natural development. Only a proportion of the conference participants are represented here. In many cases, the chapters differ substantially from the papers initially presented at the conference. Several chapters are by scholars who did not attend the conference. The book, in other words, has turned out to be not a conventional conference proceedings but an edited collection of solicited essays. In keeping with the spirit of the conference, however, our basic aim remains to encourage social anthropologists to engage with evolutionary theory and, reciprocally, to convince evolutionary biologists of the exciting challenges presented to them by the specialist study of culture.

We are especially grateful to Clive Gamble, Tim Ingold, Paul Mellars and Chris Stringer for their support in helping to publicize and organize the 1994 conference. The event also benefited much from the kind assistance and encouragement of Jonathan Benthall, Director of the Royal Anthropological Institute. Chris Knight acknowledges financial and other support from the University of East London; in particular, special thanks are due to his Research Assistant, Catherine Arthur, for her many long hours spent getting the whole volume into final shape. We would like to thank John Davey, our editor at Edinburgh University Press, for his work in shepherding the book through the editorial process. Finally, we extend our warmest thanks to all our contributors, without whose creative cultural efforts no book would have evolved.

Robin Dunbar
Chris Knight
Camilla Power

CHAPTER 1

AN EVOLUTIONARY APPROACH TO HUMAN CULTURE

CHRIS KNIGHT, ROBIN DUNBAR AND CAMILLA POWER

The past two decades have seen a resurgence in Darwinian evolutionary theory that has revolutionized our understanding of social behaviour.

Previously, it was difficult to apply a rigorous Darwinian analysis to so nebulous a phenomenon as behaviour. In consequence, students of animal behaviour were too often reduced to vague *post hoc* explanations that were largely untestable. In the 1960s, however, a number of developments including most notably William Hamilton's (1964) solution to the problem of altruism sparked an intellectual revolution which was to transform the landscape.

Hamilton clarified mathematically how to assess the costs and benefits of an individual's social behaviour in terms of that behaviour's 'fitness consequences' – its effects in getting the individual's genes into future generations. The impact on the behavioural sciences was little short of electric, precipitating a full-scale paradigm shift or 'scientific revolution' (cf. Kuhn 1970). Whole new fields of investigation opened up, with a veritable surge of empirical studies based on detailed quantification and, in some cases, experimentation. Precision in hypothesis-testing became at last a real possibility. The result was a dramatic increase in the development of explanatory theory and understanding, made possible precisely because weak or incorrect hypotheses could now be rapidly excluded by the results of carefully thought-out analyses.

The reverberations of this revolution in biology were bound to spill over into the human sciences. Though slow to get going, and often dogged by empirical underdetermination and an excess of theoretical speculation, the study of human behaviour within the new Darwinian framework has taken off during the last decade. This development has been represented by a plethora of carefully executed empirical studies in two broad areas.

One of these, often termed 'evolutionary anthropology', has involved the application of theories and methods from Darwinian behavioural

1

ecology to living and historical human social groups. The focus here has been on foraging strategies, mate choices, marriage practices, parental investment patterns and other areas of social behaviour where the fitness consequences are relatively easy to measure. Questions are asked about how individuals choose between alternative strategies in maximizing their immediate returns (energy acquired per unit time spent foraging) or their long-term 'fitness' (genetic representation in future generations). Evolutionary anthropologists are especially interested in how and why behavioural strategies vary between individuals, as well as between whole societies.

The other approach is usually referred to as 'evolutionary psychology'. This has focused less on the functional consequences of behaviour than on the cognitive mechanisms believed to underpin it. The view here is that, during the course of human evolution, natural selection has given rise to certain core elements defining the human psyche. Evolutionary psychologists see their remit as the study less of variation than of human cognitive and behavioural universals, the ultimate aim being to specify the basic design-features of the human mind. Much of this work has involved studies of the criteria used by humans in choosing mates, forming alliances, detecting and exposing cheats and so on. Evolutionary psychologists do not necessarily expect a good adaptive fit between human evolved psychology and the contemporary environment. Instead, they posit an Environment of Evolutionary Adaptedness spanning two or three million years of hominid evolution. The distinctively human mind is said to have evolved in adapting not to present conditions but to a life in which prehistoric hunter-gatherers related to one another face-to-face within small-scale cooperative bands. An obvious corollary is that the human psyche may be ill-adapted to the complex and often stressfully competitive conditions of life in modern Western societies.

Common to both perspectives, however, has been an interest in decisions about mate choice, parental investment and other forms of behaviour which can be argued to have counterparts in the animal world. By contrast, rather little attention has been devoted to those topics which form the special subject matter of social anthropology. Neither Darwinian anthropology nor evolutionary psychology has focused on how or why, over evolutionary time, humans have established, elaborated and diversified their symbolic systems, languages, rituals, gender ideologies and magico-religious myths. Topics such as 'totemism' or 'taboo' – staples of classical social anthropology – do not feature as problems within Darwinism. There have, of course, been several attempts to model cultural evolutionary processes (most successfully by Cavalli-Sforza and Feldman 1981; Boyd and Richerson 1985; Laland et al. 1995), but these have focused mainly on the rates at which cultural patterns can be expected to change over time. A further debate has concerned the relationship between cultural and genetic evolution. More recently, some evolutionary psychologists (e.g. Boyer 1994) have claimed that a knowledge of human cognitive architecture may allow us to grasp the 'naturalness' of religious ideas as 'memes' (Dawkins 1976) whose seemingly odd features in fact enhance their chances of being replicated in human minds. But a more fundamental challenge, rarely addressed by Darwinians, is to specify the concrete selection pressures which, uniquely in the case of human evolution, led to such bizarre fictions being entertained by human minds in the first place.

This book arose from a meeting organized by Chris Knight under the auspices of the Human Evolution Interdisciplinary Research Group and held at the School of Oriental and African Studies, University of London, in March 1994. The meeting's theme was 'Ritual and the Origins of Culture'. The participants included social anthropologists, archaeologists, palaeontologists, primatologists and evolutionary psychologists. Almost thirty years earlier, in June 1965, a similar focus had brought together a remarkable interdisciplinary array of ethologists, symbolic anthropologists, psychologists, classicists and art historians in a meeting organized by Julian Huxley (1966) at the Royal Society. The title of that meeting had been 'Ritualisation of Behaviour in Animals and Man'. The luminaries present included Konrad Lorenz, Robert Hinde, Victor Turner, Edmund Leach, Meyer Fortes and R. D. Laing. Perhaps the meeting proved most historic as the last occasion on which the two branches of anthropology – the biological and the social – talked to each other.

The more modest 1994 event represented an attempt to resurrect that dialogue. The chapters in this volume comprise a selection of papers from participants at that meeting, as well as some additional chapters commissioned for this volume. Although the meeting from which this book arose focused on ritual, we have broadened the scope to include also wider aspects of culture, not least because it makes little sense to discuss the evolution of ritual in isolation from the rest of symbolic culture including language.

Broadly, the present volume exemplifies two different levels of approach to cultural phenomena. One is behavioural ecological, modelling processes of social negotiation using cultural mechanisms such as gossip, dialect and other group markers. Another, more unusually, uses Darwinian models to address specific problems in symbolic culture, in line with Edmund Leach's aphorism that 'god is in the detail'. If symbolism arises as an adaptive strategy, we should be able to 'reverse-engineer' (Pinker 1997) symbolic systems in order to elucidate their adaptive function. In explaining the novelty of his approach to Central African myths, the structuralist anthropologist Luc de Heusch (1982) proclaimed:

'Instead of brutally eliminating it, for the first time we are going to take the marvellous seriously.' Darwinism has not so far devoted much time to addressing our species' more 'marvellous' creations, but this book is aimed as a step in that direction. The first part addresses the origins of society; the next asks questions about art and religion; the final part turns to the evolution of language.

The atmosphere of mistrust that had long clouded relations between the two wings of anthropology – the biological and the social – became even more deeply entrenched during the three decades from 1965 to 1994 as a result of the gene-centred developments that took place in evolutionary biology. Prior to the 'selfish gene' intellectual revolution, it had been widely assumed that cooperative behaviour in animals (including altruistic behaviour) evolved thanks to selection at the level of whole groups or species. It was argued that those groups which functioned best as harmonious wholes survived, while less cooperative groups or species became extinct, along with the genes responsible for such lack of co-operation. Such ideas attributed a kind of morality to animals, in the sense that the larger social unit was supposed to foster group-functional behaviour among its individual members. Such ideas may be seen as a misapplication to biology of something resembling Durkheimian sociology, although as Nettle (this volume) points out, Durkheim himself would never have argued that animal social systems were in any sense morally regulated. Be that as it may, the naked methodological individualism of the new 'selfish gene' Darwinism involved a rupture with Durkheimian sociology and indeed with all human-derived assumptions about morality in the social life of animals.

Initially, social anthropologists and indeed most social scientists saw the new Darwinism not as science but as right-wing ideology. They queried what they took to be the new intellectual movement's founding assumption – the dogma that human social motivations are universally reducible to the competitive maximizing of personal gain. Anthropologists who had spent their professional lives studying hunter-gatherer norms of economic or other gift-giving, sharing and generosity understandably viewed such assumptions as offensive, overgeneralized and ethnographically ill-informed. Anxious to preserve humanistic values, social anthropologists have been fighting a rearguard action to insulate their discipline from such moral contamination ever since.

Two major strategies for this insulation offered themselves. First, the new, gene-centred view of natural selection was denounced as a derivative of Western capitalist economics, inevitably tainted with political evils inherited lock, stock and barrel from 'free market' economic theory. Compounding this was the widespread view that the new Darwinism was intent on building a human origins myth which would legitimize the prevailing world order as unchangeably rooted in 'human nature' (Sahlins 1977). With the rise of postmodern influence within social anthropology during the 1970s and 1980s, not only Darwinism but Western science itself became viewed as little more than an ideological construct designed to serve the dominant political powers. This view licensed politically sensitive social anthropologists to treat social constructs as the only phenomena accessible to study. Correspondingly, the citadel into which these anthropologists retreated was the domain of constructs in general – religion, ritual, art, ideology and language. Darwinians, it was noted, generally do not 'see' collective representations or constructs, searching instead for underlying behavioural realities alleged to be masked by such myths. The final step in this chain of reasoning was to conclude that since Darwinism has nothing to say about ideological constructs – in other words, about the symbolically constituted domain – then its claims can safely be ignored by those interested in what it means to be human.

In this book, our aim is to draw on resources from evolutionary theory in making an attempt to breach social anthropology's chosen citadel. With our colleagues in the social sciences, we acknowledge that human symbolic culture is biologically unprecedented (cf. Chase, Nettle this volume). Humans inhabit a world in which promises are explicitly made, contracts symbolically formulated, taboos laid down for ritual observance, often on pain of 'supernatural' punishment. Promises, contracts, taboos, supernatural sanctions – these are all social constructs. But precisely what is a 'social construct'? Under what selection pressures did such morally compulsive intangibles become invented, believed in and held up for respect?

At this point, numerous fundamental questions arise. Is religious ideology a 'spandrel' – a mere epiphenomenon? Or did it emerge as part of an evolutionarily stable strategy linked directly with problems of subsistence and reproduction? Do humans manifest belief in supernatural beings as part of their evolved psychology? Or is it just that the human mind, as Dawkins (1993) suggests, is anomalously gullible, enabling self-replicating religious delusions to infect us like computer viruses? If gullibility is the problem, then what were the selection pressures driving humans to become so readily deceived? On face value, gullibility would hardly seem to be an ideal candidate for an evolutionarily successful strategy.

A variant of the view that religious belief is a 'spandrel', arising in the first instance as a consequence of the development of cognitive fluidity, is represented in this volume by Mithen. An alternative Darwinian approach uses models of sexual selection to explain the evolutionary emergence of a capacity for manipulating shared fictions (Miller, Power this volume). Yet another theme, recurrently explored in the chapters which follow, is the idea that for any human cooperative group, its own contractual foundations are likely to form the primary focus of linguistic, religious and other symbolic representational activity (Barnard, Chase, Knight, Nettle, Watts this volume).

In large-scale social groups, the need to cooperate in order to maintain group cohesion is continuously undermined by the tempting benefits of freeriding – accepting the benefits of cooperation while avoiding the costs (cf. Dunbar, Key and Aiello, Nettle this volume). Issues of trust and deception provide the stuff of the so-called 'Machiavellian Intelligence' or 'Social Brain' hypothesis, according to which humans evolved their unusually large brains as a result of powerful selection for social skills (Humphrey 1976; Byrne and Whiten 1988). We humans have minds which appear well-designed to read other minds from cues provided by eye movements, facial expressions, tones of voice and other bodily signals. Correspondingly, we can anticipate the effects which our movements may have in shaping others' thoughts about what we are thinking. From this, it is but a small step to the deliberate and deceptive manipulation of information.

An implication of 'Machiavellian Intelligence' theory is that it was humans' increasingly sophisticated capacity for deceiving one another which eventually gave rise to that entirely novel level of representational activity which we call 'symbolic culture'. Social deception exercises a capacity which is fundamental to symbolism – the ability to hold in mind simultaneously both a 'true' representation and also its 'false' counterpart. No Darwinian treatment of the evolution of human symbolic culture can avoid addressing the problems which must have been posed to evolving group-living humans by such devious cognitive abilities. To signal deceptively is, in principle, to concoct an imaginative scenario. Yet the paradox is that humans within symbolically constructed communities apparently delight in fictional scenarios, which are not necessarily experienced as deceitful or exploitative. Humans who participate collectively in magico-religious ritual performances do so precisely in order to instil belief in fictional 'other worlds'. Representations of such fictions are more than epiphenomenal; they are central in securing cognitive acknowledgement of and allegiance to the contractual intangibles underpinning cooperation in human social groups. Given the characteristically collaborative, cooperative nature of the rituals designed to generate such illusions, the 'deceptions' which emerge may be dubbed 'collective deceptions', corresponding to Durkheim's classic notion of 'collective representations'.

Ritual appears central among mechanisms designed to control free-riders and the rampant individualism which might otherwise cause society to disintegrate. Hunter-gatherers and others organized in pre-state social systems consistently invest enormous energies in their illusion-inducing ritual performances; it would be puzzling if the consequent religious representations – the aim of the whole exercise – were maladaptive or merely epiphenomenal. Despite using selfish-gene models, a number of chapters in this book can in fact be read as convergent with Durkheim's original thesis on the centrality of communal ritual in generating representations of a 'totem' or 'god' whose function is to provide a focus for group-level allegiance (cf. Durkheim 1915; Gellner 1989; Deacon 1997).

Although seemingly paradoxical, to model the emergence of group-level phenomena from premises in Darwinian methodological individualism is in principle nothing new. Biological processes have long been recognized as complex and multi-layered. The need to distinguish between levels of analysis, and the possibility of modelling major evolutionary transitions between levels, are notions central to modern Darwinism (Maynard Smith and Szathmáry 1995). Although genes as such are never altruistic, it is precisely gene-level 'selfishness' which has driven the emergence of altruism and cooperation at higher levels including that of the multi-cellular organism, the primate coalition or the human speech-based community. Communal rituals can be understood as an expression of human coalitionary strategies, prefigured in many respects by the coalitionary strategies of non-human primates. The apparent incompatibility between the methodological individualism of modern Darwinism and the group-level focus of much social, cognitive and symbolic anthropology is therefore illusory. In texts such as *The Elementary Forms of the Religious Life*, Durkheim (1915) himself took great care to distinguish between animal and human levels of cognition and representation, noting that 'collective representations' have no animal counterparts (cf. Nettle this volume). It is ironic that Darwinians are beginning to address such distinctions just as many social anthropologists have decided on a reverse policy, adopting a version of methodological individualism which jettisons Durkheim and group-level analysis altogether in favour of cognitive individualism (cf. Rapport 1997). This trend may explain the recent popularity of Darwinian cognitive anthropologists such as Dan Sperber and Pascal Boyer on social anthropology courses.

As the paradigm-change of which this book is a small part unfolds, social anthropology will inevitably undergo profound restructuring, particularly with respect to its relationships with neighbouring disciplines and with science in general. Yet in one sense, anthropology will remain substantively the discipline it has always been, with its traditional concerns and preoccupations. The basic gains achieved under functionalist, structuralist and more recent social anthropological paradigms will be retained and built upon rather than discarded. But more importantly, anthropology will be required to develop its own evolutionary perspective on topics of intimate concern to it precisely because none of these areas has so far been of particular interest to biologists.

But what of social anthropology's traditional concerns over the supposed moral and political implications of 'selfish gene' Darwinism? Dawkins' (1976) coining of the term 'selfishness' with respect to genes has been among the most productive of scientific metaphors. It is ironic that symbolic anthropologists and postmodern critics – scholars whose specialist area of study is the world of metaphoric constructs – should have refused to grasp this metaphor as it was intended, insisting instead on a literal interpretation. No biologist thinks that genes are literally selfish; it is just that a gene is in business to make copies of itself, not copies of its competitors. Any gene which fails to follow this imperative will simply become extinct.

Human conceptual thought is intrinsically metaphorical. Whenever we can, we approach the unique and unfamiliar using concepts already well-known and familiar to us. During the time of René Descartes, when mechanical clocks represented pinnacles of human technical ingenuity, the complexities of organic life were conceptualized through the obvious most up-to-date metaphor – animals were essentially 'clocks'. Within the past twenty years, as academics and researchers have become acquainted with modern information technology, cognitive scientists have seen the brain as a 'computer'.

It was inevitable that in modelling the evolution of animal and human social life, the unknown would likewise be conceptualized in terms of the known. When optimal foraging theory was being developed as one of the cornerstones of the evolutionary biology of behaviour during the 1960s, it was done using mathematical tools borrowed from economics. There is no doubt that the prospect of being able to apply concepts derived from modern economics to the study of animal life provided much of the initial impetus driving the 'selfish gene' revolution in the life sciences. However distant from biologists' dispassionately mathematical thinking, the metaphor of competition between genes as competition in the capitalist marketplace gave us many of the core concepts of modern Darwinism, from 'costs' and 'benefits' to 'investments', 'returns' and strategies for competitively maximizing 'gains' rendered measurable in terms of a 'common currency'.

It is only when a metaphor is exploited uninhibitedly that its limitations begin to become apparent. Superficial application of 'free market' conceptual models to palaeolithic hunter-gatherers leads to a picture of the first human societies as individualistic and competitive. But among specialist palaeoanthropologists, this position is nowadays a minority one. Key and Aiello (this volume) point to the centrality of allomothering and other forms of intra-female reproductive cooperation in driving the emergence of distinctively human forms of social organisation. Recent studies of the emergence of language (Dunbar, Hurford, Nettle this volume; see also chapters in Hurford et al. 1998) link speech closely with the evolution of cooperation.

Drawing on data from primatology and hunter-gatherer ethnography, Darwinian psychologists David Erdal and Andrew Whiten (1994, 1996) attribute the evolution of hunter-gatherer egalitarianism to a cooperative strategy of 'counter-dominance' which results from escalating Machiavellian status competition. Here, selfishness at the level of the gene leads to an evolved strategy of coalitionary resistance to subordination, driving up the costs of dominance to the point where the strategy of seeking control over others is simply no longer affordable. Erdal and Whiten describe the earliest human hunter-gatherer social systems as outcomes of such strategies, culminating in a 'don't mess with me' egalitarian ethic. An implication of all this is that while palaeolithic hunter-gatherer social systems may not have fostered competitive individualism, their methods of establishing and maintaining egalitarian, cooperative relationships can still be understood in the light of analyses derived from economic theory. Darwinian cost/benefit theory, dispassionately applied to the study of human origins, can lead to scientific conclusions not necessarily predictable in advance.

It should be stressed that borrowing methods from a neighbouring discipline need not entail wholesale acceptance of the associated conceptual baggage. When evolutionary biologists drew on the mathematics of modern economics to aid them in understanding animal behaviour, they did not thereby subordinate themselves to the economists' agendas or priorities. What were borrowed were certain of the ways in which economists think about such problems, along with their mathematical tools – much, in fact, as economists themselves had earlier borrowed these tools from physics.

Neither the problems which biologists choose to study nor the ways in which they formulate their answers have much to do with conventional economics. There is no capitalist agenda, no profit to be maximized. By the same token, as anthropology and the social sciences come to adopt the Darwinian perspective, they will not suddenly have to busy themselves with the problems which traditionally have interested biologists. What they will continue to do is anthropology, using the methods and questions of anthropology. The difference will lie in how they think about those problems.

Our appeal, then, is to common sense and to the prospects offered by new perspectives. Nothing would be gained if social anthropologists were to become biologists. Our aim in editing this volume has instead been to illustrate some of the ways in which anthropologists might do better anthropology.

REFERENCES

Boyd, R. and Richerson, P. J. (1985) *Culture and the Evolutionary Process* (Chicago: University of Chicago Press).

Boyer, P. (1994) *The Naturalness of Religious Ideas. A Cognitive Theory of Religion* (Berkeley, Los Angeles, London: University of California Press).

Byrne, R. and Whiten, A. (1988) *Machiavellian Intelligence. Social Expertise and the Evolution of Intellect in Monkeys, Apes, and Humans* (Oxford: Clarendon Press).

Cavalli-Sforza, L. L. and Feldman, M. W. (1981) *Cultural Transmission and Evolution* (Princeton NJ: Princeton University Press).

Dawkins, R. (1976) *The Selfish Gene* (Oxford: Oxford University Press).

Dawkins, R. (1993) 'Viruses of the mind', in Dahlbom, B. (ed.), *Dennett and His Critics* (Oxford: Blackwell), pp. 13–27.

Deacon, T. (1997) *The Symbolic Species. The Co-evolution of Language and the Human Brain* (London: Penguin).

Durkheim, E. (1915 [1912]) *The Elementary Forms of the Religious Life,* trans. J. W. Swain (London: Allen & Unwin).

Erdal, D. and Whiten, A. (1994) 'On human egalitarianism: an evolutionary product of Machiavellian status escalation?' *Current Anthropology* 35 (2): 175–83.

Erdal, D. and Whiten, A. (1996) 'Egalitarianism and Machiavellian intelligence in human evolution', in Mellars, P. and Gibson, K. (eds), *Modelling the Early Human Mind* (Cambridge: McDonald Institute Monographs).

Gellner, E. (1989) 'Culture, constraint and community: semantic and coercive compensations for the genetic under-determination of *Homo sapiens sapiens*', in Mellars, P. and Stringer, C. (eds), *The Human Revolution. Behavioural and Biological Perspectives on the Origins of Modern Humans* (Edinburgh: Edinburgh University Press), pp. 514–25.

Hamilton, W. D. (1964) 'The genetical evolution of social behaviour (I and II)', *Journal of Theoretical Biology* 7: 1–16; 17–52.

de Heusch, L. (1982) *The Drunken King, or, The Origins of the State* (Bloomington: Indiana University Press).

Humphrey, N. K. (1976) 'The social function of intellect', in Bateson, P. P. G. and Hinde, R. A. (eds), *Growing Points in Ethology* (Cambridge: Cambridge University Press), pp. 303–17.

Hurford, J. R., Studdert-Kennedy, M. and Knight, C. (eds) (1998) *Approaches to the Evolution of Language: Social and Cognitive Bases* (Edinburgh: Edinburgh University Press).

Huxley, J. (organizer) (1966) 'A discussion on ritualization of behaviour in animals and man', *Philosophical Transactions of the Royal Society of London,* B 251: 247–526.

Kuhn, T. (1970) 'The structure of scientific revolutions', *International Encyclo-*

pedia of Unified Science, Vol. 2, 2nd edn (Chicago: University of Chicago Press).

Laland, K. N., Kumm, J. and Feldman, M. W. (1995) 'Gene-culture co-evolutionary theory: a test case', *Current Anthropology* 36: 131–56.

Maynard Smith, J. and Szathmàry, E. (1995) *The Major Transitions in Evolution* (Oxford: N. H. Freeman).

Pinker, S. (1997) *How the Mind Works* (London: Allen Lane, Penguin).

Rapport, N. (1997) 'The "contrarieties" of Israel: an essay on the cognitive importance and the creative promise of both/and', *Journal of the Royal Anthropological Institute* (n.s.) 3: 653–72.

Sahlins, M. D. (1977) *The Use and Abuse of Biology. An Anthropological Critique of Sociobiology* (London: Tavistock).

PART I

THE EVOLUTION OF SOCIETY

CHAPTER 2

THE EVOLUTION OF SOCIAL ORGANIZATION

CATHERINE A. KEY AND LESLIE C. AIELLO

INTRODUCTION

Cooperation is a fundamental characteristic of human social life. Co-operative bonds between mothers and offspring, husbands and wives, infants and grandmothers, sisters and brothers and unrelated friends of both sexes form the backbone of our social world. Language and ritual may have evolved to help us develop and maintain our relationships with individuals whose goals and desires may be very different from our own (Dunbar 1993; Knight et al. 1995). Starting from its primate roots, this chapter explores the evolution of cooperation in humans.

One of the most distinctive features of primates is their tendency to live in social groups. While group living must confer benefits to individual members, the costs are not slight. Direct costs result from competition between group members for food, mates and other resources (van Schaik 1983, 1989). In addition, indirect costs arise as group members must coordinate and compromise their activities in order to maintain group cohesion (Dunbar 1988). To balance this competition a high degree of cooperation is required. In many primate species, position in the social hierarchy and reproductive success are dependent upon the ability to establish and maintain cooperative alliances with other group members (Chapais 1995). For instance, pairs of subordinate male baboons form partnerships in order to steal females away from more dominant males (Packer 1977; Smuts 1985; Noë 1992). Vervet females, for whom the number of allies ultimately determines position in the hierarchy, use grooming to maintain coalitions with other females. Those females who receive grooming are more likely to support the groomer during disputes (Seyfarth and Cheney 1984; Hunte and Horrocks 1987).

Of all the non-human primates, chimpanzees have the widest repertoire of cooperative behaviours. Chimpanzee males form long-term stable alliances, whose members travel together, groom each other, perform coordinated charging displays (de Waal 1992) and may hunt cooperatively (Boesch and Boesch 1988). Alpha males are dependent upon their allies to maintain their rank, and will reward their supporters with mating access

15

to the females (de Waal 1982). Cooperation is also a hallmark of bonobo life. Particularly remarkable are the high levels of cooperation between unrelated bonobo females, who share food and use sexual stimulation to reinforce friendships (Parish 1994). In both species, all members of the group are aware of who is allied with whom, and that conflict with one individual may lead to conflict with an entire coalition. Furthermore, failure to reciprocate an act of cooperation will provoke retaliation. Chimpanzees, like humans, appear to follow the rules 'you scratch my back and I'll scratch yours' and 'an eye for an eye'. Chimpanzees are reciprocal altruists (Trivers 1971; de Waal and Luttrell 1988).

The primate origins of many human cooperative behaviours, such as allocare, grandmothering, male care and food-sharing, are clear. Vervet grandmothers establish close relationships with their daughter's offspring (Fairbanks 1988). Among the New World monkeys care by female relatives, male care and food-sharing are common (Feistner and Price 1991; Khoda 1985). Among Old World monkeys females will often allomother unrelated infants (Maestripieri 1994), although male care-giving is very rare. Yet cooperation in humans involves a wider network of individuals and a greater diversity of behaviours than in any other single primate species. We develop vast cooperative networks that include non-kin as well as kin, and that cross the boundaries of both age and sex. Our network of friends and relatives is typically so large that Dunbar (1993) argues that our large brains have evolved to help us keep track of these relationships, and that we use language as an efficient method of forming and maintaining social bonds. In fact, language may be one of a number of cognitive mechanisms that have evolved to manage complex co-operative relationships.

Cooperators involved in reciprocal exchange are vulnerable to cheats. This is particularly true if the individuals involved have very different goals, if there is a large time delay between giving and receiving and if different cooperative acts are being exchanged (Boyd 1988). Male care in exchange for exclusive mating access from a female would be one such example. Complex cooperative relationships pose a cognitive challenge involving monitoring a wide number of relationships, determining when to cooperate, who is likely to cheat on you, or when it is best to cheat on someone else (de Waal and Luttrell 1988). Connor and Norris (1982) suggest that reciprocal altruism requires a 'theory of mind', the ability to infer the mental states of others and to act upon and manipulate their beliefs and desires (Premack and Woodruff 1978). Certainly, of all non-human primates, chimpanzees are the most likely to possess theory of mind and to use this ability to deceive other individuals (Byrne and Whiten 1992). But human theory of mind surpasses that of chimpanzees (Povinelli 1993) and may have evolved to further enable us to negotiate a social world in which the benefits of cooperation and the dangers of deception are profound.

Humans are particularly good at reasoning about social interactions (Cosmides 1989) and at identifying and remembering the faces of people who are likely to be cheats (Cosmides 1989; Mealey et al. 1996). After just thirty minutes of interaction, humans are adept judges of which individuals are likely to be cooperative and which are likely to cheat (Frank et al. 1993). In general, humans seem to be predisposed to cooperate. In experimental games in which there is no chance that the highest paying strategy of deception will be discovered, human subjects are still more likely to cooperate (Caporael et al. 1989; Frank 1988; Frank et al. 1993). Furthermore, discussion between subjects, and a feeling of group belonging, even on the most superficial grounds, greatly enhance cooperation (Caporael et al. 1989). The need to cooperate, and protect ourselves from individuals who could exploit our cooperation, appears to be part of our evolved psychology. Frank (1988) argues that cooperation is so important to us that emotions such as guilt and love, and social values such as trust and honesty, have evolved to prevent us from succumbing to the short-term temptation to cheat and thus protect the long-term advantages of cooperation.

Cooperative breeding, grandmothers, extensive cooperation between non-kin, food-sharing, theory of mind, guilt, love and social values define humans as much as large brains or bipedal stance. The foundations of these behaviours can certainly be found in our closest relative, the chimpanzee. Yet at some point during our evolution, cooperative relationships and the cognitive mechanisms which support them became even more extensive. Why is cooperation so important to us? When in our evolutionary history did behaviours such as allocare, grandmothering, food-sharing and male care evolve? The Prisoner's Dilemma game is an ideal model with which to explore these questions, since it encapsulates the problem of cooperation (Axelrod 1984; Axelrod and Hamilton 1981; Trivers 1971). The game is played between pairs of individuals who each have a choice: they may either cooperate with the other player, or cheat. The paradox of the game is that whatever a player assumes his or her opponent will do, the highest paying strategy is always to cheat; however, if both players cheat they both score poorly. In the long term, players will achieve higher scores if they both cooperate, but it is difficult to overcome the short-term temptation to cheat. Key and Aiello (in press) have used computer simulations of the Prisoner's Dilemma to explore the conditions under which cooperation evolves. The model shows how sex differences in the energetic cost of reproduction can affect decisions about when to cooperate and when to cheat.

The energetic cost of reproduction is the amount of energy that an individual must invest in order to successfully reproduce and then raise a single offspring to maturity. For female primates, who bear the responsibility of gestation, lactation and an extensive period of infant dependency, the energetic costs of reproduction are always likely to be high. Mean calorific intake increases by 66–188 per cent in lactating compared to non-lactating females (Clutton-Brock 1991) and females lose weight during lactation in most wild populations (Altmann 1980; Bercovitch 1987). For males, the energetic cost of reproduction is more likely to be dependent upon the energy spent in finding, attracting and guarding mates. In sexually dimorphic species, where males must maintain a large body mass, energetic costs may be as high as, or even higher than, female costs (Key 1998). In rhesus macaques, Bercovitch and Nürnberg (1996) have shown that males who successfully sire offspring have twice as much body fat at the start of the mating season compared with un-successful males. By the end of the season sires and non-sires have equal amounts of body fat, indicating high levels of energy expenditure on the part of the sires.

For both males and females, energetic costs are likely to be important determinants of behaviour (Wrangham 1987). In particular, the mag-nitude of the energetic cost of reproduction can affect decisions about when to cooperate and with whom. In the following sections, the evol-ution of cooperation between females, and between males and females, will be discussed. It will be shown that intra-female cooperation is most likely when energetic costs of reproduction are high and when individuals are dependent upon a meat-based diet. Male and female inter-sexual strategies of cooperation and competition will be shown to be highly sen-sitive to sex differences in the energetic cost of reproduction. Specifically, when female energetic costs are relatively higher than male energetic costs, the evolution of paternal care may occur. Thus, studies of both intra-female and male–female cooperation point to the importance of energetic costs in understanding the development of cooperative strategies. With this in mind, the final section looks at the ways in which the nature of energy intake and expenditure may have changed during hominid evol-ution. Central to this discussion will be the implications of a shift to a meat-based diet. It is these shifting patterns in energy utilization that may have fuelled the development of the cooperative strategies currently seen in humans, and their supporting psychological mechanisms.

THE EVOLUTION OF ALLOCARE

Prisoner's Dilemma models were used to examine the conditions under which cooperation is most likely (Key and Aiello, in press). It was found that the likelihood of cooperation increases as the energetic cost of reproduction increases. At very high energetic costs, cooperation in the form of reciprocal altruism, or 'tit-for-tat', evolves in almost every experiment. Furthermore, regardless of how high or low the cost of reproduction is for males, the model predicts that cooperation is far more likely to arise between females, especially when energetic costs are great.

Female cooperation is widely reported in the wild, usually in the context of infant care. Females from species as diverse as elephants, bats, lions and red foxes are known to suckle infants other than their own (Davis et al. 1962; Douglas-Hamilton and Douglas-Hamilton 1975; Ewer 1973; Schaller 1972). Babysitting is an effective form of female cooperation in many species including African wild dogs, gray wolves, golden jackals, coyotes, lions, mongooses, coatis, vespertilionid bats, elk, bison, pronghorns, mountain sheep and dolphins (Riedman 1982). In the vespertilionid bats *Myotis thysanodes* and *Antrozous pallidus*, O'Farrell and Studier (1973) found that babysitting was such a successful strategy that infant postnatal mortality was only 1 per cent.

Female cooperation is widespread in mammals, and primates are no exception. Female cooperation is particularly common among Old World monkeys, but the prevalence of female philopatry means that cooperation is usually kin-directed (this is not always the case – see, for example, Schaub 1996 and Seyfarth and Cheney 1984). Thus, inclusive fitness effects increase the benefits of cooperation. But even among the apes, in which females migrate from their natal group, female cooperation is strong. For instance, chimpanzee females band together to protect themselves against overly aggressive males (de Waal 1984) while bonobo females partake in food-sharing and genito-genital rubbing (Parish 1994). As in other mammals, female primates cooperate in infant care. While such cooperation often involves family members, as in marmosets and tamarins (Goldizen 1987a, b), this is not always the case. For example, in langurs adult females will help unrelated females in infant care (Stanford 1992). While the costs and benefits of allomaternal care are still under debate (see, for example, Hrdy 1976, 1977; Nishida 1983; Stanford 1992), in many cases it is beneficial to both the mother and her offspring in terms of rapid infant growth, and shortened inter-birth intervals (Mitani and Watts 1997).

Babysitting behaviour is also common in primates, having been reported for patas monkeys (Hall and Mayer 1967), rhesus macaques (Rowell 1963), vervets (Lancaster 1971), Nilgiri langurs (Poirier 1968), hanuman langurs (Hardy 1977), mantled howlers (Glander 1974) and squirrel monkeys (Rosenblum 1971). In the ring-tailed lemur, *Lemur catta*, Klopfer and Boskoff (1979) suggest that babysitters may be particularly important for providing protection for the infant during terrestrial feeding.

There is, however, one type of female cooperation that is very unusual: provisioning of offspring. While there are exceptions among the calli-trichids (Feister and Price 1991) food-sharing between adults and young is very rare in primates. This behaviour is also uncommon among non-primates (Lewis and Pusey 1997) with a single notable exception, the social carnivores (Macdonald and Moehlman 1982). Why this should be is clearly demonstrated in the brown hyena.

Brown hyenas live in clans of several adult females, a dominant male, and several subordinate males, adolescents and infants. Emigration and immigration by both sexes means that not all clan members are related. All infants older than three months are raised in a communal den (Owens and Owens 1979, 1984). Owens and Owens describe female cooperation as the glue that holds the clan together, and all females participate in off-spring care, regardless of rank or kinship. Lactating females suckle all cubs, regardless of whether they are their own, and all clan females bring food to the communal den, feeding pups undiscriminatingly. As in many primate species, the social life of the hyena is of paramount importance. Strong bonds develop between group members and protracted greeting and appeasement displays maintain group harmony. It is the hyena's dependence upon meat that appears to make cooperation a vital part of their reproductive strategy. Meat is an elusive resource, and scavenger hunts may take females more than thirty kilometres away from the den. Furthermore, it takes a long time to become an effective hunter or scavenger, which means that weanlings are unable to acquire food for themselves and are reliant on adults for up to two years. Without com-munal provisioning, few hyena pups would survive. Similar reasoning has been used to explain communal living in many species of carnivore (Riedman 1982) as well as in raptors (Thiollay 1991) and blackbacked jackals (Moehlman 1979) in which helpers not only provision infants, but also teach them hunting techniques.

Both theoretical models and field observations point to the importance of female cooperation in many mammalian species. Since female mam-mals are responsible for gestation and lactation their reproductive costs are likely to be high. Harsh breeding seasons and high infant mortality have also been suggested as factors that may further increase female repro-ductive costs (Emlen 1982; Ligon 1991). Primate species show an exten-sion of the mammalian pattern of high female investment, since female primates must also provide social stimulation for their infants throughout long periods of infant dependency (Smuts 1997). However, among the wide range of cooperative behaviours seen in both primates and non-primates, the provisioning of offspring is highly unusual except in the social carnivores. Dependence upon a meat-based diet may be a key factor favouring this behaviour.

THE EVOLUTION OF PATERNAL CARE

Female–female cooperation is the easiest type of cooperation to establish, since females share a common goal, namely to provide their infants with the best possible resources. Females can exchange similar altruistic acts, such as suckling or provisioning of meat, which are easier to monitor than non-symmetrical exchanges of different goods or services (Boyd 1992). Cooperation between males and females is much more difficult to establish and is likely to be much less common than intra-female cooperation since the currencies of exchange are usually very different. For instance, Ligon (1991) suggests that males may exchange offspring care for mating rights from the female. But the female has no guarantee that the male will provide post-partum care for her offspring, and the male has no guarantee that he is the father of the female's offspring. Since even in supposedly monogamous species the level of paternity certainty can be very low indeed (Dixon et al. 1994; Freeman-Gallant 1997; Whittingham and Lifjeld 1995) cooperation between the sexes may be a very risky strategy.

Simulations based on the Prisoner's Dilemma indicate that under certain conditions males will cooperate with females, even when females do not reciprocate this cooperation. This unconditional cooperation on the part of the male is analogous to male investment in the female and her offspring. Two factors are required in order to establish this behaviour (Key and Aiello, in press). Firstly, female energetic costs must be much higher than male energetic costs. Secondly, females must develop strategies whereby males who fail to cooperate unconditionally are severely punished by a long-term refusal to cooperate. Importantly, the initial conditions for male investment in females and their offspring do not require any level of paternity certainty. When male energetic costs are low in comparison to those of females, males will invest in females as long as doing so does not jeopardize their ability to mate with at least one other female (similar results were obtained by Maynard Smith 1977 and Werren et al. 1980).

If males are investing in females and their offspring, it is to their advantage to try to target those in which they have a direct reproductive interest. Cooperation and reproduction may become closely associated as in chimpanzees and bonobos, where food exchange and copulation sometimes occur simultaneously (Kuroda 1984; de Waal 1987). The likelihood is that once paternal care arises, males will adopt strategies that increase their paternity certainty. If this occurs, simulations strongly suggest that male investment will increase, even when male energetic costs are quite high.

Hypotheses regarding the evolution of male care generally focus only on female energetic costs (Wright 1984; Dunbar 1988). Wright (1990) points out that the energetic costs of infant transport are relatively higher in arboreal primates, especially those of small body size which tend to have proportionately bigger infants. Simulations suggest that patterns of cooperation, including male care, are dependent upon the relationship between both male and female energetic costs. Estimates of energetic costs for males and females of a wide number of primate species suggest that female energetic costs in species with high levels of male care, such as the callitrichids, are indeed high relative to male costs (Key 1998).

ENERGY USE AND THE EVOLUTION OF HUMAN COOPERATION

Human cooperative behaviours are, at least partly, a legacy of our primate origins. Coalitions of females form the basic structure of many primate groups, especially Old World monkeys. Male care-giving is observed in 15 per cent of primate species, most notably the callitrichids and cebids. It is rare to find both intra-female cooperation, especially among non-relatives, and male care in the same social group. Yet, this is exactly the pattern of cooperative bonds that we find in humans. In fact, humans have a unique social structure in which males and females form pair bonds which involve extensive amounts of cooperation, within the context of a large multi-male, multi-female group (Deacon 1997). Paternal care-giving is very unlikely within such a framework, since the opportunities for extra-pair matings are great. Infant protection by male chacma baboons (Busse and Hamilton 1981) and infant carrying by Barbary macaques (Taub 1980) have both been cited as examples of male care within the context of a multi-male, multi-female social structure. Yet, both these cases may be interpreted as agonistic buffering (Deag and Crook 1971) and evidence suggests that the males involved are unrelated to the infants (Paul et al. 1992).

The structure of human social groups emerges from strong cooperative bonds between individuals of both the same sex and different sexes. The challenge, then, is to understand how this highly unusual social system may have arisen. The discussions above suggest that patterns of cooperation are dependent upon the energetic costs of reproduction of males and females. Thus, if it is possible to make predictions about the energetic costs of reproduction from fossil and archaeological material, it may then be possible to speculate on the evolution of cooperation in the ancestral hominids. As will be shown below, both postcranial and cranial evidence provide valuable clues as to how the energetic demands of the hominids may have changed over time.

The energetic cost of reproduction is defined as the sum of the energetic costs of every activity that contributes to the production of a single surviving offspring (Key 1998). For females these costs will primarily be associated with the production of gametes, gestation, lactation and child care. Male costs arise from the production of gametes, courtship, male–male competition and, in some instances, child care. For both sexes, body condition is also an important determinant of reproductive success (Bercovitch and Nürnberg 1996; McFarland 1997). Since the costs of body maintenance are closely related to body size, the relationship between male and female energetic costs is largely related to differences in body mass. In species where males and females have similar body mass, the energy requirements of females are greater than those of males due to the demands of direct parental care. However, when males are at least 50 per cent larger than females, the energetic costs to the male of maintaining a larger body balance the female's energetic costs, so that the total cost of reproduction for each sex is more or less equal (Key 1998). In short, female energetic costs are highest, relative to male energetic costs, in species with the lowest levels of body mass dimorphism.

Changes in sexual dimorphism in body mass can be determined from the fossil record (McHenry 1992a, 1992b, 1996). McHenry (1996) estimates that males were around 50 per cent larger than females in *Australopithecus afarensis* and 40 per cent larger in *Australopithecus africanus*. The most significant change in body mass dimorphism occurs with the appearance of early *Homo*. *Homo erectus* males were just 20 per cent heavier than females, indicating an important shift in the balance of energetic costs between the sexes. It is significant that the change in sexual dimorphism in *Homo erectus* is the result of changes in both male and female body size. Both sexes increased in size, with the greatest increase occurring in females, possibly in response to thermoregulatory demands (Aiello 1996a, 1996b; Wheeler 1994). It seems unlikely that the decrease in sexual dimorphism was in response to a change in social system involving reduced intra-sex competition (as suggested by, for example, Deacon 1997) since this would be expected to involve changes in male body size alone. However, changes in sexual dimorphism that increased the relative energetic load on the female may have contributed to a change in social behaviour involving more cooperation both between females and between males and females.

Gross changes in the overall energy demands of humans, due to changes in body size, have been accompanied by a fundamental change in the way that energy is utilized. Over the course of human evolution there has been a threefold increase in the size of the brain, a change which has important energetic implications (Aiello and Wheeler 1995; Aiello 1997). The brain is one of the most energetically expensive organs in the body. Brain tissue has over twenty-two times the mass specific metabolic rate of skeletal muscle. Other energetically expensive organs are the gastrointestinal tract, heart, liver and kidney which, together with the brain, are responsible for nearly 70 per cent of the human body's energy requirements (Aiello and Wheeler 1995; Aiello 1997). However, while humans have larger brains than would be expected for an average primate of our body mass, the mass of the gastrointestinal tract is only 60 per cent of the size expected. It appears that in humans the high metabolic costs of having a large brain are balanced by a reduction in the energetic costs of the gastrointestinal tract. Aiello and Wheeler (1995) argue that a change in gut size must have been accompanied by a change in diet to a less bulky, more digestible food source. Animal-based products (e.g. meat or bone marrow) would satisfy this criterion.

The adaptive complex of an increase in brain size and a reduction in gut size, mediated by a change to an animal-based diet, implies a profound change in the energetic costs of reproduction for females. Firstly, an increase in brain size directly increases the energetic load on the mother, since the main period of brain growth occurs in utero and during the post-natal period prior to weaning (Martin 1981, 1983, 1996). Foley and Lee (1991) estimate that up to the age of eighteen months human infants are around 9 per cent more energetically costly than chimpanzee infants. Secondly, a change to a diet with a high meat component requires that females provision their offspring until they have gained the necessary skills to acquire meat for themselves (Aiello in press a). The dual loads of extensive food-sharing between mother and offspring, and the training necessary for the offspring to find its own resources, would significantly increase the period of maternal investment beyond the weaning period.

In short, there is every reason to believe that the energetic loads on *Homo* females were much greater than had been the case for their smaller-bodied, more sexually dimorphic, smaller-brained ancestors. In the previous discussion it was argued that intra-female cooperation is most likely when female energetic costs are high. In particular, it was shown that female cooperation in the care and feeding of offspring is especially important in social carnivores. Similarly, the combination of high energetic costs and a shift to a meat-based diet in *Homo* seems very likely to have been accompanied by an increase in female–female cooperation. Hawkes et al. (1997a, b, c) suggest that menopause and long post-menopausal lifespans may have evolved as part of such a cooperative strategy. They found that senior post-menopausal Hadza women play an important role in provisioning their daughter's offspring. The benefits of this are clear for the child, the mother and the grandmother. With more provisioning the child would be expected to have higher survival. The mother is relieved of some of the burden of providing food, reducing her energetic stress and shortening her inter-birth interval. Finally, the decreased mortality of the child and the increased fecundity of the mother equate to higher inclusive fitness for the grandmother.

The changes in sexual dimorphism in body mass and an increase in brain size seen in *Homo erectus* are indicative of a fundamental change in energetic requirements. At the very least, it seems likely that *Homo erectus* females were highly cooperative, particularly with respect to infant care. There may have been selection for menopause and increased post-reproductive lifespans (Aiello in press a, in press b) as well as other features such as concealed ovulation, reproductive synchrony and increases in subcutaneous fat (Power and Aiello 1997; Power et al. 1997; Stern and McClintock 1998). However, female energetic costs were not only increasing in absolute terms, but also with respect to male energetic costs. This would suggest that there would also be selection for increased paternal investment. In *Homo erectus*, this imbalance in male and female energetic costs may have been adequately buffered by female cooperation. However, between 500,000 and 100,000 years ago there was an exponential increase in brain size which would have escalated female energetic costs far beyond those found in *Homo erectus*. During this time period, the first unequivocal evidence of large game hunting also appears in the archaeological record, the earliest finds at Schöningen and Boxgrove dating to between 500,000 and 400,000 years ago (Thieme 1997). It seems likely that during this period there would have been strong selection for male cooperation, particularly for providing animal food for females and their offspring (Aiello in press a, in press b).

Hawkes (1990, 1991, 1993; see also Hawkes et al. 1991) argues that large animal hunting by males is not a paternal care strategy at all. Rather, it is a method of intra-sexual competition, whereby successful hunters hope to gain status and attract mates. Hawkes and her co-workers show that among the Hadza, hunting large game benefits the group as a whole by providing more calories per head than other hunting or foraging strategies. But, at an individual level, it is a risky strategy, as the likelihood of catching an animal on any given day is very low. Hunting small game would be a more reliable strategy; moreover, since small animals are not shared with the whole group (as large animals are), the entire product of the hunt goes to the hunter's family. Hawkes argues that since men do not pursue small game, the purpose of hunting is to 'show off' to potential mates.

That hunting may be used to reap social rewards does not necessarily exclude the possibility that it may further function as a mechanism of male investment. The degree to which this might be the case is strongly dependent on specific habitat conditions. For example, Hill et al. (1987; see also Hawkes et al. 1997c) found that Ache men contribute greater than 85 per cent of the total caloric intake of the group. Bleige Bird and Bird (1997) have found the presence of both male strategies ('showing off' and provisioning) among the Merriam of the Torres Strait. A large part of the

Merriam diet is made up of turtle meat, and turtle-hunting is carried out all year round. During the turtle's feeding and mating season, turtle-hunting can be risky and expensive, involving 'long travel times, high speed pursuits in motorised craft and dangerous hand-capture methods' (Bliege Bird and Bird 1997: 54). Only a few, usually young, males participate in these hunts and the fruits of their labour are widely shared during feasts, rather than being used for household consumption. During the nesting season, the energetic costs of hunting and risks involved are low, since turtles are easy to find and capture. During this season the majority of the turtle meat is shared only with close neighbours for household consumption. Bleige Bird and Bird conclude that Merriam men practise two different reproductive strategies, which are associated with age and marital status. Young, unmarried men engage in high-risk hunting from which they gain very little nutritional reward but great social status through their generous distribution of the meat. Married men, on the other hand, concentrate on low-risk hunting through which they can provide meat for their family and closest neighbours.

The two hunting strategies described above correspond well with the two sexual strategies identified by Buss and Schmitt (1993; see also Buss 1989). Males may be short-term strategists pursuing short-term relationships with the aim of mating with as many females as possible. Alternatively, they may be long-term strategists investing heavily in a single female with a view to long-term, exclusive mating access. Both long-term and short-term strategies have costs and benefits (Buss and Schmitt 1993), and both strategies may be practised by a single male at different life stages. The presence of two male strategies presents complex reproductive scenarios for both sexes. It is important for females to be able to distinguish between short-term and long-term male strategists. A female who mates with a short-term strategist faces high costs, since there will be little investment from the male and she may deter long-term strategists. The ideal scenario for a female may be to mate with a short-term strategist (for his 'good genes') but to form a more lasting relationship with a long-term strategist (for his investment). This in turn presents a conundrum for male long-term strategists who must avoid being cuckolded, a strong possibility in a large, mixed-sex group. The social dilemmas faced by individuals in this context are immense. Theory of mind would play a vital role in ascertaining the true desires of potential mates. Furthermore, Frank (1988) proposes that emotions such as love and guilt may play a very important role in maintaining cooperative bonds between males and females by constraining the temptation to give in to the benefits of short-term matings.

CONCLUSIONS

This chapter has examined the primate origins of human social structure, concentrating on the evolution of cooperation between females and between males and females. There has been much debate in the current literature regarding the function of cooperation in human societies (Blurton-Jones 1987; Hawkes 1993; Hill et al. 1987; Hill and Kaplan 1994; Wilson 1998). Male hunting behaviour has been the focus of much of this attention, in particular whether it is a reciprocal behaviour or a male mating strategy. However, whatever function may be ascribed to cooperation, it is clearly a central feature of human society, to such an extent that we have even evolved specialized psychological mechanisms to negotiate our complex social networks. The development of pair-bonding and paternal care within the context of large multi-male, multi-female groups placed unique cognitive demands upon our hominid ancestors, elevating our capacity for altruism, deception, culture, communication and knowing other peoples' minds beyond anything yet observed in non-human primates. We conclude that these human patterns of cooperation are the result of changes in the energetic costs of producing large-brained offspring for males and females in association with a change to an animal-based diet.

REFERENCES

Aiello, L. C. and Wheeler, P. (1995) 'The expensive tissue hypothesis: the brain and the digestive system in human evolution', *Current Anthropology* 36: 199–221.

Aiello, L. C. (1996a) 'Hominine preadaptions for language and cognition', in Mellars, P. and Gibson, K. (eds), *Modelling the Early Human Mind* (Cambridge: McDonald Institute Monograph Series), pp. 89–99.

Aiello, L. C. (1996b) 'Terrestriality, bipedalism and the origin of language', in Maynard Smith, J. (ed.), *Evolution of Social Behaviour Patterns in Primates and Man* (London: Proceedings of the British Academy).

Aiello, L. C. (1997) 'Brains and guts in human evolution: the expensive tissue hypothesis', *Brazilian Journal of Genetics* 20: 141–8.

Aiello, L. C. (in press a) 'The expensive tissue hypothesis and the evolution of the human adaptive niche: a study in comparative anatomy', in *Proceedings of the Science in Archaeology Conference*, HBMC Archaeology Reports Series, English Heritage.

Aiello, L. C. (in press b) 'The foundations of human language', in Jablonski, N. and Aiello, L. C. (eds), *The Origin and Diversification of Language* (San Francisco: California Academy of Sciences).

Altmann, J. (1980) *Baboon Mothers and Infants* (Cambridge, Mass.: Harvard University Press).

Axelrod, R. (1984) *The Evolution of Cooperation* (London: Penguin).

Axelrod, R. and Hamilton, W. D. (1981) 'The evolution of cooperation', *Science* 211: 1390–6.

Bercovitch, F. B. (1987) 'Female weight and reproductive condition in a population of olive baboons (*Papio anubis*)', *American Journal of Primatology* 12: 189–95.

Bercovitch, F. B. and Nürnberg, P. (1996) 'Socioendocrine and morphological correlates of paternity in rhesus macaques (*Macaca mulatta*)', *Journal of Reproduction and Fertility* 107: 59–68.

Bliege Bird, R. L. and Bird, D. W. (1997) 'Delayed reciprocity and tolerated theft: the behavioural ecology of food-sharing strategies', *Current Anthropology* 38: 49–78.

Blurton-Jones, N. G. (1987) 'Tolerated theft, suggestions about the ecology and evolution of sharing, hoarding and scrounging', *Social Science Information* 26: 31–54.

Boesch, C. and Boesch, H. (1988) 'Hunting behaviour of wild chimpanzees in the Taï National Park', *American Journal of Physical Anthropology* 78: 547–73.

Boyd, R. (1988) 'Is the repeated Prisoner's Dilemma a good model of reciprocal altruism?' *Ethology and Sociobiology* 9: 211–22.

Boyd, R. (1992) 'The evolution of reciprocity when conditions vary', in Harcourt, A. H. and de Waal, F. B. M. (eds), *Coalitions and Alliances in Humans and Other Animals* (Oxford: Oxford University Press), pp. 473–89.

Buss, D. M. (1989) 'Sex differences in human mate preferences: evolutionary hypotheses tested in 37 cultures', *Behavioural and Brain Sciences* 12: 1–49.

Buss, D. M. and Schmitt, D. P. (1993), 'Sexual strategies theory: an evolutionary perspective on human mating', *Psychological Review* 100: 204–32.

Busse, C. D. and Hamilton III, W. J. (1981) 'Infant carrying by male chacma baboons', *Science* 212: 1282–3.

Byrne, R. W. and Whiten, A. (1992) 'Cognitive evolution in primates: evidence from tactical deception', *Man* 27: 609–27.

Caporael, L. R., Dawes, R. M., Orbell, J. M. and van de Kragt Alphons, J. C. (1989) 'Selfishness examined: cooperation in the absence of egoistic incentives', *Behavioural and Brain Sciences* 12: 683–739.

Chapais, B. (1995) 'Alliances as a means of competition in primates: evolutionary, developmental and cognitive aspects', *Yearbook of Physical Anthropology* 38: 115–36.

Clutton-Brock, T. H. (1991) *The Evolution of Parental Care* (Princeton, NJ: Princeton University Press).

Connor, R. C. and Norris, K. S. (1982) 'Are dolphins reciprocal altruists?' *American Naturalist* 119: 358–74.

Cosmides, L. (1989) 'The logic of social exchange: has natural selection shaped how humans reason? Studies with the Wason selection task', *Cognition* 31: 187–276.

Davis, R. B., Herreid II, C. F. and Short, H. L. (1962) 'Mexican free-tailed bats in Texas', *Ecological Monograph* 32: 183–200.

Deacon, T. (1997) *The Symbolic Species* (London: W. W. Norton).

Deag, J. M. and Crook, J. H. (1971) 'Social behaviour and "agonistic buffering" in the wild barbary macaque, *Macaca sylvana*', *Folia Primatologica* 14: 183–200.

Dixon, A., Ross, D., Omalley, S. L. C. and Burke, T. (1994) 'Paternal investment inversely related to degree of extra-pair paternity in the reed bunting', *Nature* 371: 698–9.

Douglas-Hamilton, I. and Douglas-Hamilton, O. (1975) *Among the Elephants* (New York: Viking Press).

Dunbar, R. I. M. (1988) *Primate Social Systems* (London: Croom Helm).

Dunbar, R. I. M. (1993) 'Co-evolution of neocortex size, group size and language in humans', *Behaviour and Brain Sciences* 16: 681–735.

Emlen, S. T. (1982) 'The evolution of helping: an ecological constraints model', *American Naturalist* 119: 29–39.

Ewer, R. F. (1973) *The Carnivores* (Ithaca, NY: Cornell University Press).

Fairbanks, L. A. (1988) 'Vervet monkey grandmothers – effects on mother–infant relationships', *Behaviour* 104: 176–88.

Feistner, A. T. C. and Price, E. C. (1991) 'Food-sharing in cotton-top tamarins (*Saguinus oedipus*)', *Folia Primatologica* 54: 34–45.

Foley, R. A. and Lee, P. C. (1991) 'Ecology and energetics of encephalization in hominid evolution', *Philosophical Transactions of the Royal Society of London*, B 334: 223–32.

Frank, R. H. (1988) *Passions within Reason* (New York: W. W. Norton).

Frank, R. H., Gilovich, T. and Regan, D. T. (1993) 'The evolution of one-shot cooperation: an experiment', *Ethology and Sociobiology* 14: 247–56.

Freeman-Gallant, C. R. (1997) 'Extra-pair paternity in monogamous and poly-gynous Savannah sparrows *Passerculus sandwichensis*', *Animal Behaviour* 53: 397–404.

Glander, K. E. (1974) 'Baby-sitting, infant sharing and adoptive behaviour in mantled howling monkeys', *American Journal of Physical Anthropology* 41: 482 (abstract).

Goldizen, A. (1987a) 'Facultative polyandry and the role of infant-carrying in wild saddle-back tamarins (*Saguinus fusciollis*)', *Behavioural Ecology and Sociobiology* 20: 99–109.

Goldizen, A. (1987b) 'Tamarins and marmosets: communal care of offspring', in Smuts, B. et al. (eds), *Primate Societies* (Chicago: University of Chicago Press), pp. 34–43.

Hall, K. R. L. and Mayer, B. (1967) 'Social interactions in a group of captive patas monkeys (*Erythrocebus patas*)', *Folia Primatologica* 5: 213–36.

Hawkes, K. (1990) 'Why do men hunt? Some benefits for risky strategies', in Cashdan, E. (ed.), *Risk and Uncertainty* (Boulder, Colo.: Westview Press:), pp. 145–66.

Hawkes, K. (1991) 'Showing-off: tests of a hypothesis about men's foraging goals', *Ethology and Sociobiology* 12: 29–54.

Hawkes, K. (1993) 'Why hunter-gatherers work: an ancient version of the prob-lem of public goods', *Current Anthropology* 34: 341–61.

Hawkes, K., O'Connell, J. F. and Blurton Jones, N. G. (1991) 'Hunting income patterns among the Hadza: big game, common goods, foraging goals, and the evolution of the human diet', *Philosophical Transactions of the Royal Society of London*, B 334: 243–51.

Hawkes, K., O'Connell, J. F. and Blurton Jones, N. G. (1997a) 'Menopause: evolutionary causes, fossil and archaeological consequences', *Journal of Human Evolution* 32: A8–A9 (abstract).

Hawkes, K., O'Connell, J. F. and Blurton Jones, N. G. (1997b) 'Hadza women's time allocation, offspring provisioning, and the evolution of long post-menopausal lifespans', *Current Anthropology* 38: 551–77.

Hawkes, K., O'Connell, J. F. and Rogers, L. (1997c) 'The behavioral ecology of modern hunter-gatherers, and human evolution', *Trends in Ecology and Evolution* 12: 29–32.

Hill, K. and Kaplan, H. (1994) 'On why male foragers hunt and share food', *Current Anthropology* 34: 701–6.

Hill, K., Hawkes, K., Kaplan, H. and Hurtado, A. M. (1987) 'Foraging decisions among Ache hunter-gatherers: new implications for optimal foraging models', *Ethology and Sociobiology* 8: 1–36.

Hrdy, S. B. (1976) 'Care and exploitation of nonhuman primate infants by conspecifics other than the mother', in Rosenblatt, J., Hinde, R., Shaw, E. and Bier, C. (eds), *Advances in the Study of Behaviour*, Vol. 6 (New York: Academic Press), pp. 101–58.

Hrdy, S. B. (1977) *The Langurs of Abu* (Cambridge, Mass.: Harvard University Press).

Hunte, W. and Horrocks, J. A. (1987) 'Kin and non-kin interventions in the aggressive disputes of vervet monkeys', *Behavioural Ecology and Sociobiology* 20: 257–63.

Key, C. A. (1998) *Cooperation, paternal care and the evolution of hominid social groups*, PhD dissertation (London: University of London).

Key, C. A. and Aiello, L. C. (in press) 'A Prisoner's Dilemma model of the evolution of paternal care', *Folia Primatologica*.

Khoda, M. (1985) 'Allomothering behaviour of new and old world monkeys', *Primates* 26: 28–44.

Klopfer, P. H. and Boskoff, K. (1979) 'Maternal behaviour in prosimians', in Doyle, G. A. and Martin, R. D. (eds), *The Study of Prosimian Behaviour* (New York: Academic Press), pp. 123–56.

Knight, C., Power, C. and Watts, I. (1995) 'The human symbolic revolution: a Darwinian account', *Cambridge Archaeological Journal* 5: 75–114.

Kuroda, S. (1984) 'Interactions over food among pygmy chimpanzees', in Susman, R. (ed.), *The Pygmy Chimpanzee* (New York: Plenum), pp. 301–24.

Lancaster, J. (1971), 'Play-mothering: the relations between juvenile females and young infants among free-ranging vervet monkeys (*Cercopithecus aethiops*)', *Folia Primatologica* 15: 161–82.

Lewis, S. E. and Pusey, A. E. (1997) 'Communal care in plural breeding mammals', in Solomon, N. G. and French, J. A. (eds), *Cooperative Breeding in Mammals* (Cambridge: Cambridge University Press), pp. 335–63.

Ligon, J. D. (1991) 'Cooperation and reciprocity in birds and mammals' in

Hepper, P. G. (ed.), *Kin Recognition* (Cambridge: Cambridge University Press), pp. 30–59.

Macdonald, D. W. and Moehlman, P. D. (1982) 'Cooperation, altruism and restraint in the reproduction of carnivores', in Bateson, P. P. G. and Klopfer, P. H. (eds), *Perspectives in Ethology, Vol. 5: Ontogeny* (New York: Plenum Press), pp. 433–67.

McFarland, R. (1997) 'Female primates: fat or fit?' in Morbeck, M. E., Galloway, A. and Zihlman, A. L. (eds), *The Evolving Female* (Princeton, NJ: Princeton University Press), pp. 163–78.

McHenry, H. M. (1992a) 'Body size and proportion in the early hominids', *American Journal of Physical Anthropology* 86: 407–31.

McHenry, H. M. (1992b) 'How big were early hominids?' *Evolutionary Anthropology* 1: 15–19.

McHenry, H. M. (1996) 'Sexual dimorphism in fossil hominids and its socio-ecological implications', in Steele, J. and Shennan, S. (eds), *The Archaeology of Human Ancestry* (London: Routledge), pp. 91–103.

Maestripieri, D. (1994) 'Social structure, infant handling, and mothering styles in group-living old world monkeys', *International Journal of Primatology* 15: 531–53.

Martin, R. D. (1981) 'Relative brain size and metabolic rate in terrestrial vertebrates', *Nature* 393: 57–60.

Martin, R. D. (1983) *Human Brain Evolution in an Ecological Context*. 52nd James Arthur Lecture on the Evolution of the Brain, American Museum of Natural History.

Martin, R. D. (1996) 'Scaling of the mammalian brain: the maternal energy hypothesis', *News in Physiological Sciences* 11: 149–56.

Maynard Smith, J. (1977) 'Parental investment: a prospective analysis', *Animal Behaviour* 25: 1–9.

Mealey, L., Daood, C. and Krage, M. (1996) 'Enhanced memory for faces of cheaters', *Ethology and Sociobiology* 17: 119–28.

Mitani, J. C. and Watts, D. (1997) 'The evolution of non-maternal caretaking among anthropoid primates: do helpers help?' *Behavioural Ecology and Sociobiology* 40: 213–20.

Moehlman, P. D. (1979) 'Jackal helpers and pup survival', *Nature* 277: 382–3.

Nishida, T. (1983) 'Alloparental behaviour in wild chimpanzees of the Mahale Mountains, Tanzania', *Folia Primatologica* 41: 1–33.

Noë, R. (1992) 'Alliance formation among male baboons: shopping for profitable partners', in Harcourt, A. H. and de Waal, F. B. M. (eds), *Coalitions and Alliances in Humans and Other Animals* (Oxford: Oxford University Press), pp. 285–321.

O'Farrell, M. J. and Studier, E. H. (1973) 'Reproduction, growth and development in *Myotis thysanodes* and *M. lucifugus* (Chiroptera: Vespertilionidae)', *Ecology* 54: 23–30.

Owens, D. D. and Owens, M. J. (1979) 'Communal denning and clan associations in brown hyenas (*Hyaena brunnea*, Thunberg) of the central Kalahari Desert', *African Journal of Ecology* 17: 35–44.

Owens, D. D. and Owens, M. J. (1984) 'Helping behaviour in brown hyenas', *Nature* 308: 843–5.

Packer, C. (1977) 'Reciprocal altruism in *Papio anubis*', *Nature* 265: 441–3.

Parish, A. R. (1994) 'Sex and food control in the uncommon chimpanzee – how bonobo females overcome a phylogenetic legacy of male dominance', *Ethology and Sociobiology* 15: 157–79.

Paul, A., Kuester, J. and Arnemann, J. (1992) 'DNA fingerprinting reveals that infant care by male barbary macaques (*Macaca sylvanus*) is not paternal investment', *Folia Primatologica* 58: 93–8.

Poirier, F. E. (1968) 'The Nilgiri langur (*Presbytis johnii*) mother–infant dyad', *Primates* 9: 45–68.

Power, C. and Aiello, L. C. (1997) 'Female proto-symbolic strategies', in Hager, L. D. (ed.), *Women in Human Origins* (London: Routledge), pp. 153–71.

Power, C., Arthur, C. and Aiello, L. C. (1997) 'On seasonal reproductive synchrony as an evolutionarily stable strategy in human evolution', *Current Anthropology* 38: 88–91.

Povinelli, D. J. (1993) 'Reconstructing the evolution of mind', *American Psychologist* 5: 492–509.

Premack, D. and Woodruff, G. (1978) 'Does the chimpanzee have a theory of mind?' *Behavioural and Brain Sciences* 1: 1–26.

Riedman, M. L. (1982) 'The evolution of alloparental care and adoption in mammals and birds', *Quarterly Review of Biology* 57: 405–35.

Rosenblum, L. A. (1971) 'Infant attachment in monkeys', in Shaffer, R. (ed.), *The Origins of Human Social Relations* (New York: Academic Press), pp. 85–109.

Rowell, T. E. (1963) 'The social development of some rhesus monkeys' (1961 seminar), in Foss, B. M. (ed.), *Determinants of Infant Behaviour Vol. II* (London: Methuen), pp. 35–49.

van Schaik, C. P. (1983) 'Why are diurnal primates living in groups?' *Behaviour* 87: 120–44.

van Schaik, C. P. (1989) 'The ecology of social relationships amongst female primates', in Standen, V. and Foley, R. A. (eds), *Comparative Socioecology: The Behavioural Ecology of Humans and Other Mammals* (Oxford: Blackwell), pp. 195–218.

Schaller, G. B. (1972) *The Serengeti Lion: A Study of Predator–Prey Relations* (Chicago: University of Chicago Press).

Schaub, H. (1996) 'Testing kin altruism in long-tailed macaques (*Macaca fascicularis*) in a food-sharing experiment', *International Journal of Primatology* 17: 445–67.

Seyfarth, R. M. and Cheney, F. L. (1984) 'Grooming alliances and reciprocal altruism in vervet monkeys', *Nature* 308: 541–3.

Smuts, B. B. (1985) *Sex and Friendship in Baboons* (New York: Aldine).

Smuts, B. B. (1997) 'Social relationships and life histories of primates', in Morbeck, M. E., Galloway, A. and Zihlman, A. L. (eds), *The Evolving Female* (Princeton, NJ: Princeton University Press), pp. 60–8.

Stanford, C. B. (1992) 'Costs and benefits of allomothering in wild capped langurs (*Presbytis pileata*)', *Behavioural Ecology and Sociobiology* 30: 29–34.

Stern, K. and McClintock, M. K. (1998) 'Regulation of ovulation by human pheromones', *Nature* 392: 177–9.

Taub, D. M. (1980) 'Testing the "agonistic buffering" hypothesis I. Dynamics of participation in the triadic interaction', *Behavioural Ecology and Sociobiology* 6: 187–97.

Thieme, H. (1997) 'Lower palaeolithic hunting spears from Germany', *Nature* 385: 807–10.

Thiollay, J. (1991) 'Foraging, home range use and social behaviour of a group-living rainforest raptor, the red-throated Caracara *Daptrius americanus*', *IBIS* 133: 382–93.

Trivers, R. L. (1971) 'The evolution of reciprocal altruism', *Quarterly Review of Biology* 46: 35–57.

de Waal, F. B. M. (1982) *Chimpanzee Politics* (London: Allen & Unwin).

de Waal, F. B. M. (1984) 'Sex differences in the formation of coalitions among chimpanzees', *Ethology and Sociobiology* 5: 239–55.

de Waal, F. B. M. (1987) 'Tension regulation and nonreproductive functions of sex among captive bonobos', *National Geographic Research* 3: 318–35.

de Waal, F. B. M. (1992) 'Coalitions as part of reciprocal relations in the Arnhem chimpanzee colony', in Harcourt, A. H. and de Waal, F. B. M. (eds), *Coalitions and Alliances in Humans and Other Animals* (Oxford: Oxford University Press), pp. 233–57.

de Waal, F. B. M. and Luttrell, L. M. (1988) 'Mechanisms of social reciprocity in three primate species: symmetrical relationship characteristics or cognition?' *Ethology and Sociobiology* 9: 101–18.

Werren, J. H., Gross, M. R. and Shine, R. (1980) 'Paternity and the evolution of male parental care', *Journal of Theoretical Biology* 82: 619–31.

Wheeler, P. (1994) 'The thermoregulatory advantages of heat storage and shade-seeking behaviour to hominids foraging in equatorial savannah environments', *Journal of Human Evolution* 26: 339–50.

Whittingham, L. A. and Lifjeld, J. T. (1995) 'Extra-pair fertilizations increase the opportunity for sexual selection in the monogamous House Martin *Delichon urbica*', *Journal of Avian Biology* 26: 283–8.

Wilson, D. S. (1998) 'Hunting, sharing and multi-level selection: the tolerated-theft model revisited', *Current Anthropology* 39: 73–98.

Wrangham, R. W. (1987) 'Evolution of social structure', in Smuts, B. et al. (eds), *Primate Societies* (Chicago: University of Chicago Press), pp. 282–96.

Wright, P. C. (1984) 'Biparental care in *Aotus trivirgatus* and *Callicebus moloch*', in Small, M. (ed.), *Female Primates: Studies by Women Primatologists* (New York: Alan R. Liss), pp. 59–75.

Wright, P. C. (1990) 'Patterns of paternal care in primates', *International Journal of Primatology* 11: 89–101.

CHAPTER 3

SYMBOLISM AS REFERENCE AND SYMBOLISM AS CULTURE

PHILIP G. CHASE

INTRODUCTION

It has been argued that the transition from Middle to Upper Palaeolithic, particularly in Europe, was characterized by the first solid archaeological evidence for the use of symbols (e.g. Byers 1994; Chase and Dibble 1987, 1992; Davidson and Noble 1989; Mellars 1973, 1991, 1996: 369–83; Stringer and Gamble 1993: 203–7; White 1982). This view has been challenged by a number of authors (e.g. Bednarik 1992, 1995; Duff et al. 1992; Holloway 1969; Knight et al. 1995; Lindly and Clark 1990; Marshack 1976, 1988, 1990; Schepartz 1993). The question is important because of what it says about the evolution of human culture, communication and information processing, and the debate has been lively and sometimes acrimonious. It has for the most part hinged either on the interpretation of specific objects (or configurations of objects) as either symbolic or else utilitarian or natural, or else on the role of taphonomy in concealing early evidence for symbolism. In other words, the debate has concentrated primarily on the archaeological record itself.

In this chapter, I would like to step back from the particulars of the archaeological record and take a fresh look at just what symbolism is and what it means, both for human adaptation and for our interpretation of the archaeological record. It appears to me that as it exists today (i.e. among living and historically known peoples), symbolism really consists of two different phenomena. The first of these is symbolic reference, the use in language and elsewhere of arbitrary (i.e. conventional) signs to refer to things or concepts. The second, which I will call 'symbolic culture', is the extension of symbolism beyond reference to the creation of an intellectual environment populated by phenomena that owe their very existence to symbolism and where every thing and every action has significance in an all-encompassing symbol system. These two phenomena are inextricably linked today, but that does not mean we can assume that they appeared simultaneously in the course of human evolution.

I will therefore do three things in the pages that follow. I will first define what I mean when I refer to symbolism as two phenomena; I will describe what I see as the adaptive advantages of the phenomenon I call symbolic culture; and I will discuss the possible role of genetic evolution in the appearance of symbolic culture. My purpose here is not to argue that those on one side of the current debate are right and those on the other side are wrong, but rather to help clarify exactly what the debate is about.

TWO KINDS OF SYMBOLISM

SYMBOLIC REFERENCE

I will begin with Peirce's (1932/1960) definition of symbolism as reference by arbitrary convention. In his terminology, a symbol is one kind of sign – that is, something (a gesture, sound, object, image, etc.) that refers to something else. Some signs point to their referents by association, as smoke indicates fire. Others point to their referents by resemblance, as certain paintings at Lascaux resemble horses or a pantomime may resemble the behaviour of a fleeing man. Symbols, however, refer to things by arbitrary convention. The red, green and yellow of a traffic light, the badge of a policeman, and the sounds of the word 'table' are all symbols because their meaning is essentially arbitrary.

Symbolism, defined this way, is of great importance to human behaviour because it lies at the heart of language. Language consists of more than just symbolic reference, but such reference is fundamental to it. This is true of semantics, where words or morphemes consist of sequences of sounds that have nothing to do with their referents except by arbitrary convention. Symbolic reference also lies at the heart of syntax. Syntax, in Peirce's terminology, consists of the relationships between signs rather than between signs and referents. However, in language, the syntactic links among symbols are used to refer to similar links in the mind of the speaker between the referents of those symbols. Thus syntax, like semantics, is referential in the sense that arbitrary, conventional forms of signs or arbitrary, conventional relationships among signs are used to express relationships among their referents.

Because symbolic reference makes possible much more efficient and complex communication than is possible in its absence, that function alone could explain its evolution. This means that we must at least consider the possibility that during the Palaeolithic there was a time when symbolic reference, both in semantics and syntax, played an important part in hominid adaptation, but when symbolism did not fulfil some of the other functions it plays in our lives today.

SYMBOLIC CULTURE

Among living and historically known humans, symbolism goes far beyond reference, a point made quite clearly by Byers (1994). As a purely referential phenomenon, symbols merely stand for things that would exist anyhow in the absence of symbolism. These referents may be natural objects or phenomena. They may be emotions or sensations. They may also be concepts or ideas, but in this case they are the kinds of concepts or ideas that would exist without symbolism. For example, referential symbols might permit a mother to explain to her child that a termite-fishing stick should be straight and not crooked if it is to be efficient. However, this is merely a matter of communicating something that a chimpanzee mother knows without symbolism.

We humans, however, construct an amazing repertoire of 'things' that have no existence outside a symbolic context, things that depend on symbolism for their very existence. The game of chess, for example, is a set of definitions and rules that have no reference to anything in the real world.[1] Chess has its origin in the context of symbolism and does not and cannot exist outside that context. Moreover, it is not itself essentially a referential symbol. It may be used as one, but only after the fact. It was not invented in order to refer to something else. Such symbolic 'things' pervade the entire environment in which we live our lives. They come in an almost infinite variety: beings (deities, ghosts), social roles (presidents, bridesmaids), objects (sceptres, stop signs), concepts (sin, authority), acts (baptizing, promising), values (virtuous, chic) and so forth.

Moreover, such symbolic phenomena do not exist in isolation from one another, but are integrated into overarching systems of symbols. Different symbolic entities are related to one another in ways defined within the symbolic realm. Thus, for example, food taboos may be related to totemic concepts linked to culturally defined social structures, and may be backed up by mythical explanations and reinforced by rituals. This is not to say that all such symbol systems are necessarily either internally consistent or inherently stable. Especially in times of social stress and culture change, the contrary may be true. Nevertheless, changes in one part of the symbol system will have repercussions elsewhere in the system.

Moreover, symbolic culture is all-encompassing. As Byers points out, almost nothing we do can be separated from its place in the symbol system, because that system now provides rules for defining what is or is not appropriate, or for what symbolic meaning any act or artifact has beyond its purely practical purpose. A garment may be made to keep one warm, but the details of its appearance also provides symbolic (i.e.

---

1. This is so in spite of chess terminology – in the real world, castles cannot move about and 'capture' bishops.

arbitrarily coded) information about the wearer. Thus any action, large or small, is now judged not only in terms of its practical consequences, but also in terms of its meaning and value within the larger symbol system.

This situation, where not only are symbols in common use, but where symbolism goes beyond reference and where all actions and all things are caught up in a web of symbolic meanings, is what I refer to when I use the term 'symbolic culture'.

WHY SYMBOLIC CULTURE?

If symbolic culture is an integral part of the modern human way of life, its evolution begs explanation. Learning one's culture is a burdensome affair, and it is not immediately apparent either how it helps individuals or groups to solve concrete practical problems or why it is needed for social interaction. After all, other species get along perfectly well socially without it. It might seem that symbolic culture is merely an accidental epiphenomenon of language, symbolism run wild.

However, there is one thing that extant humans can do that other primate species cannot do. We organize very large social systems, networks of interaction that require cooperation between individuals who may never have seen one another before and who may expect never to see one another again. It is not at all clear that humans could do this without symbolic culture. It will be worthwhile, therefore, to investigate how such large social systems can be formed and if in fact it is symbolic culture that makes them possible.

SOURCES OF COOPERATION

Cooperation that involves no sacrifice is easy to understand. Wolves may find it easier to run down and kill a moose if they work together rather than individually. If we assume that a moose carcass provides plenty of meat for all, it is understandable why they would hunt together. However, such cases represent a minority of the cooperation among humans. The real problem is explaining altruism, action (or perhaps inaction) by one individual that, in the short run, will benefit another but will result in a less than optimal return for the actor. Why does a chimpanzee who succeeds in killing a monkey share its meat with other chimpanzees when he could instead eat the whole monkey himself? In evolutionary terms, this would seem to be counterproductive, since it would seem to decrease his survival and reproductive potential. However, two explanations for such altruism have been proposed.

COOPERATION IN SMALL GROUPS

First, evolution involves the survival and reproduction not of individuals but of genes. Therefore, if our chimpanzee gives meat to a close relative with whom he shares a large proportion of his genotype, he is in fact contributing to the survival of his own genes (Dawkins 1976; Hamilton 1964), even if they are being carried in another body. Whether the positive effects of this contribution outweigh the negative effects of his own deprivation will depend on a number of circumstances, circumstances that can be modelled mathematically and tested empirically. Nevertheless, the principle remains, that it is possible to explain the evolution of altruism toward kin by invoking the fact that close relatives share a large fraction of their genotypes.

However, it is clear from the ethological literature that cooperation based on altruism extends beyond the individual's close kin (Cheney and Seyfarth 1990: 67–71; Packer 1977; de Waal 1989; Walters and Seyfarth 1987). This cooperation often involves a certain sacrifice or risk-taking on the part of the one individual, without any immediate return. Nevertheless, even cooperation with non-kin can be explained. It makes sense for an individual to make a certain sacrifice for another if in the long run the other will reciprocate. Even if, in the short run, one's cooperative actions produce a less than optimal return, altruism that is reciprocated may in the long run yield better returns than selfish orientation toward short-term goals. That cooperation can evolve in this way has been shown theoretically, empirically and in computer gaming (Axelrod 1984; Trivers 1971). However, it can do so only when cheating can be eliminated, that is, when those who put short-term benefits ahead of cooperation are punished by being deprived of the cooperation of others. Normally, this can occur only when all individuals in a relationship expect to interact fairly frequently in the future. When this is not the case, then cheating is always the most productive strategy for an individual.

COOPERATION IN LARGE SOCIAL NETWORKS

The problem, then, is not explaining cooperation itself, but rather how cooperation can be extended beyond close kin and beyond those with whom one interacts frequently. This is actually something that no primates other than humans do, yet it is commonplace among living and historically known peoples. The trouble is that as group size increases, or as the mobility of individuals increases, the number of individuals with whom one interacts also increases, and the probability that one will have few or no future interactions with some of them increases. In such a situation, the best evolutionary strategy is to cheat on strangers or semi-strangers. In fact, it can be shown, theoretically at least, that as either the size of a group or the mobility of its members increases, it becomes increasingly difficult, indeed impossible, to account for cooperation (Boyd and Richerson 1988, 1989; Enquist and Leimar 1993). The fact that only humans seem to have developed cooperation under such circumstances lends empirical support to these theoretical findings, implying that something special is happening among humans.

Let us imagine a situation where resources, although plentiful in absolute terms, are unevenly and unpredictably distributed over a very large area. This is likely to be the case, for example, in tundra or steppes where the main resource is mobile herds of large ungulates. Whallon (1989) sees the late Pleistocene colonization of Siberia and Australia as evidence of an ability to adapt to such environments, and these are essentially the circumstances that Gamble (1982) invoked to explain the origins of art. As Whallon points out, in such a situation, a limited territory will not provide enough resources for survival on a reliable basis. The only alternative is to have a very large territory. However, if a large territory is to be monitored, then it will have to be inhabited by a large but dispersed population, whose members are highly mobile, moving as individuals or small subgroups that come together and split up frequently. These are exactly the circumstances – large population and high mobility – that most encourage cheating and most discourage cooperation. Yet as Whallon (1989) has pointed out, only by sharing territory, resources and information about resources can a population efficiently exploit resources under such circumstances, and this requires a means of ensuring that all members of a population, not just the first to find them, will be given access to resources.

Thus, the problem of explaining cooperation beyond a limited scope is not one of determining how such cooperation could be advantageous for a *group*. Rather, the problem lies in understanding how an *individual* can be motivated to make sacrifices when such sacrifices cannot be counted on to be reciprocated.

SYMBOLIC CULTURE AND COOPERATION

What is needed to extend cooperation to complete or relative strangers is some factor that can provide the individual with rewards and punishments that the natural circumstances themselves cannot provide. No well adapted animal will find in its natural physical and social environment any reason to make sacrifices for a stranger. This means that if an individual can be motivated to behave in such an unnatural way, he or she must be acting in the context of an unnatural environment. Symbolic culture provides just such an environment.

By 'stranger' I mean anyone an individual does not know personally or with whom interactions are rare – too infrequent for the benefits of reciprocity to outweigh those of cheating. This means that strangers may include individuals who are culturally recognized as kinsmen. In fact, cooperation with strangers is usually made possible by incorporating them into culturally defined categories with whom cooperation is mandated culturally, or as Whallon (1989: 438) put it, '... individuals are identified not as unique persons but in terms of symbolic categories, among which mutual rights and obligations are defined by the system, whatever the history of actual interpersonal encounters among the members of the group sharing that system.' Among hunter-gatherers, this very often takes the form of extending kinship ties artificially, well beyond the limits of kin selection.

There are four aspects of symbolic culture that enable it to provide an environment in which cooperation with strangers is not only possible but potentially even required of the individual.

1. SYMBOLIC CULTURE PROVIDES CULTURAL IMPERATIVES FOR COOPERATION

As Lieberman (1991: 196–9) has noted, altruism beyond the ordinary primate level is usually enjoined by moral imperatives, often in a religious context. Cultural imperatives (whether or not one wishes to call them 'moral') are one of those classes of 'things' that make up symbolic culture, things that can only be created in the context of symbolism and that belong entirely to the symbolic realm. Genetic imperatives requiring co-operation with strangers cannot survive natural selection. All such impera-tives must therefore be constructed culturally rather than genetically and depend on symbolism for their existence.

2. SYMBOLIC CULTURE JUSTIFIES CULTURAL IMPERATIVES FOR COOPERATION

This symbolic web includes the rules, definitions and the like that explain *what* one is expected to do. However, it usually also involves a set of symbolic concepts, usually embedded in mythology, that explain *why* one must do what is expected. That is to say, cultural imperatives, especially the most important ones, are not seen by members of the culture as merely arbitrary rules. Rather, they are embedded in a world-view that justifies their existence and that adds weight to concepts such as good and evil, or required and forbidden, and all of these will be parts of a world-view, usually defined in terms of mythology, that explains and justifies their existence and that reinforces their demands.

A good illustration of this point comes from the Murngin of Australia, who were described by Warner (1937/1958) when they were living by hunting and gathering in an environment marked by extreme seasonal fluctuations in rainfall. These seasonal changes were stressful but essential to the Murngin adaptation. The Murngin world-view incorporated the seasons, the entire natural environment and the social structure in a system of principles, institutions such as the moiety and clan, obligations and prohibitions expressed in mythology and supported by ritual. In fact, ritual was believed necessary to the proper operation of the natural as well as the social world:

> That which organizes the two categories (the seasonal reproductive cycle of nature and the male-cleanliness female-impurity dichotomy of society) into one is the totemic symbol which can be manipulated by ritual and gives man an effective control over nature and an effective negative sanction over members of his society. The rituals must be properly conducted yearly to keep the group and its individuals ritually clean; and in these rituals the manipulation of the sacred totem insures the proper function of the seasons, a sufficient production of food, and a continuation of the natural surroundings proper for man. Thus that which is beyond man's technology or beyond his real powers of control becomes capable of manipulation because its symbols can be controlled and manipulated by the extraordinary powers of man's rituals. At the same time the identification, in the totemic concept, of the male and female principles with the seasonal cycles gives the adult men's group the necessary power to enforce its sanctions; the providing world of nature will not function if the rules of society are flouted and man's uncleanliness contaminates nature. Hence everyone must obey. If he does not by his own volition, then he must be forced to ...
>
> Warner 1937/1958: 396

3. SYMBOLIC CULTURE PROVIDES FOR SOCIAL ENFORCEMENT OF COOPERATION

As the above quote illustrates, this same symbolic context also provides society with a justification for enforcing culturally dictated behaviour by its members. Without symbolic culture, one individual has no motivation and no reason to interfere with the behaviour of another unless it threatens his own self-interest, either directly or indirectly by threatening the interests of a relative or personal ally. In the context of symbolic culture, however, as we have just seen in the Murngin example, not only are there rules that must be obeyed for purely cultural reasons, but there are rules that must be enforced as well. A Murngin need not injure another person's welfare in any concrete manner in order to be punished by society. Because any violation of the symbolic rules of conduct threaten the well-being of society (as seen through the filter of Murngin symbolic culture), such violations must be sanctioned.

4. SYMBOLIC CULTURE PROVIDES EMOTIONAL REINFORCEMENT OF COOPERATION

Finally, symbolism provides the means for emotionally reinforcing culture's demands. It takes a great deal to make people sacrifice their own selfish good for an abstract concept, as is clear to anyone who observes the real behaviour of people today compared to cultural ideals. But culture constantly provides strong emotional reinforcement for its demands and for its world-view through myth and ritual. The result is that people living in the context of symbolic culture are emotionally involved in it, and that when they ignore its demands they are likely to suffer negative emotions that have no source in their genetically programmed attachment to another individual. Stefánsson (1913/1962: 272) describes an example that is so common as to be thoroughly hackneyed: an Eskimo hunter who, having failed to notify his fellow hunters when he killed a bearded seal and having kept all the meat for himself, felt bitter remorse and blamed on his selfishness the blindness that later befell him. By the same token, adherence to cultural norms brings positive emotional rewards.

A NEW ENVIRONMENT FOR ACTION

These four aspects of symbolic culture, taken together and viewed in an evolutionary perspective, constitute a revolutionary adaptation. They create a whole new context in which all action must be planned, executed and evaluated. No longer is behaviour to be judged only by the concrete results it produces. Rather, its symbolic meanings and symbolic (cultural) results are equally important – and often more so. Action is motivated by culture; action is justified by culture; action is even defined by culture. When social relationships are built on face-to-face contacts, what you can do in a social relationship depends on your personal strength and personal alliances. It is only in the context of an extended symbol system that symbols justify action. Without it, an individual's right to act in a certain way is determined by what he can get away with; in the context of a symbol system, it is determined by the badges, uniforms, warrants and other symbols conferred by society ritually or in other symbolic acts (Byers 1994). A chimpanzee who steals another's fruit is simply obtaining food. In human society, however, a repossessor who, armed with the proper documents, takes another person's automobile is acting justifiably, while a citizen without such documents would be open to both censure and prosecution for theft.

This means that one's rewards and punishments are largely defined in terms of symbolic culture. This may be very direct. The young Victorian woman who refrained from premarital sex usually did so out of a simultaneous fear of damnation and hope for salvation, even though marriage, damnation and salvation are all culturally defined concepts and even though the natural world provides no punishment (especially in evolutionary terms) for such behaviour. Moreover, because one's peers now have reason to approve or disapprove of what one does, even when it does not concern their own immediate interests, one is rewarded or punished by one's peers for things that no other species would reward or punish. This means that even when one does not share all or part of society's symbolic beliefs, one is subject to punishment for purely cultural transgressions that do no one else any concrete harm. Even if the wayward daughter in a Victorian melodrama were an atheist, she would still have risked being driven from her parents' home in a blizzard with her illegitimate baby in her arms.

Thus symbolic culture provides just the 'unnatural' environment needed to enforce cooperation beyond the scope of one's kin and acquaintances: an intellectual and emotional context in which the rewards and punishments for one's actions stem not just from their practical and 'natural' social consequences but from their consequences in terms of an overarching, all-encompassing system of symbolic meanings, values and the like.

ARE GENETICS INVOLVED?

This is actually two separate questions.

1. Can genetic evolution alone produce an equivalent situation, in which one is rewarded for cooperation or punished for failure to cooperate with relative strangers?
2. Was the appearance of symbolic culture due to an underlying genetic change?

Probably neither question can be answered with any certainty given the current state of our knowledge. However, I suspect, tentatively, that the answer to both is negative.

PUNISHMENT AND COOPERATION
WITH STRANGERS

Boyd and Richerson (1992) have argued that in theory any behaviour, including cooperation with strangers, can evolve if it does so in conjunction with a propensity to punish cheaters. According to their mathematical model, the circumstances are fairly complex. The punishment must be real retribution, not just the withholding of cooperation. Nor can the targets of punishment by one individual be limited to those who have failed to cooperate with just that individual. There must, from the beginning, be individuals who not only punish non-cooperators but also punish those who fail to punish non-cooperators.

As we have seen above, symbolic culture provides exactly this, a motivation to punish those who do not live up to cultural norms. However,

Boyd and Richerson's work indicates that such a propensity might, at least theoretically, evolve genetically as well. That is, the motivation for punishing both non-cooperators and those who failed to punish non-cooperators might arise not from a cultural dictate but from a genetic mutation. Thus in theory, the formation of large social networks might be a product of genetic evolution.

However, our species appears to be the only one that forms large social networks based on cooperation with strangers or partial strangers. Many species, for example bees and ants, form very large colonies based on altruism and cooperation, but in these all the members are closely related genetically (Boyd and Richerson 1989: 213–14). Other species may form large schools, herds or flocks, but these do not constitute networks based on altruistic cooperation. Humans, of course, do form such networks, but in the context of symbolic culture. Thus, while it can perhaps not be proven that the origins of extended altruism among humans did not involve a mutation or mutations for such cooperation combined with a mutation or mutations for punishing failure to cooperate *and* for punishing failure to punish non-cooperators, the evidence taken at face value would probably indicate that the enabling factor was the development of symbolic culture.

There is a second possibility to consider. Lieberman, as I mentioned above, indicated that cooperation beyond the scope explainable by reciprocal altruism usually involves moral imperatives of the kind provided by symbolic culture, moral imperatives made possible by human linguistic and cognitive abilities. However, he also seems to invoke another genetic character, albeit in a supporting role: 'In my view, this "higher" human altruism evolved from human cognitive and linguistic ability *acting on a preadaptive "emotional" base*' (Lieberman 1991: 166, emphasis added). In other words, it may be that symbolic culture builds on a tendency to sympathy, a tendency that evolved in the context of altruism toward one's kin. There are, however, two problems with invoking it as a basis for human cooperation with strangers. First there is the theoretical problem discussed above, that any genetic propensity for altruism toward strangers or partial strangers is evolutionarily maladaptive, not adaptive, when the likelihood of reciprocity is low. Symbolic culture, however, by enforcing norms of altruistic behaviour can both help overcome any natural tendency not to act altruistically and, for the same reason, give some expectation of reciprocity. Second, there is the fact that while culture may demand sympathy and altruism toward relative strangers, it just as often demands brutality, or at least callousness toward others. One may be punished for not assisting a stranger. One may just as easily be punished for giving aid and comfort to society's enemies – even those, such as heretics, who are defined in entirely symbolic terms and even when those enemies of society may be one's own kin or close associates.

It would seem, then, that the construction of large social networks based on extended cooperation is based not on any genetically coded tendency to cooperate with strangers, but rather on symbolic culture, which provides the motivation for such cooperation. However, this leaves the question of whether or not the appearance of symbolic culture reflects some other evolutionary change in the human gene pool.

SYMBOLIC CULTURE

Lieberman (1991: 166) points out that 'human language and cognition are necessary conditions for moral sense', which is entirely correct if we take 'moral sense' to mean an attitude stemming from symbolic culture. However, there are two further questions to consider. First, could symbolic reference in semantics and syntax have evolved before symbolic culture, or must the two have evolved in tandem? In other words, is symbolic culture a necessary and simultaneous by-product of symbolic reference? If the answer is yes, then those genetic changes that produced human language must also be directly responsible for the evolution of symbolic culture. If the answer to this first question is no, then the second question arises. Given the existence of symbolic communication as an integral part of human adaptation at some point in the Palaeolithic, was any further genetic change necessary in order to produce symbolic culture? Could this way of life have been 'invented' independently of genetic evolution, at different times in different parts of the world in response to local conditions, and have then diffused from several centres, much as plant cultivation and animal husbandry were 'invented' independently in different parts of the world (and independently of any genetic change in the human cognitive capacity)?

The answer to either of these questions is beyond the scope of archaeology alone to answer. I will not attempt to do so here. I will, however, argue that it would be highly detrimental to the cause of investigating such questions if one were simply to *assume* that symbolic reference and symbolic culture must have evolved or appeared together in the Pleistocene, just because they are closely associated today. Until a case is made (on solid psychological or neurological grounds) that the one produces the other by inevitable causation, it is better to assume that they *could* have arisen one after the other, because at least then one will be led to investigate the question.

CONCLUSION

Symbolism is a crucial part of the human way of life. For this reason, archaeologists have been arguing for a long time about what the archaeological record tells us about the origins of symbolism. We have not, however, fully addressed the question of what symbolism really is or the possible alternative trajectories its evolution could have taken. Because we have not paid enough attention to what it is, we have not really been in a position to decide what the archaeological correlates of symbolism really are. In attempting to address this problem, I have made four different suggestions.

First, I have argued that symbolism is not a simple unitary phenomenon, but that at least in theory one can separate purely referential symbolism from the more complex phenomenon I have called symbolic culture. It may be that from a psychological or neurological perspective, this distinction may turn out to be untenable, but I believe that given the present state of our knowledge we are not justified in assuming that the two phenomena had to evolve simultaneously.

Second, I have presented a hypothesis that would explain the appearance of symbolic culture. This hypothesis is open to testing, but whatever the outcome, such testing does not affect the first argument, that symbolic reference and symbolic culture are not necessarily one and the same thing.

Third, arguing on the basis of the above hypothesis, I have suggested, albeit tentatively, that the appearance of symbolic culture as an adaptation probably had more to do with local environmental and historical factors than with any genetic change (beyond those earlier changes that made symbolic reference possible). Again, the validity of this argument remains open to testing, but its resolution need have no bearing on either of the first two points.

The separation of symbolism into referential symbolism and symbolic culture has major implications in terms of our interpretation of the archaeological record. Let me briefly explain what I think these implications would be.

Let us assume that there were two ways of life in the Late Pleistocene. In the first, people were intelligent and were making full use of referential symbolism but symbolic culture was absent. In other words, in this one respect their way of life was like that of other primates, but in all other respects it was like our own. The second way of life included symbolic culture and therefore resembled that of ethnographically and historically known hunter-gatherers. What would be the archaeological correlates of each?

I strongly suspect that, in the absence of symbolic culture, a people would rarely, if ever, use their material culture to express symbolic meanings. Purely referential symbolic artifacts are very rare among hunter-gatherers. It is only with agriculture and writing that referential symbolism appears in a durable rather than ephemeral medium. The existence of symbolism would therefore be essentially invisible archaeologically.[2]

By contrast, in the context of symbolic culture, material objects automatically have symbolic meaning, and this is likely to be manifest in their appearance. Moreover, symbolic culture provides many motivations either for making material objects of purely symbolic function or of adding symbolic decoration to utilitarian objects. Rituals that explain and reinforce the imperatives of culture demand such objects. So too does the public advertisement by what Byers calls warrants of culturally defined status or culturally defined rights and duties.

In the first paragraph of this chapter I described the debate about the kinds of artifacts and other evidence that some authorities cite as evidence for symbolism and that others explain in other ways. While I have not here contributed to solving that debate, what I hope I have done is to raise the possibility that this debate is about the earliest evidence for symbolic culture, not about the earliest evidence for referential symbolism. Evidence for the origins of language as a purely referential phenomenon may be unobtainable from the archaeological record, in which case we will need to rely on other disciplines such as human palaeontology, linguistics, comparative neuroanatomy, etc.

One thing is certain. Archaeology alone cannot solve the problem of symbolism. We must work with fields such as psychology and neurology, because in large measure the phenomena we are wrestling with are psychological and neurological ones. However, symbols are social inventions and therefore cultural phenomena, so that the problem of symbolism must also be seen as an anthropological one. Any attempt to understand culture that excludes an anthropological perspective is bound to fail. Moreover, only archaeology and human palaeontology have evidence concerning what happened in prehistory, and any attempt to understand human evolution that excludes the evidence they have to offer will also fail. Thus we are still only at the starting point, but as long as the effort is truly multidisciplinary, we can hope to make progress.

2. There is one possible exception to this. There are those (notably Noble and Davidson 1996) who see symbolism both as a fundamentally important cognitive tool (for scenario-building, mental manipulation of possibilities, etc.) as well as a tool for social communication. If they are right, then the mental processes involved in making certain artifacts such as boats (Davidson and Noble 1992) may have involved symbolism, and evidence for such technical abilities would then also constitute evidence for referential symbolism. This is a question I will have to leave to the psychologists and neuroscientists.

ACKNOWLEDGEMENTS

I would like to thank Harold Dibble and Simon Holdaway for reading drafts of this article.

REFERENCES

Axelrod, R. (1984) *The Evolution of Cooperation*. (New York: Basic Books).

Bednarik, R. G. (1992) 'Palaeoart and archaeological myths', *Cambridge Archaeological Journal* 2: 27–57.

Bednarik, R. G. (1995) 'Concept-mediated marking in the Lower Palaeolithic', *Current Anthropology* 36: 605–34.

Boyd, R. and Richerson, P. J. (1988) 'The evolution of reciprocity in sizeable groups', *Journal of Theoretical Biology* 132: 337–56.

Boyd, R. and Richerson, P. J. (1989) 'The evolution of indirect reciprocity', *Social Networks* 11: 213–36.

Boyd, R. and Richerson, P. J. (1992) 'Punishment allows the evolution of co-operation (or anything else) in sizeable groups', *Ethology and Sociobiology* 13: 171–95.

Byers, M. (1994) 'Symboling and the Middle–Upper Paleolithic transition: a theoretical and methodological critique', *Current Anthropology* 35: 369–400.

Chase, P. G. and Dibble, H. L. (1987) 'Middle Paleolithic symbolism: a review of current evidence and interpretations', *Journal of Anthropological Archaeology* 6: 263–96.

Chase, P. G. and Dibble, H. L. (1992) 'Scientific archaeology and the origins of symbolism: a reply to Bednarik', *Cambridge Archaeological Journal* 2(1): 43–51.

Cheney, D. L. and Seyfarth, R. M. (1990) *How Monkeys See the World* (Chicago: University of Chicago Press).

Davidson, I. and Noble, W. (1989) 'The archaeology of perception. Traces of depiction and language', *Current Anthropology* 30: 125–55.

Davidson, I. and Noble, W. (1992) 'Why the first colonisation of the Australian region is the earliest evidence of modern human behaviour', *Archaeology in Oceania* 27: 135–42.

Dawkins, R. (1976) *The Selfish Gene* (New York: Oxford University Press).

Duff, A. I., Clark, G. A. and Chadderdon, T. J. (1992) 'Symbolism in the Early Paleolithic: a conceptual odyssey', *Cambridge Archaeological Journal* 2: 211–29.

Enquist, M. and Leimar, O. (1993) 'The evolution of cooperation in mobile organisms', *Animal Behaviour* 45: 747–57.

Gamble, C. (1982) 'Interaction and alliance in palaeolithic society', *Man* 17: 92–107.

Hamilton, W. D. (1964) 'The genetical evolution of social behavior I, II', *Journal of Theoretical Biology* 7: 1–52.

Holloway, R. L. (1969) 'Culture: a human domain', *Current Anthropology* 10: 395–412.

Knight, C., Power, C. and Watts, I. (1995) 'The human symbolic revolution: a Darwinian account', *Cambridge Archaeological Journal* 5(1): 1–27.

Lieberman, P. (1991) *Uniquely Human: The Evolution of Speech, Thought, and Selfless Behavior* (Cambridge, Mass.: Harvard University Press).

Lindly, J. and Clark, G. (1990) 'Symbolism and modern human origins', *Current Anthropology* 31: 233–61.

Marshack, A. (1976) 'Some implications of the Paleolithic symbolic evidence for the origins of language', *Current Anthropology* 17: 274–82.

Marshack, A. (1988) 'Neanderthals and the human capacity for symbolic thought: cognitive and problem-solving aspects of Mousterian symbol', in Otte, M. (ed.), *L'Homme de Néandertal, Vol. 5: La Pensée* (Liège: Université de Liège), pp. 57–92.

Marshack, A. (1990) 'Early hominid symbol and evolution of the human capacity', in Mellars, P. (ed.), *The Emergence of Modern Humans: An Archaeological Perspective* (Ithaca, NY: Cornell University Press), pp. 457–98.

Mellars, P. (1973) 'The character of the middle-upper palaeolithic transition in south-west France', in Renfrew, C. (ed.), *The Explanation of Culture Change* (London: Duckworth), pp. 255–76.

Mellars, P. (1991) 'Cognitive changes and the emergence of modern humans in Europe', *Cambridge Archaeological Journal* 1: 63–76.

Mellars, P. (1996) *The Neanderthal Legacy. An Archaeological Perspective from Western Europe* (Princeton, NJ: Princeton University Press).

Noble, W. and Davidson, I. (1996) *Human Evolution, Language and Mind: A Psychological and Archaeological Inquiry* (Cambridge: Cambridge University Press).

Packer, C. (1977) 'Reciprocal altruism in olive baboons', *Nature* 265: 441–3.

Peirce, C. S. (1932/1960) 'The icon, index, and symbol', in Hartshorne, C. and Weiss, P. (eds), *Collected Papers of Charles Sanders Pierce, Vol. II* (Cambridge, Mass.: Harvard University Press), pp. 156–73.

Schepartz, L. (1993) 'Language and modern human origins', *Yearbook of Physical Anthropology* 36: 91–126.

Stefánsson, V. (1913/1962) *My Life with the Eskimo* (New York: Collier Books).

Stringer, C. and Gamble, C. (1993) *In Search of the Neanderthals: Solving the Puzzle of Human Origins* (London: Thames & Hudson).

Trivers, R. L. (1971) 'The evolution of reciprocal altruism', *Quarterly Review of Biology* 46: 35–57.

de Waal, F. (1989) *Chimpanzee Politics: Power and Sex among Apes* (Baltimore, Md.: Johns Hopkins University Press).

Walters, J. R. and Seyfarth R. M. (1987) 'Conflict and cooperation', in Smuts, B., Cheney, D. L., Seyfarth, R. M., Wrangham, R. W. and Struhsaker, T. T. (eds), *Primate Societies* (Chicago: University of Chicago Press), pp. 306–17.

Warner, W. L. (1937/1958) *A Black Civilization: A Social Study of an Australian Tribe* (revised edn) (Chicago: Harper and Bros).

Whallon, R. (1989) 'Elements of cultural change in the later Palaeolithic' in Mellars, P. and Stringer, C. (eds), *The Human Revolution* (Edinburgh: Edinburgh University Press), pp. 433–54.

White, R. (1982) 'Rethinking the Middle-Upper Paleolithic transition', *Current Anthropology* 23(2): 169–92.

CHAPTER 4

MODERN HUNTER-GATHERERS AND EARLY SYMBOLIC CULTURE

ALAN BARNARD

Hunter-gatherers have evolved diverse understandings of the relationship between themselves and the worlds they live in. Sometimes these differ substantially from the understandings of people such as ourselves. In particular, hunter-gatherers often construct the category 'nature' differently than do people in other societies. They view their relation to the environment differently, and therefore they understand the relation between the environment and the cosmos differently. However, not all hunter-gatherers are in agreement, either as individuals or, more particularly, as exponents of their traditional, cultural understandings of such relations. In many ways, African and Australian hunter-gatherers have developed rather different views of the world.

In order to probe the origins of symbolic behaviour, it is useful to engage ourselves in some symbolic thought. We need to consider the potential relations between nature and culture, and between one human and another, as these may have been conceived by early man. We also need to consider the place of our ideas in the history of anthropological and archaeological thought. Our generation is not the first to speculate on the origins of language, culture or ritual. The data presented in this volume may be new, but many of the ideas are old. The debates which engaged our ancestors, both 100,000 years ago and 100 years ago, should engage us today.

In this chapter, I shall begin by considering the problem in its historical context, before considering the principal features of human foraging societies in general and the features of Australian and southern African foraging societies. Within the history of anthropological thought, different positions have emerged about whether the world-views of African or Australian hunter-gatherers present the best models for the reconstruction of early culture. Broadly, the Australianist view has dominated evolutionist thinking in social anthropology since the late nineteenth century (in so far as social anthropologists have been concerned with evolution at all). However, the earlier and most commonly cited alternative, the Africanist one, is now gaining ground as a result of new work in genetics and archaeology, and is the one I favour as the more likely. The decision must rest not merely on which might be geographically appropriate but on which has the greater propensity to define the necessary social and cosmological order while allowing flexibility for cultural adaptation. (Other possibilities, including Amazonian or Inuit world-views, have not been part of this debate and will not be dealt with here.)

SOCIETY, LANGUAGE, TOTEMISM AND EXOGAMY

The preoccupations of seventeenth- and eighteenth-century thinkers were, among other things, with matters relating society to the individual and language to society. Then, especially in the late nineteenth century, the narrower concerns of totemism and exogamy took over as major interests.

The seventeenth-century legal theorists Hugo Grotius and Samuel Pufendorf, among others, regarded society as the natural condition of humankind. In contrast, Thomas Hobbes and Jean-Jacques Rousseau, despite their differences on the goodness of human nature, regarded the individual as prior and solitude as natural (see, for example, Slotkin 1965: 143–74, 320–41). In the nineteenth century, Sir Henry Maine (1861) was, for the time being, to solve the problem through his argument that the family, and not a literal 'social contract', is the basis of society.

On language, there were debates as early as the seventeenth century on universal grammar versus a *tabula rasa*. There were debates about whether language originated in warning calls or in proper names. There were also debates on which came first, language or society. Rousseau (1966 [1791]), for example, held that they emerged simultaneously. Lord Monboddo (1773) argued that society had to come first; part of his proof was the existence of what he called the 'Orang Outang' – the speechless but supposedly gregarious 'Man' of South East Asia and central Africa (not the same species as the orang-utan we know today!). Those seventeenth- and eighteenth-century notions are important, as we shall see, because they have something to tell us about two other alternatives: evolution and revolution.

Meanwhile, through the late nineteenth century and well into the twentieth century, many of the great anthropological theorists have grappled with the origin of totemism, the origin of exogamy, and the relation between them (see, for example, Kuper 1988: 76–122). J. F. McLennan had a theory; W. Robertson Smith had a theory; E. B. Tylor, Edward Westermarck, Andrew Lang, Sigmund Freud, Émile Durkheim and others were all involved in heated debate. A. R. Radcliffe-Brown had two theories of totemism, and Sir James Frazer had at least three. Significantly, Alexander Goldenweiser and, following him, Claude Lévi-Strauss, argued that the monolithic concept of 'totemism' had no basis. Yet most theorists accepted its utility and most based their ideas of totemism primarily on the ethnography provided by Spencer and Gillen (1899, 1904) on the Arunta (Aranda) and other tribes of central and northern Australia.

Durkheim's theory (especially 1898) had interesting parallels with Knight's (1991, this volume) – Durkheim believed that primitive men were in awe of blood and refused to cohabit with females of their respective clans, since their totemic gods were thought to inhabit this clan blood. In contrast, Lang and Frazer emphasized the consubstantial relation between a man and his totem. Tylor saw totemism simply as a special case of ancestor worship. Yet whatever their considerable disagreements, almost all theorists saw a relation between totemism and exogamy, and most of them held that totemism had evolved first. And, by implication at least, almost all of them saw this as an answer to the problem of primal human society, because they believed that Australian Aboriginal culture represented a survival of early culture.

In a crude sense, virtually all of them, including Durkheim, saw some aspect of belief as prior to social institutions (totemism prior to exogamy). However, it is common to single out Durkheim (especially 1915 [1912]) as asserting, against Frazer in particular, that religious belief only exists in a social context. It is not an individual's relation to his or her totem which is important, but the relation between social groups represented by totemism, or, ultimately (according to both Radcliffe–Brown and Lévi-Strauss), the symbolic and mythological relations between the totemic species themselves.

I propose we reject the constellation of nineteenth-century ideas which necessarily drew together totemism, exogamy, the incest taboo and ritual, and keep an open mind about the general relation between society and cosmology. Frankly, I agree with Frazer (for example 1910: IV) that totems may well have once been edible species that had become forbidden; that where totemism and exogamy coexist, as among the Aranda, they can be quite separate; that totemism may have originated in many places independently; and that it may precede but nevertheless spur on the evolution of systems of food production. In the last instance, it is noteworthy that African totemism tends to be found in pastoralist societies, where it provides a separation of symbolic from productive activities. Of course, Frazer's notions are not any more verifiable than Durkheim's, but they should be falsifiable through counter-example.

Now consider a debate of our own time: that between Claude Lévi-Strauss and Robin Fox on the place of the incest taboo as the bridge between nature and culture (see Figure 4.1). According to Lévi-Strauss

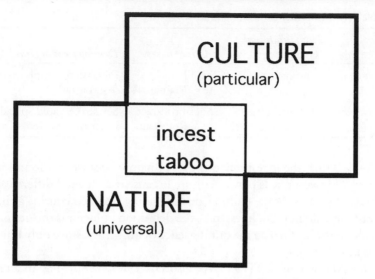

Claude Lévi-Strauss (1969 [1949])

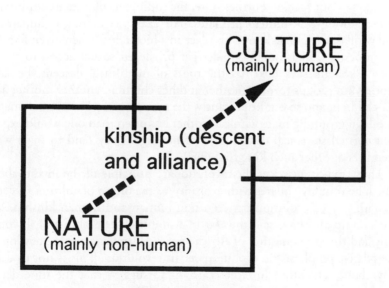

Robin Fox (1975)

Fig. 4.1 *Lévi-Strauss versus Fox.*

Table 4.1 *Evolution versus revolution*

	Human/animal 'kinship'	Basis of society	Development of ritual
Evolution	Continuity (e.g. Fox)	Family (e.g. Maine)	Increasing complexity (e.g. Frazer)
Revolution	Discontinuity (e.g. Lévi-Strauss)	Social contract (e.g. Rousseau)	Sex strike, rapid spread of totemism, etc. (e.g. Knight)

(1969 [1949]), the incest taboo is part of nature because it is found in all cultures. However, it is part of culture because it is defined differently by different cultures. Some cultures define mating between cousins as incestuous; some do not. So, in essence, the definition of incest is the definition of culture itself. It is also the quintessence of humanity, since only humans have incest taboos.

However, Robin Fox (1975; see also Fox 1983 [1980]) has an alternative view. Fox's division of culture from nature has an area of overlap, just like Lévi-Strauss's, but his area of overlap is but a blur. He takes the view that human kinship systems are partly cultural intrusions onto human nature, and partly expressions of human nature, that is, of the natural propensities of our species. Furthermore, the rudiments of human kinship are found among non-human primates. For example, among chimpanzees and gorillas, each male knows his place in a hierarchy. When given females are in oestrus, high-ranking males get privileged sexual access to them. Such a system, says Fox, has the roots of matrilineal descent. Female-centred kin groups form: a mother and her children, another mother and her children, and so on. Importantly, the members of a given, small matrilineal kin grouping mate with each other less often than one would expect in a normal statistical distribution of matings. They tend to mate with members of other such kin groupings.

Thus Lévi-Strauss sees the revolutionary principle of the incest taboo, which he roughly equates with exogamy, as the origin of culture. Fox sees a continuity of evolution between non-human and human kinship. We can sum up all I have said thus far in a simple chart (Table 4.1). I would only add that the question of Africa versus Australia is also a question of the relative emphasis on evolution versus revolution. This is not to deny a symbolic revolution in either case, or to suggest that the time depth would be any different. The fundamental difference between the two is that African hunter-gatherer society is based on flexible accommodation between society, nature and the universe, whereas Aboriginal Australian cosmology assumes an exact fit which is quite foreign to African notions of the relation between social and cosmological spheres. Essentially, to support an Africanist model implies a greater emphasis on evolution from higher primate society, whereas to support an Australianist model implies a greater emphasis on the human revolution.

SIMILARITIES BETWEEN HUNTING-AND-GATHERING SOCIETIES

The precise definitions and exact time depths of our genus and species have long been matters of hot debate. The timing and cause of the origin of culture are the subjects of related debates. Yet none deny that only relatively little of humankind's time on earth has been spent in any subsistence activities other than hunting, gathering and fishing. Let us take that as a baseline.

Living hunter-gatherers are largely confined to parts of the world which are inaccessible or unattractive to agricultural peoples. They are found in the deserts of Australia and southern Africa, in the frozen wastes of the Arctic, and in the jungles of central Africa and Southeast Asia. Hunting and gathering activities are successful adaptations to harsh environments, and the way in which living hunter-gatherers explain their relation to the environment can be extremely revealing.

Hunter-gatherers exhibit a variety of different forms of social structure. However, there are a number of attributes which are common to most hunter-gatherer societies and which serve to differentiate them both from most non-foraging human societies and from the social groupings of non-human higher primates. One may quibble over details, but in essence there are some ten central, differentiating attributes of human hunter-gatherer societies. These are as follows: (1) large territories for the size of population and notions of territorial exclusivity; (2) a nested social organization with the band as the primary unit and further units both within and beyond the band; (3) a lack of social stratification except as regards sex (or gender) and age; (4) sexual differentiation in activity and in rituals (which take specific forms, for example emphasizing hunting) to mark initiation into adult gender roles; (5) mechanisms for the redistribution of accumulated resources; (6) universal kinship, that is the recognition of kin beyond the band to the limits of human interaction; (7) structures which relate humans to animals or to animal species; (8) a world order based on even, as opposed to odd, numbers; (9) a world order founded on symbolic relations within and between levels; (10) flexibility. Let us look at each one in turn.

1. Each hunter-gatherer population occupies a relatively large, recognized territory. In other words, they have a very low population density compared to non-hunter-gatherers; hunting and gathering are not labour-intensive activities, but they are land-intensive.

Non-human primates may also have relatively low population densities and defend their territories, but human hunter-gatherers, in addition, have the capability of expressing, through verbal and often symbolic means, the boundaries between their group and some other, similar group.

2. A band level of social organization, with both larger and smaller units, is typical of human hunter-gatherers. They live in small groups of twenty or thirty people (for example, in the case of most African, South Asian and Australian peoples), or a maximum of a few hundred people (in the case of northern North American Indians and other temperate-climate populations). The larger groups often form only seasonally, and such 'composite' bands afterwards break down into smaller units to hunt in their own separate territories. Similarly, some smaller bands, such as those of the G/wi and the !Xō Bushmen, break down into family units to exploit resources separately within band territories. Likewise, all 'band societies' recognize units larger than the band, such as the macro-band or band cluster or the language group.

3. Hunter-gatherer societies generally exhibit a lack of social hierarchy except, sometimes, through age and sex. Where social stratification exists, it tends to be where hunting and gathering are accompanied by fishing as a major subsistence activity, especially where there are rich fishing grounds (for example, in Northwest Coast North America). Generally, hunter-gatherers have no class structure, and they give little formal recognition to leadership roles. Indeed, when compared both to non-human primates and to human non-foragers, there tends to be relative equality between the sexes, though with sexual differentiation in subsistence activities. Strict age and gender hierarchy are characteristic mainly of Australian Aboriginal societies. In this sense, they may indeed resemble non-foragers, as suggested by James Woodburn's (1980: 108–9) description of Aborigines as people who 'farm out' their women and therefore are not good examples of immediate-return economy.

4. Hunter-gatherers the world over do recognize a distinction between men and women in subsistence and in ritual. In subsistence, men hunt (or fish) and women do most of the gathering of wild plants, firewood and water. In ritual, there are separate initiation ceremonies for boys and for girls. Girls' initiation stresses sexuality over subsistence or non-sexual knowledge, and girls are generally initiated individually (at the time of their first menstrual period). Boys' initiation, on the other hand, tends to be collective (more than one boy being initiated at a time), often involves the teaching of hunting skills and the transmission of secret knowledge, and not infrequently the two

are linked. It can have a sexual aspect as well, but this is rarely its main purpose. Only in Australia is genital mutilation common.

5. Hunter-gatherers also have mechanisms to distribute the produce of their hunting and gathering activities, not only to the immediate family of the procurer, but also to his or her relatives and other members of the band (cf. Bird-David 1992). They do not accumulate a surplus. As they are nomadic, it is useless for them to accumulate more than they can carry. Also, accumulation incurs an obligation to give things away, so there is neither the incentive nor even any real possibility to accumulate wealth. What a person or group cannot use, they often share out immediately, through systems of rules which determine who gets what. Among various Kalahari Bushman groups, for example, a man gives his parents-in-law the best parts of the hind quarters of any large game animal he shoots. He gives other parts to other relatives, depending on kin relationship and on their participation in the hunt. Among several Bushman groups, non-consumable movable property, in turn, is distributed in an elaborate system of formalized exchange. Australian Aboriginal peoples also share the meat of the hunt, though in place of formalized gift-giving, gambling is common. There is however, far from a clear-cut distinction between Africa and Australia here, as East African foragers gamble and Aborigines do exchange their most valuable commodity – their relatives – in very elaborate networks indeed.

6. Hunting and gathering societies are usually based on a universal system of kinship classification (Barnard 1978). In other words, they classify all members of society as 'relatives', some being 'husbands' or 'wives' and others 'brothers' or 'sisters', some being 'parents' or 'children' (usually a relatively formal relationship) and others 'grandparents' or 'grandchildren' (often a more casual and indulgent relationship). Hunting and gathering societies have evolved various mechanisms for this beyond simple genealogical ties. Among the Ju/'hoansi (!Kung) and Nharo Bushmen, for example, people bear their grandparents' names, and namesakes are treated as 'grandrelatives'. A sister's namesake is treated as a 'sister', a brother's namesake as a 'brother', and so on. Among Australian Aborigines, the key mechanism through which classification takes place is the moiety, section or subsection system. Through universal kinship, the incest taboo is generated and maintained – a point I will return to.

7. There are also structures which relate humans to animals or to animal species. Especially in the Arctic, animals and humans are thought to be in communication. Elsewhere, such as in the Kalahari, animals possess essences which are released by the hunter upon killing. In some societies, universal kinship is carried through to domestic

animals; Australian Aborigines classify their dogs as 'sisters', 'wives' and so on. And, of course, there can be totemistic relations between an individual and a species and totemic relations between a group and a species.

8. On a horizontal plane, that is any given level of the world-view, symbolic order is generally present in the form of binary oppositions or sets of such oppositions forming an order defined through an even number of elements. There are cultures in which threes, fives, sevens, and nines are important (Needham 1979: 6–15). Odd-number-conscious societies tend to be stratified, agricultural ones, where odd numbers are used to express differences between groups: our group, the group above us, the group below us, and so on. Hunter-gatherer societies, in contrast, tend to be egalitarian, and most operate in some multiple of two. This can include such sociocentric divisions as genders and moieties, and it can also include egocentric categories such as alternate generations and the distinction between a woman's classificatory brothers and her potential husbands.

9. Hunter-gatherers recognize a world order which expresses comparable symbolic relations within and between levels. It is conventional for us to think of these levels as comparable to the environment, society and cosmology, though hunter-gatherers themselves do not necessarily see the world order in quite this way; I will come back to this point later. Within one hierarchical sphere or level, say that of heavenly bodies, there will be relations which mimic those of another, say the animal world or the human world. Gender differentiation exists at all these levels. Interestingly, in light of Knight's theory of the origin of culture, hunter-gatherers the world over consider the moon as male or masculine and the sun as female or feminine. Non-foragers have almost invariably reversed this relation, with the moon as female and the sun as male, though why this should be is a subject beyond the scope of the present paper (but see Power and Watts 1997).

10. All these attributes are combined with a degree of flexibility which is rare in non-foraging societies. This flexibility is manifest in band migrations from waterhole to waterhole and in seasonal aggregations and dispersals which occur according to the availability of resources. It is also apparent in the freedom of individuals to move from place to place and even to change band membership. Because of the flexibility in intra-group relations, modern hunter-gatherers are able to take advantage of scattered and often meagre resources which non-hunter-gatherers could not hope to utilize.

The flexibility discussed in the final point above has enabled modern hunter-gatherers to retain aspects of their cultures, even when living on the fringe of areas exploited by pastoral and agricultural peoples. Indeed some hunter-gatherers in both central and southern Africa have been able to move between a hunting-and-gathering lifestyle and a farming or herding lifestyle, depending on season and on the relative abundance of traditional resources from year to year. Some anthropologists would exclude such part-time foragers from the category 'hunter-gatherers', while others see this flexibility as an aspect of the *hunting-and-gathering*, or more broadly, the *foraging* lifestyle itself (see Barnard 1993).

Arguably, flexibility stretches even in some cases to the construction of a flexible or 'fluid' cosmological system. Bushmen, for example, develop their own, individualistic understandings of the world. Even the same individual can employ diverse and seemingly contradictory notions about deities and mythological figures in order to express different views of the world according to circumstances (Guenther 1979; Barnard 1988). Other hunter-gatherers, especially Australian Aborigines, have cosmologies which are more ordered. Yet even here, the ways in which categories are combined and recombined, in which symbolic associations are made between seemingly disparate objects within them (for example, people, animals or heavenly bodies), and in which individuals manipulate the rules of categorization, all betoken a flexibility too. Order and flexibility are not entirely opposites, and can at times be complementary.

Finally, the flexibility inherent in hunter-gatherer social organization, together with the very long time span that often separates even adjacent groups of hunter-gatherers, has generated a diversity within culture areas which is sometimes overlooked. The Kalahari Bushmen are not just one people, but indeed represent literally dozens of quite distinct ethnic groups who speak just as many languages and dialects. The Australian Aborigines are even more linguistically and culturally diverse. They speak languages of several different indigenous families (within one super-family), and the time depth which marks the divergence of Australian peoples – some 40,000 years – is far greater than that which separates the languages of the Indo-European language family, and certainly the cultures of the European nations.

DIFFERENCES BETWEEN ABORIGINES AND BUSHMEN

The similarities between Australian Aborigines and southern African Bushmen are not inconsiderable. Both populations live primarily in desert environments. Their foraging strategies, their seasonal aggregations and dispersals, and their group size and social interactions are similar. Yet they are very different in a number of respects. I would isolate six central differences, which are mainly ways in which the Aborigines differ from virtually all other modern hunter-gatherers: (1) their belief in the Rainbow Serpent and the Dreaming; (2) their spiritual relation to the land; (3) their spiritual relation to other species (through totemism); (4) their relation to each other through unilineal descent and strong clan ties; (5) a system of negative and positive marriage rules related to such ties and to divisions of society into moieties, semi-moieties, sections and subsections; (6) a parallel division of the universe into such categories. The existence of these features and, more importantly, the unity of cosmology with social forms they create imply if anything the reverse of what nineteenth-century writers thought. The Australian Aboriginal world-view is the most coherent, or perhaps more precisely the most *structurally evolved*, the world has yet seen (cf. von Brandenstein 1970; Turner 1993).

1. The belief in the Rainbow Serpent, and more particularly the Dreaming, provides a common mythological basis for society across Australia. It also provides Aborigines with a coherent explanation of the relations between time and place, land and society, humans and animals, and indeed the order of the universe. (Although Rainbow Serpent-type creatures feature too in African mythology and rock art, they do not carry this symbolic weight; and there is no African equivalent to the Dreaming.) As flexibility is the hallmark of foraging society in general, order is the hallmark of Aboriginal society in particular.

2. In terms of their *use of the land*, Australian groups are not unlike Bushmen. Desert groups on the two continents live in similar-size units (twenty-five or fifty people in a band, depending on resources). In each case there are groups who live outside desert areas, and rely on fishing and a variety of seasonal adjustments depending on flooding as well as rainfall. In each case also, there is a high degree of flexibility in living arrangements. Yet, while their use of the land is similar, their *relation to the land* is very different. Aborigines recognize a spiritual relation to the land which is vested particularly in sacred sites. Sometimes these are areas where spirits are said to be especially present, where they emerged from the ground in the Dreaming. Specific groups are associated with specific pieces of land and with sacred sites, of which they are custodians, and the relation between groups of men and their land and sacred sites is represented ritually through initiation ceremonies. It is also represented even through 'kinship' – among the Aranda, in the form of 'conception' clans which complement matrilineal and patrilineal clans (see, for example, Strehlow 1947: 86–96).

3. Spiritual relations to other species are represented through totemism. Totemism is found in many societies, and this was of course a reason why nineteenth-century writers dwelt on it. Yet in Australia, totemic relations are much more elaborated than elsewhere, whereas in Africa

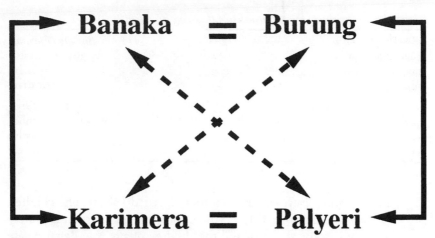

Fig. 4.2 *A representation of Kariera rules of marriage and descent.*

totemism is associated with non-foraging societies and not generally with hunter-gatherers. Late in his life, Frazer (1937: 406–8) expressed his delight at the 'discovery' of totemism among Bushmen in the eastern Kalahari, but he apparently did not realize that these Hiechware Bushmen had probably borrowed the custom from their Bantu-speaking neighbours.

4. Australian Aborigines have rights and obligations through their totemic clans, rights and obligations over clans to which they are related (such as in bestowal and in funeral and reburial rituals), and relations between groups ordered through rigid systems which define each person's place in the social order. There is flexibility, but it is flexibility to account for 'wrong' marriages, flexibility to fit one's own culturally-determined divisions into those of one's neighbouring tribe, flexibility to bend the rules – not flexibility to dispense with the categories. I once argued that perhaps Bushmen had been on their way to inventing an Australian-like world order when they were interrupted by outside forces (Barnard 1975), but the fact is they never developed even the clan system, much less a system of cross-cutting clans, sections and so on.

5. Australian Aborigines have the most elaborate marriage rules of any society. What is more, these rules exist within systems, which themselves exist within a continent-wide system of mathematical precision (see, for example, Maddock 1973). This fact was well known to Radcliffe-Brown, Lévi-Strauss and others, and has been an object of both fascination and terror to generations of anthropology students. In the classic case of the Kariera, for example, the world was divided into four sections: Banaka, Burung, Karimera and Palyeri (see Figure 4.2).

Table 4.2   *Kariera totemic associations (after von Brandenstein 1970)*

Banaka (Pannaga)	*Burung (Purunu)*
savage goanna (dry)	lazy goanna (moist)
active	passive
abstract	abstract
Karimera (Karimarra)	*Palyeri (Palt'arri)*
plains kangaroo (fierce)	hill kangaroo (mild)
active	passive
concrete	concrete

Banaka married Burung, and Karimera married Palyeri. The children of a male Banaka were Palyeri (these forming one patrilineal moiety and set of patrilineal clans), and the children of a female Banaka were Karimera (these forming one matrilineal moiety which, in the mind of the anthropologist if not those of the Kariera, bisected the patrilineal moieties to form the four sections). The sections are also united by an alternating-generation principle: Banaka and Burung in one, and Palyeri and Karimera in the other. Kinship terms map directly onto the sections; though terms for parents and children are different, terms for grandparents are the same as those for grandchildren (see, for example, Romney and Epling 1958). Thus egocentric categories like 'grandfather', which are common to all kinship systems, are amplified by their congruence with the sociocentric categories of the section system, namely the four sections themselves.

6. Above all, Aborigines classify their world as they classify their relatives. The categories of marriage are the categories of totemic relations, and these also map onto the categories of night and day, moon and sun, fresh water and sea water, activity and passivity, abstractness and concreteness, and a host of cross-cutting as well as coinciding binary oppositions. The totemic associations may embody these, creating a world order in which animals may represent not only social groups but the entire structure of the universe (see Table 4.2).

Yet a further question to be considered here is how the Aborigines see this world order. Briefly, I would suggest that most social anthropologists see the relation between society and the rest of the world order in a hierarchical and essentially Durkheimian way, with society sandwiched between the environment and the cosmology, and with a causal or transformative relation between these elements as indicated in Figure 4.3. (At least within the British tradition, most would emphasize the relationship between society and cosmology over that between the environment and society.)

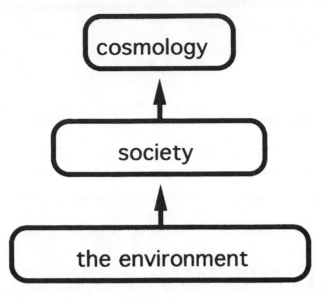

Fig. 4.3 *An anthropological model of the relation between the environment, society and cosmology.*

In Aboriginal thought, all these elements are so interrelated that it becomes difficult to separate them and certainly difficult to give priority to material causation or social behaviour over cosmological assumptions. It has recently been argued that in Aboriginal thought, form is prior to content and thus, as Frazer suggested, society can only reflect the natural order (Turner 1991). What separation there is involves a horizontal distinction between land and people, with totemic spirits associated with particular groups of people, and these spirits in turn associated with particular plots of land. Indeed, there is a direct association between spirits and land. Cosmology (as a belief system) is not necessarily dependent upon people or society if it is taken as representing the true nature of the world, which to Aborigines it of course does. There is also a sense in which society itself rests simultaneously on both the environment and the spirits which are associated with it (cf. Maddock 1973: 21–44). What that implies is a reversal of the Durkheimian notion that society is the source of cosmology. It also reverses ideas held by many ecological anthropologists that the main features of social organization in foraging societies simply spring from the environment. To put it simply, Aborigines see their society as founded on natural associations which are spiritually manifest. This view is represented in Figure 4.4.

So, why not Australian models? There are essentially two interrelated reasons. First, Australian models are virtually unique to Australia. No

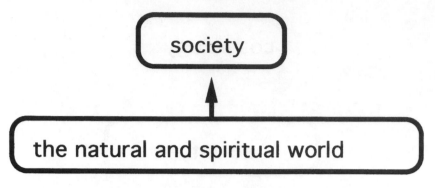

Fig. 4.4 *An Aboriginal model of the relation between the environment, society and cosmology.*

other continent, as far as we know, has produced quite the degree of cosmological structure or structural uniformity as has Australia. Although structures such as those Aborigines possess may once have had a wider distribution, nevertheless no unified system has existed within the historical record in Africa, Asia, Europe or the Americas. Nor is it necessary to have evolved moiety or section systems in order to classify the central elements of one's cosmology or to classify individuals of opposite sex as possible or not possible as mates. Although it has been argued that a four-section system might be considered *logically* simpler for classifying kin than one based on egocentric categories alone (e.g. Allen 1986), it seems unlikely that such logical simplicity would have evolved or diffused everywhere, only to be replaced by more flexible systems as technology advanced.

Secondly, Australian models are too elaborate to be the basis of early culture. They relate to social divisions which are necessary only when form becomes an end in itself. Some of the more elaborate systems were, apparently, only being worked out in the nineteenth century, when Europeans were arriving. Further, Australian models require the investment of too much intellectual energy for them to be primal. With due respect to Aboriginal thinkers, in my view their cosmological system is self-defining. That is, it finds order in order, as much as it finds order in the external world. Pantheism and 'primitive monotheism', which are not incompatible, characterize the rest of the religions of the world's hunting-and-gathering peoples even better than do animism and totemism, let alone a religion based on form alone.

In contrast, the Bushman world-view is based on one simple principle: an extreme flexibility at all levels. In relation to the six attributes of the Aboriginal world-view, we have six alternative ones: (1) a belief in one or many deities as well as spiritual essences ascribed to things; (2) a connection to the land through an intimate knowledge coupled with a belief in ancestral right; (3) emotional, but not totemic, relations to animals hunted; (4) a lack of clan organization, but wide cognatic kin networks; (5) marriage rules which follow egocentric means of universal kin category extension; (6) a complete separation between levels, that is no uniform division of the world. This last attribute reflects the greater flexibility inherent in Bushman society. I will touch just briefly on each (see, for example, Barnard 1992 for ethnographic details and further references).

1. Bushmen generally believe in one main deity. Though essentially male, often he is divided into male and female halves, sometimes into good and evil halves. Or the male and female, the good and evil, are all considered part of a pantheon of deities which are not definite in number. They merge with other things; they are represented, for example, in the moon or the sky.
2. Bushmen do not have a spiritual relation to the land in the same sense that Aboriginal peoples do. Nevertheless, Bushman groups do occupy delimited territories. Families, bands and band clusters can all be territorially based. People change band membership, but bands, as corporate entities, retain rights over resources. The core members may be any who are descended from putative band founders, and not just those in a single line of descent. Indeed, lines of (unilineal) descent are essentially foreign to Bushman ideology.
3. Bushmen may have relations to the animals they hunt, for example through the spiritual force called *n!ow* among the Ju/'hoansi (Marshall 1957). Only a small number of groups are totemic, like the Hiechware – the example used by Frazer. Totemism is not a necessary feature of exogamy, nor of food exchange. Bushmen, of course, maintain both egocentrically defined marriage rules and various forms of exchange without totemic beliefs.
4. Bushman groups generally lack clan structures. Again, those which exist, in the eastern Kalahari, resemble those of the neighbouring Bantu-speaking herding peoples and not the clan structures of the Khoekhoe, who are related to the Bushmen and who themselves lack totemism. Nevertheless, Bushmen extend kinship widely. Ju/'hoansi and Nharo do it through namesake links, G/wi and G//ana do it simply through friendship links. Among the Nharo one's namesake is classified as one's 'grandrelative'. Even ethnographers can be incorporated into the system of universal kinship by being given a Nharo name. This brings everyone into the same 'kinship' system. Consequently, one may distinguish from 'kinship' those relationships which make up voluntary giving and receiving networks, called *hxaro*

in Ju or *//aî* in Nharo, and those within a separate, non-kinship sphere.

5. Universal kinship is often the mechanism of determining the choice of spouse. Far from *not* having elementary structures, several Bushman groups indeed do have them in the sense that they possess positive marriage rules. One must marry a member of the category 'grand-relative' among Central Bushmen (Nharo, G/wi, G//ana, etc.) including the classificatory 'cross-cousin'. They share this particular attribute with Australian Aborigines; what they do not share is a sociocentric means of classification. They do not need it because universal kin category extension can and does function independently both of group structure and of the world order.

6. Thus the world order has no singular coherence. Its basic property is its flexibility.

For me, the existence of universal kinship structures, without the constraints imposed by totemism, is of prime importance. If, as Dunbar (1993) suggests, a turning point in evolution was marked by the development of language and the expansion of groups to a size of about 150 with a recognition of that as a social unit, then I would suggest that the further expansion of such groups through kin category extension marks an equally significant event. It is also a related event, for with mechanisms such as namesake equivalence (or indeed sections and subsections) one does not need to keep track of ancestors. If people are named after their relatives, as happens among Ju/'hoansi and Nharo, then they may all be presumed descended from an original namesake ancestor whose essence they share (cf. Marshall 1976: 202–3). This is at least as good a model of the origin of human culture as any other.

ACKNOWLEDGEMENTS

Nick Allen, Chris Knight, Adam Kuper and an anonymous reader have all made helpful comments on earlier drafts. However, none of them is responsible for my position, which, I suspect, differs from each of theirs as much as their respective positions differ from each other.

REFERENCES

Allen, N. J. (1986) 'Tetradic theory: an approach to kinship', *Journal of the Anthropological Society of Oxford* 17(2): 97–109.

Barnard, A. (1975) 'Australian models in the South West African highlands', *African Studies* 34: 9–18.

Barnard, A. (1978) 'Universal systems of kin categorization', *African Studies* 37: 69–81.

Barnard, A. (1988) 'Structure and fluidity in Khoisan religious ideas', *Journal of Religion in Africa* 28: 216–36.

Barnard, A. (1992) *Hunters and Herders of Southern Africa: A Comparative Ethnography of the Khoisan Peoples* (Cambridge: Cambridge University Press).

Barnard, A. (1993) 'Primitive communism and mutual aid: Kropotkin visits the Bushmen', in Hann, C. M. (ed.), *Socialism: Ideals, Ideologies, and Local Practice*, ASA Monographs 31 (London: Routledge), pp. 27–42.

Bird-David, N. (1992) 'Beyond "The Original Affluent Society": a culturalist reformulation', *Current Anthropology* 33: 25–47.

von Brandenstein, C. G. (1970) 'The meaning of section and section names', *Oceania* 41: 39–49.

Dunbar, R. I. M. (1993) 'Co-evolution of neocortex size, group size and language in humans', *Behaviour and Brain Sciences* 16: 681–735.

Durkheim, É. (1898) 'La prohibition de l'inceste et ses origines', *L'Année sociologique* I: 1–70.

Durkheim, É. (1915 [1912]) *The Elementary Forms of the Religious Life*, trans. Swain, J. W. (London: Allen & Unwin).

Fox, R. (1975) 'Primate kin and human kinship', in Fox, R. (ed.), *Biosocial Anthropology*, ASA Studies 1 (London: Malaby Press), pp. 9–35.

Fox, R. (1983 [1980]) *The Red Lamp of Incest: An Enquiry into the Origins of Mind and Society* (Notre Dame, Ind.: University of Notre Dame Press).

Frazer, J. G. (1910) *Totemism and Exogamy: A Treatise on Certain Early Forms of Superstition and Society*, 4 vols (London: Macmillan).

Frazer, J. G. (1937) *Totemica: A Supplement to Totemism and Exogamy* (London: Macmillan).

Guenther, M. (1979) 'Bushman religion and the (non)sense of anthropological theory of religion', *Sociologus* 29: 102–32.

Knight, C. D. (1991) *Blood Relations: Menstruation and the Origins of Culture* (New Haven, Conn./London: Yale University Press).

Kuper, A. (1988) *The Invention of Primitive Society: Transformations of an Illusion* (London: Routledge).

Lévi-Strauss, C. (1969 [1949]) *The Elementary Structures of Kinship*, revised edn, trans. Bell, J. H., von Sturmer, J. R. and Needham, R. (Boston, Mass.: Beacon Press).

Maddock, K. (1973) *The Australian Aborigines: A Portrait of Their Society* (London: Allen Lane, Penguin).

Maine, H. S. (1861) *Ancient Law: Its Connection with the Early History of Society and Its Relation to Modern Ideas* (London: John Murray).

Marshall, L. (1957) 'N!ow', *Africa* 27: 232–40.

Marshall, L. (1976) *The !Kung of Nyae Nyae* (Cambridge, Mass.: Harvard University Press).

Monboddo, J. Burnet, Lord (1773) *Of the Origin and Progress of Language*, Vol. I (Edinburgh: A. Kincaid and W. Creech/London: T. Cadell).

Needham, R. (1979) *Symbolic Classification* (Santa Monica, Calif.: Goodyear).

Power, C. and Watts, I. (1997) 'The woman with the zebra's penis: gender, mutability and performance', *The Journal of the Royal Anthropological Institute* (n.s.) 3: 537–60.

Romney, A. K. and Epling, P. J. (1958) 'A simplified model of Kariera kinship', *American Anthropologist* 60: 59–74.

Rousseau, J. J. (1966 [1791]) 'Essay on the origin of languages', in *On the Origin of Language: Two Essays by J. J. Rousseau and J. G. Herder*, trans. Moran, J. H. and Gode, A. (New York: Frederick Ungar), pp 1–83.

Slotkin, J. S. (ed.) (1965) *Readings in Early Anthropology* (Chicago: Aldine).

Spencer, B. and Gillen, F. J. (1899) *The Native Tribes of Central Australia* (London: Macmillan).

Spencer, B. and Gillen, F. J. (1904) *The Northern Tribes of Central Australia* (London: Macmillan).

Strehlow, T. G. H. (1947) *Aranda Traditions* (Melbourne: Melbourne University Press).

Turner, D. H. (1991) 'Australian Aboriginal religion as "world religion"', *Studies in Religion/Sciences Religieuses* 20: 165–80.

Turner, D. H. (1993) 'The religious forms of the elementary life: Durkheim revisited', *Culture* 13(1): 37–42.

Woodburn, J. (1980) 'Hunters and gatherers today and reconstruction of the past', in Gellner, E. (ed.), *Soviet and Western Anthropology* (London: Duckworth), pp. 95–117.

PART II

THE EVOLUTION OF ART AND RELIGION

CHAPTER 5

SEXUAL SELECTION FOR CULTURAL DISPLAYS

GEOFFREY F. MILLER

Friedrich Nietzsche, male, aged twenty-seven, published his first book *The Birth of Tragedy* in January 1872, barely a year after Charles Darwin published *The Descent of Man and Selection in Relation to Sex*. Both books viewed human culture as a natural outcome of human sexuality and animal instinct. Although both were widely read and discussed, their views on the origins of human culture were widely forgotten. The assumption they were attacking, that culture is an autonomous sphere of human activity and belief above the biology of behaviour and instinct, persists as the dominant framework for thinking about the evolution of culture. That framework has provoked much writing about cultural transmission, memes and gene-culture co-evolution. However, it has signally failed to deliver a good theory about what evolutionary selection pressures actually shaped the human capacity for producing and understanding concrete instances of 'culture'. This chapter suggests that, a century and a quarter after Nietzsche and Darwin, cultural theory and sexual selection theory have advanced enough that we should once more consider their subversive idea: cultural behaviour is very much more instinctive in nature and sexual in function than most cultured people would care to admit.

Nietzsche (1872) distinguished two modes of culture: the Apollonian (individual, rational, technical, cognitive, useful, hierarchical) and the Dionysian (collective, emotional, sexual, mystic, fertile, revolutionary). Most Darwinian theories have tried to explain the evolution of human culture through a strange combination of Apollonian technology, utility and hierarchy, and Dionysian collectivity and ritual. Typically, this entails trying to find survival benefits for group cultural traditions. By contrast, this chapter emphasizes Apollonian individuality and Dionysian sexuality, seeing whether culture may have evolved mostly through reproductive benefits for individual displays of 'cultural' behaviours.

Culture, rather than a system for transmitting useful technical knowledge and group-benefiting traditions down through the generations, can be considered an arena for various courtship displays in which individuals try to attract and retain sexual partners (Miller 1997, 1998, in press).

When a young male rock star stands up in front of a crowd and produces some pieces of human 'culture' known as songs, he is not improving his survival prospects. Nor is he engaging in some bizarre maladaptive behaviour that requires some new process of 'cultural evolution' to explain. Rather, he is doing something that fulfils exactly the same function as a male nightingale singing or a male peacock showing off his tail. He is attracting sexual partners. As we will see later, the fact that most publicly generated 'cultural' behaviour is produced by young males points towards its courtship function.

This cultural courtship model proposes that sexual selection through mate choice by both our male and female ancestors was a major evolutionary force in shaping human culture, i.e. the genetically inherited capacities for behaviours such as language, art and music (Miller 1997, 1998, in press). These behaviours, according to this model, function mainly as courtship displays to attract sexual partners and show many of the same design features shared by other courtship displays in other species. In short, human culture is mainly a set of adaptations for courtship. This hypothesis doesn't really come from Nietzsche, of course, or from Freud. Rather, it is a relatively simple application of standard Darwinian sexual selection theory to a somewhat puzzling set of behavioural phenomena in one rather pretentious species of primate.

This chapter examines what kind of data would be most relevant to testing competing evolutionary hypotheses about culture and reviews sexual selection theory as a possible explanatory framework. It then introduces my cultural courtship model where cultural displays function as sexually-selected indicators of phenotypic and genetic quality, and presents some data on the demographics of cultural production that seem better explained by a sexual selection model than by standard survival selection models.

WHY CULTURAL ANTHROPOLOGY WON'T TELL EVOLUTIONISTS WHAT WE NEED TO KNOW ABOUT CULTURE

Explaining the 'evolution of culture' is shorthand for explaining the genetic evolution, through natural selection and sexual selection, of the human mental adaptations that generate, learn, modify and produce those behaviours that sustain 'cultural' phenomena (Tooby and Cosmides 1992). At first glance, it would seem obvious that this explanatory project should take seriously everything that anthropologists have learned about cultural phenomena. Shouldn't the evolutionary psychology of culture take cultural anthropology as its starting point?

Unfortunately, cultural anthropology can't tell evolutionists the most important things we need to know, because its concerns have pulled in different directions. Evolutionists need thorough functional descriptions of the mental adaptations underlying culture, their specialized features, their survival and reproductive benefits and costs, their phylogeny, their phenotypic variability between humans, their genetic heritability, their lifespan development and their strategic flexibility in response to various ecological, demographic, social and sexual contexts. These are the basic kinds of data that biologists would routinely collect as a first step to determining why something evolved in any other species. These are the kinds of data that evolutionary psychologists are starting to collect for other human mental adaptations.

But cultural anthropologists have not usually collected that sort of data on human culture. Most cultural anthropology relies on qualitative description of cultural patterns. Where anthropologists have collected quantitative data on culture, it has generally been at the level of aggregate group data, measuring things like divisions of labour, rates of polygyny and durations of initiation rituals. These sorts of group averages do not reveal who is producing or receiving particular exemplars of culture, ideological or material.

Crucially, group aggregate data cannot reveal how individual heritable variation in the capacity for various cultural behaviours co-varies with various components of biological fitness. Thus, group average data permits only very weak and indirect tests of competing hypotheses about cultural evolution. Stronger tests would require knowing exactly what fitness pay-offs accrued to individuals who generated particular kinds of behaviours that sustained various kinds of cultural phenomena, not merely knowing what those phenomena are. For example, ornithologists test hypotheses about the functions of bird song mostly by looking at how individual variation in song production co-varies with individual variation in survival and reproduction (Catchpole and Slater 1995), not by derived predictions about emergent group-level song patterns from their hypotheses and comparing these predictions to group aggregate data.

There are special methodological problems in studying the possible courtship functions of human cultural behaviour. The 'participant observation' method allows anthropologists to share in a group's survival behaviours but usually excludes them from courting or copulating with the people they are studying. With direct experience of a group's economic, social and even ritual activities, but less experience with their mating activities, the survival functions of culture may have been better appreciated than the courtship functions. Also, humans are often secretive and misleading about their sexual behaviour to other members of their own group, and may be even more so to visitors (Freeman 1983). This opens even classic sexual ethnographies such as Bronislaw Malinowski and Margaret Mead to serious doubt.

It may be more productive to shift our attention from cultural anthropology to sexual selection theory itself, to see how far it can take us in explaining what we do know about human culture. Some useful tests of the cultural courtship model may then be found right under our noses, not in hunter-gatherer ethnographies, but in evidence about cultural production in our own post-industrial societies.

SEXUAL SELECTION THEORY

If the courtship model is right, the best tools for understanding human culture can be found in sexual selection theory, as first developed by Darwin (1859, 1871) and revived in the last twenty years (Andersson 1994; Cronin 1991; Miller 1998; Miller and Todd 1998). Darwin recognized that evolution is fundamentally reproductive competition, not just Spencer's 'survival of the fittest'. Natural selection for survival ability is certainly important, but sexual selection for attracting mates is often more important. Darwin understood that in most sexually reproducing species, there would be strong incentives for choosing one's sexual mate carefully, because one's offspring would inherit their traits, good or bad, along with one's own traits. Bad mate preferences would find themselves in poor-quality offspring, and would eventually die out. Equally, poor courtship displays that attracted few mates would also die out over generations. Thus, a process of sexual selection will tend to arise in many sexually-reproducing animals, whereby individuals display their attractiveness, health, status, fertility, genetic quality and other reproductively important traits, and individuals select their mates based on such displays. As Darwin (1871) noted, female animals are often choosier about their mates than males, and males often display more intensely than females. However, sexual selection does not necessarily produce or depend on sex differences; it could equally apply to hermaphrodites.

Victorian biologists generally rejected the idea that mate choice by females could be a major force in evolution, so the core idea in Darwin's sexual selection theory fell into disrepute for many decades. Sexual selection has been revived only in the last two decades because evolutionary theorists finally figured out how to use analytical proofs and computer simulations to show some of the counter-intuitive ways that sexual selection can work, and animal behaviour researchers figured out how to demonstrate mate preferences experimentally in the lab and the field (Andersson 1994). Especially in the last decade, sexual selection theory and animal mate choice research have dominated the best journals in biology and evolutionary psychology (see Miller and Todd 1998).

The strange history of sexual selection theory is important to appreciate because virtually all of twentieth-century anthropology, psychology and cultural theory developed when the theory was in scientific exile. Lacking an appreciation of how mate choice shapes behavioural evolution, evolution-minded social scientists searched for survival functions for the more puzzling human cultural behaviours, largely without success.

SEXUAL SELECTION FOR INDICATORS OF PHENOTYPIC AND GENOTYPIC QUALITY

So, how does mate choice shape courtship displays? Biologists such as Alfred Russell Wallace, George Williams and William Hamilton have long argued that mate choice should often favour cues that indicate a prospect's phenotypic quality, including health, fertility, parasite resistance, parenting abilities and genotypic quality or heritable fitness (Cronin 1991; Andersson 1994). However, this idea that mate choice favours 'indicators' rather than arbitrary, aesthetic traits was not widely considered until 1975, when Amotz Zahavi stirred intense controversy with his 'Handicap Principle' (Zahavi and Zahavi 1997). Zahavi proposed that the only way to reliably demonstrate one's quality during courtship is to display a high-cost signal such as a heavy peacock's tail, an exhausting bird-song concert or an expensive sports car. Only these costly 'handicap' signals are evolutionarily stable indicators of their producer's quality, because cheap signals are too easy for low-quality imitators to fake (Zahavi and Zahavi 1997).

Many sexual cues in many species have now been shown to function as indicators: they have high growth and maintenance costs, their size and condition correlates with their owner's overall fitness and genetic quality, and they influence mating decisions (Andersson 1994). Sexual selection theorists now believe that many sexual cues, both bodily ornaments and courtship behaviours, function as reliable indicators of an individual's quality. Such indicators, while improving reproductive prospects, actually impair survival chances, so are fairly easy to distinguish from naturally-selected traits shaped for survival. Many empirical methods have been developed to test whether a particular trait is a sexually-selected indicator, but these methods have almost never been applied in studies of human culture.

A key question is whether sexually-selected indicators reveal just environment-influenced phenotypic quality, or heritable genotypic quality as well. Until recently, many biologists and evolutionary psychologists believed that fitness must not be heritable in most species most of the time, because natural selection should tend to eliminate any genetic variation in traits that influence survival or reproduction ability (Tooby and Cosmides 1990). However, theorists realized that mutation pressure, spatial and temporal variations in selection and migration tend to maintain heritable fitness (see Andersson 1994; Rowe and Houle 1996; Pomiankowski and Moller 1995). Also, every human mental trait ever studied by behaviour geneticists shows significant heritability, even traits that must have been strongly fitness-related such as general intelligence and other capacities fundamental to cultural behaviour (Jensen 1997; Plomin et al. 1997).

Many biologists now agree that fitness often remains substantially heritable in most species most of the time (Moller and Swaddle 1997; Rowe and Houle 1996; for review see Miller and Todd 1998). Thus, our mate choice strategies probably evolved to focus on sexual cues that advertise heritable fitness. From a selfish gene's point of view, mate choice is supremely important because mate choice determines whose genes it will have to collaborate with in all succeeding generations.

The most dramatic examples of human culture, such as ritual, music, art, ideology and language-play, seem like energetically expensive wastes of time, to someone thinking in terms of the survival of the fittest. From the viewpoint of indicator theory, that sort of wasteful display is exactly what we would expect from traits shaped for reproductive competition.

SEXUAL SELECTION FOR OTHER FEATURES OF COURTSHIP DISPLAYS

Courtship displays can reveal quality in an almost limitless number of ways, because all they need to do is have high marginal fitness costs in all domains other than courtship. Thus, the indicator function vastly underdetermines the details of courtship displays, and other sexual selection processes can become important. For example, the peacock's tail needs to be large, heavy and expensive to grow to function as an indicator, but its indicator function doesn't determine its exact colours, patterns and movements.

R. A. Fisher (1930) proposed a 'runaway' model of sexual selection that could favour courtship features that are not indicators. In the runaway process, a heritable mate preference (e.g. a preference for a longer-than-average peacock tail) becomes genetically correlated with the heritable trait it favours (e.g. a longer-than-average tail), because offspring tend to inherit both the preference and the trait as a package. The result is an evolutionary positive-feedback loop that drives both the preference and the trait to an extreme. Because the runaway process is extremely sensitive to initial conditions, its evolutionary outcome is hard to predict. Given two similar species living in similar econiches, runaway might lead them to evolve very different courtship displays (Miller and Todd 1995; Todd and Miller 1997).

Recent theorists have also suggested that perceptual biases (e.g. greater responsiveness to large, bright, high-contrast, loud, rhythmic or novel stimuli) can influence the direction of sexual selection and the details of courtship displays (e.g. Endler 1992; Ryan and Keddy-Hector 1992; for review see Miller 1998). Small differences between species in these perceptual biases may lead to large differences in the courtship displays they evolve.

THE CULTURAL COURTSHIP MODEL

In my cultural courtship model, 'culture' subsumes a variety of specific human behaviours such as telling stories, wearing clothes, dancing, making music, decorating artifacts, expressing belief in certain ideas and so forth. The human capacity for culture, then, is not a single adaptation, but a set of interrelated adaptations that may have evolved under different selection pressures to fulfil different biological functions (Tooby and Cosmides 1992). Our unique human capacities for language, art, music and ideology may be distinct mental modules that evolved at different times, develop according to different life histories, operate according to different psychological principles and contribute in different ways to biological fitness. In this rather modular view of mental evolution, culture does not come for free as a side-effect of having a large brain, general-purpose learning and imitation abilities, or general intelligence (Pinker 1997).

However, there may be a common theme running through these cultural capacities. They are self-expressive. They cost time and energy. Most of them have no clear survival benefits. They are unique to our species. They show strong individual differences, with some people much better at them than others. They require intelligence, creativity and health. They play upon the perceptual and cognitive preferences of spectators. These are all the hallmarks of adaptations that have been shaped as courtship ornaments by Darwin's process of sexual selection through mate choice.

CULTURAL DISPLAYS AS
SEXUALLY-SELECTED INDICATORS

Cultural displays such as productions of language, art, music and ideology may function in courtship as sexually-selected indicators of phenotypic and genotypic quality. This idea may explain not only behavioural differences between humans and other primates, but also the easily observed differences between individual humans in their capacity for producing impressive, attractive cultural behaviour. The whole point of indicators is to amplify perceivable differences between individuals, to make heritable differences in health, intelligence, creativity and other traits more apparent and easier to judge during mate choice (see Andersson 1994; Pomian-kowski and Moller 1995; Rowe and Houle 1996; Zahavi and Zahavi 1997). Almost all other evolutionary theories of culture (e.g. Dissanayake 1992; Knight, Power and Watts 1995) would be expected to produce very small differences between modern humans in their cultural capacities, because they assume survival selection for culture, and survival selection tends to eliminate genetic variation much faster than sexual selection.

If cultural displays evolved as sexually-selected indicators of intelligence and creativity, this may also explain why many building-blocks of cultural displays are so highly ritualized while many higher-order structures are so variable. Comparison between courtship displays is easier if the displays share many elements in common so deviations indicating inferior pro-duction ability can be easily noticed. For example, ritualization of vocabu-lary, pronunciation and grammar makes it easy to tell who is good at language and who is not. Ritualization of timbre, rhythm and tonality makes it easy to tell who is good at music (Miller in press). This is why most people dislike abstract art, atonal music and modernist architecture: these styles avoid just those recognizable, ritualized elements that indicate whether their creators are any good at the basics of their craft.

But individuals can display their creativity in addition to their virtuosity by recombining these basic cultural elements in novel patterns (Catchpole and Slater 1995; Miller 1997; Werner and Todd 1997). Such new patterns can yield new emergent meanings that capture attention, excite the im-agination and remain memorable. This is why people during courtship tell new stories using old words, rather than expecting a sexual prospect to be impressed by a string of newly invented words. Standardized cultural elements allow easy comparisons of behavioural virtuosity, while protean cultural patterns allow easy assessment of behavioural creativity (Miller 1997).

SEXUAL FUNCTIONS VERSUS SEXUAL MOTIVES

Culture as a set of adaptations for courtship does not mean that the production of cultural behaviour stems from some kind of Freudian sublimated sex drive. Sexually-selected adaptations do not need to feel very sexy to their users. A trait shaped by sexual selection does not have to include a little copy of its function inside, in the form of a conscious or subconscious sexual motivation (see Tooby and Cosmides 1992). The male human beard, although almost certainly an outcome of sexual selection through female mate choice, is not a jungle of hidden, illicit motives. It simply grows and displays that its possessor is a sexually mature male without having any idea why it's doing that. Even psychological adaptations like music production may work similarly, firing off at the appropriate age and under the right social circumstances without their possessor having any idea why they suddenly feel 'inspired' to learn the guitar and play it where single people of the opposite sex happen to congregate. The cultural courtship model does not reduce culture to a crude sex drive any more than natural selection models of cultural evolution reduce culture to a crude survival drive.

WHY SEXUAL SELECTION DOESN'T CARE WHETHER MYTHS ARE TRUE

Anthropology textbooks (e.g. Haviland 1996) present many functions for art, music, myth, ritual and other cultural phenomena, such as 'imposing order on the cosmos', 'coping with the unpredictability of life', 'appeasing ancestral spirits' and 'maintaining tribal identity'. To an evolutionary biologist, none of these even come close to qualifying as reasonable adaptive functions for costly, complex, evolved behaviours. In a strictly Darwinian framework, behaviours only evolve when their fitness benefits exceed their fitness costs. Fitness almost always relates directly to individual survival and reproduction in the real, objective econiche that a species faces, not in an imagined world of spirits and cultural meanings. The single thing we must demand of any theory concerning the evolution of human culture is: show me the fitness!

Showing the fitness benefits for many cultural behaviours is hard because they create and transmit fictional mindscapes that are not accurate models of biological reality (Knight, Power and Watts 1995). The almost unbeatable advantage the courtship model has in this regard is that cultural displays must be honest only as reliable indicators of their producer's fitness, not as accurate mental models of the world. Mate choice doesn't care whether a story told during courtship is literally true; it only cares whether the story is good enough to prove the intelligence and creativity of its narrator. Indeed, the more fantastic, baroque, outlandish and counter-factual the tale, the better an indicator of heritable mental capacity it may be. Without sexual selection, it seems impossible to explain why so much human culture represents the world so inaccurately, and why fiction outsells non-fiction by such a large margin.

Language did not evolve just so we could tell each other amusing fictions. It clearly shows some design features for communicating useful, true information to others very quickly and efficiently when necessary (Pinker 1994). The survival and social benefits of complex information-transfer from one mind to another would have been substantial. However, the courtship benefits of being able to activate complex mental representations inside the minds of sexual prospects must also have been substantial, a revolutionary advance over tickling their eyes or ears with meaningless colours and sounds as all other species are limited to doing.

Both the survival and courtship models for language evolution face the same difficult problem of explaining why language evolved only once, in our species, if it was so useful for either function. Here the courtship model has the advantage that sexual selection is a highly stochastic process, extremely sensitive to initial conditions and unpredictable in outcome, whereas natural selection is a relatively more predictable hill-climbing process that often produces convergent evolution on the same adaptation in many lineages (Miller and Todd 1995).

WHY SEXUAL SELECTION IS AS SMART AS WE ARE

Sexual selection is a very powerful process, not just evolutionarily (see Miller and Todd 1995; Todd and Miller 1997), but epistemologically. Sexual selection through mate choice can potentially explain anything you can ever notice about evolved human behaviour as something that needs explaining. This is because anything you can notice about other people, your ancestors could have noticed too, and perhaps favoured in picking their sexual mates. While natural selection is so often blind and dumb, sexual selection is as smart as the individuals making the mate choices. Our ancestors were very smart indeed, according to the dominant social intelligence theory of human brain evolution. So, if we are even capable of noticing that someone else is wonderfully creative in their cultural efforts, that perceptual capacity itself is good evidence that mate choice could have shaped the very phenomenon we are admiring. Sexual selection through mate choice can reach as far into the minds of others as our own social intelligence can reach, and can potentially explain whatever we find admirable there.

WHY SEXUAL SELECTION PRE-EMPTS NATURAL SELECTION

A second immodestly powerful feature of sexual selection is that it tends to hijack whatever natural selection pressures are already shaping a species (Miller and Todd 1995; Todd and Miller 1993). This is because there are such large incentives to avoid mating with individuals whose offspring would stand little hope given whatever natural selection is happening. For example, suppose the capacity for social imitation happened to confer some survival advantage on our ancestors. If social imitation abilities remained subject to natural selection over many generations, it seems likely that mate preferences would evolve to favour individuals who displayed above-average social imitation abilities. Those mate preferences in turn would favour the evolution under sexual selection of courtship displays that reliably indicated one's social imitation abilities. The result would be a set of costly, exaggerated displays of one's social-imitation ability, such as a talent for humorous impersonations of sexual competitors. These displays might look vaguely related to traits useful for survival, but their principal function would be courtship. This same argument applies to any other behavioural capacity: if it was really useful for survival, mate preferences would have evolved to 'realize' that and favoured elaborate advertisements of the capacity that do not, in themselves, contribute to survival. Theories of culture evolution that stress pure survival advantages need to explain why cultural behaviours would be uniquely immune to this sort of hijacking, amplification, subversion and complexification by sexual selection.

DARWINIAN DEMOGRAPHICS OF CULTURAL DISPLAY

The courtship hypothesis makes a simple prediction that the amount of cultural production in many domains should depend heavily on the age and sex of the producer. Specifically, cultural production should increase rapidly after puberty, peak at young adulthood when sexual competition is greatest, and gradually decline over adult life as parenting eclipses courtship. Males should also show much higher rates of cultural production than females, because they are competing more intensely for mates (see Andersson 1994; Cronin 1991; Ridley 1993). Daly and Wilson (1986) found that homicide follows exactly this pattern across many different cultures and historical epochs, suggesting that violent competition is largely sexual competition. I was curious whether quantifiable types of cultural production would show the same demographic profile, suggesting similar evolutionary origins in sexual selection.

An initial sample of over 16,000 items of culture from diverse media showed the demographic profile predicted by the courtship hypothesis (Miller submitted). The method relied on finding reference works such as music discographies, museum catalogues of paintings and writer's directories that include very large samples of cultural works for which the age and sex of their producer can be identified. From these references, large random samples were obtained, and the number of cultural works produced by individuals of a particular age and sex were counted and plotted. The method works best for discrete, easily counted cultural productions such as paintings, books, music albums and plays. Reference works were chosen that aimed to exhaustively list all works that fit some well-defined objective criteria rather than small samples based on some author's quality judgements. For this short chapter, only a few example studies can be reviewed, analyzing the production demographics for jazz albums, modern paintings and modern books.

Figure 5.1 plots 1,892 jazz albums by age and sex of their principal musician/composer, reflecting a random sample of about 20 per cent of the albums documented in Carr, Fairweather and Priestly (1988), an exhaustive reference that includes every commonly recognized jazz musician and album. The data points represent how many jazz albums (as an absolute frequency) were released by musicians of a particular age (displayed along the x-axis from age 0 to age 90) and sex (distinguished by rhomboid symbols for men and circles for women). Two striking features are apparent from the figure. First, there is an enormous sexual dimorphism in cultural production, with 1,800 albums by 685 men, and 92 albums by 34 women. Males produced about twenty times as many total jazz albums as females, and produced them at a much higher rate for every age. Second, male productivity peaks very sharply at thirty years of age, rising steeply from age twenty upwards, and falling off steeply until age fifty, and then more slowly until age seventy. While homicide rate typically peaks in the early twenties (Daly and Wilson 1986), the later peak for jazz album production suggests that it takes longer to learn to play good music than to kill someone, and longer between composing music and releasing the album than between pulling a trigger and committing a murder.

Figure 5.2 plots 3,374 modern paintings from *The Tate Gallery Collections* (1984), an exhaustive sample of every painting owned by one of Britain's major national museums. The sample includes all datable works in the collection done by every artist with a last name beginning A through K. The sample yielded 2,979 paintings by 644 men and 395 paintings by 95 women, showing an eightfold sexual dimorphism. Here, cultural productivity for both sexes peaks in their mid to late thirties, following a gradual rise from age twenty, with a slower decline from forty into the eighties.

Figure 5.3 plots 2,837 English-language books published in the twentieth century, a random sample of about 2 per cent of all books listed in *The Writers Directory* (1992). This includes 2,213 books by 180 men and 624 books by 49 women, with males still producing over three times as many books as females. The age peaks are later for books, around forty-three for males and fifty for females, with the first hint of a sex difference in age profiles.

Similar results were obtained in other studies of over 2,500 rock albums from Strong (1993), 3,800 major works of classical music from Sadie

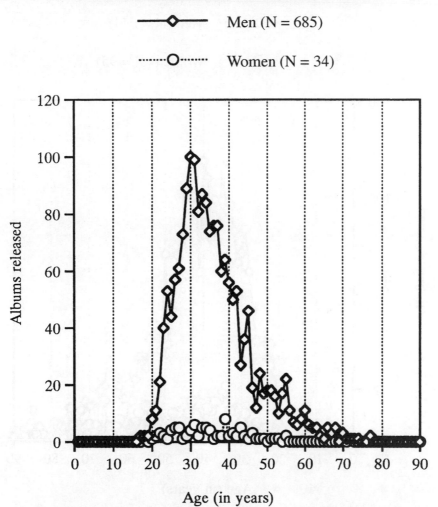

Fig. 5.1 *Jazz albums: output of jazz albums as a function of age and sex of the principal musician/composer, reflecting a random sample of 1,892 albums by 719 musicians from Carr, Fairweather and Priestly (1988). The data points represent how many jazz albums (as an absolute frequency) were released by musicians of a particular age (displayed along the x-axis, from age 0 to age 90) and sex (with rhomboids representing men and circles representing women). The sample consists of full-length LP records released between the 1940s and 1980s in the US or Britain.*

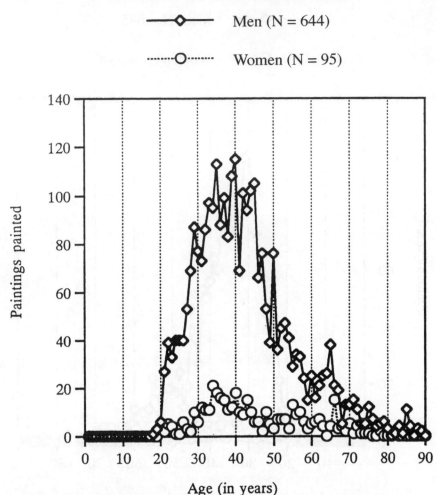

Fig. 5.2 *Modern paintings: output of modern paintings as a function of age and sex of the painter, reflecting an exhaustive sample of 3,274 paintings by 739 artists from* The Tate Gallery Collections *(1984). The data points represent how many paintings (as an absolute frequency) were produced by artists of a particular age (displayed along the x-axis, from age 0 to age 90) and sex (with rhomboids representing men and circles representing women). The sample is the exhaustive set of every datable painting owned by the Tate Gallery, London, as of 1984, where the artist's last name began with A through K, and where the artist's sex could be determined by first name. The sample includes mostly twentieth century British paintings.*

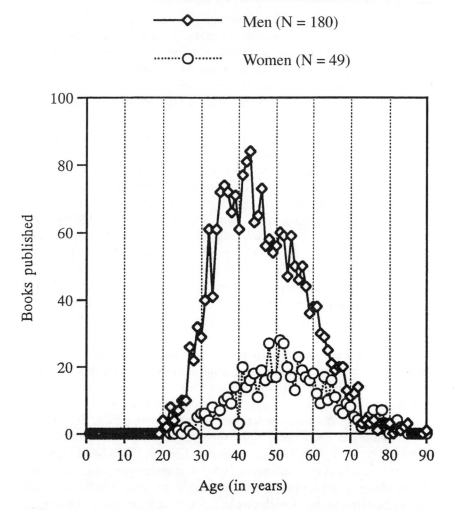

Fig. 5.3 *Books: output of books as a function of age and sex of the writer, reflecting a random sample of 2,837 books by 229 writers from* The Writers Directory *(1992). The data points represent how many books (as an absolute frequency) were produced by writers of a particular age (displayed along the x-axis, from age 0 to age 90) and sex (with rhomboids representing men and circles representing women). The sample includes twentieth century English-language works of both fiction and non-fiction, spanning all genres; most of the writers were British or American.*

(1993), 850 old paintings from the *National Gallery: Illustrated General Catalogue* (1986), 250 plays from Crystal (1993) and 150 major philosophical tracts from Collinson (1987) – Nietzsche, male, aged twenty-seven, was a typical culture-producer (see Miller, submitted, for details). In every case, cultural production was much greater for males than for females, and showed the same general age profile, though with somewhat different age peaks depending on the medium.

A single pattern seems to pervade the age–sex profiles of cultural production across quite different media from different cultures and historical epochs. Human males and females show a virtually identical age profile for cultural production: a rapid rise following late adolescence, a peak around age thirty (plus or minus a few years), and a roughly exponential decline throughout the remainder of life, with the most rapid productivity loss between ages forty and sixty, followed by a more gradual decline until death. This age pattern for cultural production resembles that found for many other domains of display behaviour (Simonton 1988). Though this age profile looks positively skewed if chronological age is plotted on a linear axis, it looks like an almost perfect normal distribution if age is plotted on a logarithmic axis, with the production peak midway between puberty and death.

The second major result is the persistent sexual dimorphism in cultural production rates, with males producing about ten times more cultural output, across all media, than females. This male domination of public culture has been widely recognized by both evolutionary psychologists (e.g. Ellis 1934) and feminist scholars (e.g. Battersby 1989; Russ 1983), but is almost entirely ignored in theories of cultural evolution (e.g. Dissanayake 1992). Given observations by Darwin (1871) and hundreds of other researchers (see Andersson 1994) that male courtship displays are almost always more frequent, more energetic, brighter, louder and more strongly motivated than female displays, the most parsimonious biological interpretation of the cultural dimorphism is this: human cultural production functions largely as a courtship display, and the persistent sex difference in public cultural production rates reflects an evolved sex difference in courtship strategies.

There are also strong incentives for females to display cultural creativity during courtship to attract high-quality male mates. But the costs of male sexual harassment probably favoured a female display strategy of targeting desired prospects rather than broadcasting one's fertility and attractiveness to all males indiscriminately. Also, we would expect much of female 'courtship' to occur after a sexual relationship forms and even after children are produced, with the cultural displays directed specifically at one's partner and designed to solicit his continued attention and investment. These arguments suggest a sexually dimorphic motivational system, with equal capacities for cultural production in both sexes, but with males much more prone to publicly broadcast their cultural production and thereby to leave their mark on historical records of culture.

DO THESE AGE–SEX DEMOGRAPHICS DESCRIBE PRODUCTION OF OTHER KINDS OF HUMAN CULTURE?

The three figures shown, plotting cultural production as a function of age and sex of producer, could be termed 'display profiles'. Though they show some variation, there is a general pattern of much more public display by males than by females, and display rates that increase markedly after puberty, peak in young adulthood and decline slowly with decreasing fertility. There may be a universal display profile that shows these features across many different domains and styles of cultural production. A strong version of my cultural courtship model would make the following prediction: this universal profile will be found for every quantifiable human behaviour that is public (i.e. perceivable by many potential mates) and costly (i.e. not affordable by all sexual competitors). This universal profile may even apply to evolutionarily novel behaviours such as skydiving, playing one's car stereo at high volume and constructing an elaborate 'home page' on one's Internet web site. If the universal profile is replicated for other genres, other media, other cultures and other historical epochs, it could be interpreted as an evolved, species-typical, sexually dimorphic, life-history adaptation, shaped by sexual selection and fundamental to understanding the distribution of cultural behaviour in our species.

A different version of the cultural courtship model could emphasize sex differences not in display rates, but in display channels that show off particular components of phenotypic quality desired by the opposite sex. For example, one could take the standard evolutionary psychology view that males pay relatively more attention to youth and physical attractiveness in mate choice than females do (Buss 1989) to predict that body ornamentation (e.g. cosmetics, jewellery, costly clothes) will show a display profile with a similar age peak, but with more ornamentation worn by females than by males. However, the definition of body ornamentation depends on where one draws the border around an individual's 'extended phenotype' (Dawkins 1982). If women wear more red ochre or lipstick, but high-status men 'wear' more sports cars, bodyguards, country estates and corner offices with skyline views, how do we quantify their relative amounts of phenotypic ornamentation? Developing better methods for measuring cultural production and reception will be necessary for testing more sophisticated models of cultural evolution.

This courtship hypothesis is bound to stir some scepticism, but we must be clear about whether such scepticism concerns the validity of the production data or their interpretation as serving a courtship function. If culture theorists do not believe that the universal display profile proposed here will apply to their favourite type of public cultural behaviour, I would invite them to measure production of that behaviour, using objective, replicable, quantitative methods in a large random sample of people from their favourite culture, and see if the profile holds. The universal display profile may not be truly universal, but trying to see whether it is may be useful in distinguishing between different hypotheses about cultural evolution. At least, standard survival-benefit or group-benefit models of cultural evolution have no reason to predict sex differences in display profiles, whereas sexual selection models do.

On the other hand, some may claim that this display profile, though a possibly valid description of public cultural behaviour, is a self-perpetuating artifact of patriarchy rather than an evolved aspect of human nature (e.g. Battersby 1989; Russ 1983). In that case, one would have to explain why it is sensible to explain similar profiles in bird song production (e.g. Catchpole and Slater 1995) and other courtship behaviour in other species using a different theory than one invokes for human cultural behaviour. Parsimony demands that if we see the same age and sex profiles for animal courtship behaviour and for human public cultural production, and if these behaviours show many of the same design features (e.g. high cost, aesthetic appeal, heritable variation in production ability, importance in mate choice), we should admit that the same theory, sexual selection through mate choice, might explain both phenomena.

CONCLUSION

Human culture does not make much sense as a set of survival adaptations shaped by natural selection. Too much of cultural behaviour, such as art, music, ritual, ideology, myth, humour and story-telling, seems so expensive in terms of time, energy and practice costs, and so useless for survival. Anthropologists have struggled for a century to find plausible survival functions for such cultural behaviours and have not succeeded to their general satisfaction. Indeed, the difficulty of finding survival functions for much of human culture has led many cultural anthropologists to abandon evolutionary explanation altogether as irrelevant and distracting.

This pessimism is misplaced because it ignores the astonishing revival of Darwin's sexual selection theory in biology over the last two decades. That revival has not been taken seriously by cultural theorists, but it seems to offer their best hope for a fruitful connection with human evolutionary psychology. Human culture makes a great deal of sense as a set of courtship adaptations shaped by sexual selection through mate choice. The costs and aesthetics of cultural behaviour that make it so inexplicable in survival terms make it perfect as a set of reliable fitness indicators that help advertise one's superiority over sexual competitors. This hypothesis offers a natural way of explaining the distinctive age and sex patterns of human cultural production.

This chapter is just a first attempt at tracing the implications of sexual selection for understanding human culture, and a plea for grounding any evolutionary discussion of culture in an up-to-date knowledge of evolutionary theory combined with rigorous quantitative measurements of the cultural behaviours to be explained. The evolutionary significance of culture lies not in its subjective meaning, but in its objective fitness costs and benefits. Subjective meaning is simply what our would-be mates use to excite and entertain us during courtship.

REFERENCES

Andersson, M. B. (1994) *Sexual Selection* (Princeton, NJ: Princeton University Press).

Battersby, C. (1989) *Gender and Genius* (London: Women's Press).

Buss, D. M. (1989) 'Sex differences in human mate selection: evolutionary hypotheses tested in 37 cultures', *Behavioral and Brain Sciences* 12(1): 1–49.

Carr, I., Fairweather, D. and Priestley, B. (1988) *Jazz: The Essential Companion* (London: Paladin).

Catchpole, C. K. and Slater, P. J. B. (1995) *Bird Song: Biological Themes and Variations* (Cambridge: Cambridge University Press).

Collinson, D. (1987) *Fifty Major Philosophers: A Reference Guide* (London: Routledge).

Cronin, H. (1991) *The Ant and the Peacock: Altruism and Sexual Selection from Darwin to Today* (Cambridge: Cambridge University Press).

Crystal, D. (1993) *The Cambridge Factfinder* (Cambridge: Cambridge University Press).

Daly, M. and Wilson, M. (1988) *Homicide* (New York: Aldine).

Darwin, C. (1859) *On the Origin of Species by Means of Natural Selection, or, The Preservation of Favoured Races in the Struggle for Life* (London: John Murray).

Darwin, C. (1871) *The Descent of Man, and Selection in Relation to Sex*, 2 vols (London: John Murray).

Dawkins, R. (1982) *The Extended Phenotype: The Gene as the Unit of Selection* (Oxford: W. H. Freeman).

Dissanayake, E. (1992) *Homo aestheticus: Where Art Comes From and Why* (New York: Free Press).

Ellis, H. (1934) *Man and Woman: A Study of Secondary and Tertiary Sexual Characteristics*, 8th edn (London: W. Heinemann).

Endler, J. A. (1992) 'Signals, signal conditions, and the direction of evolution', *American Naturalist* 139: S125–S153.

Fisher, R. A. (1930) *The Genetical Theory of Natural Selection* (Oxford: Clarendon Press).

Freeman, D. (1983) *Margaret Mead and Samoa: The Making and Unmaking of an Anthropological Myth* (Cambridge, Mass.: Harvard University Press).

Haviland, W. A. (1996) *Cultural Anthropology*, 8th edn (New York: Harcourt Brace College Publishers).

Jensen, A. (1997) 'The neurophysiology of *g*', in Cooper, C. and Varma, V. (eds), *Processes in Individual Differences* (London: Routledge).

Knight, C., Power, C. and Watts, I. (1995) 'The human symbolic revolution: a Darwinian account', *Cambridge Archaeological Journal* 5(1): 75–114.

Miller, G. F. (1997) 'Protean primates: the evolution of adaptive unpredictability in competition and courtship', in Whiten, A. and Byrne, R. W. (eds), *Machiavellian Intelligence II: Extensions and Evaluations* (Cambridge: Cambridge University Press), pp. 312–40.

Miller, G. F. (1998) 'How mate choice shaped human nature: a review of sexual selection and human evolution', in Crawford, C. and Krebs, D. (eds), *Handbook of Evolutionary Psychology: Ideas, Issues, and Applications* (Mahwah, NJ: Lawrence Erlbaum Associates), pp. 87–129.

Miller, G. F. (in press) 'Evolution of human music through sexual selection', in Wallin, N. L., Merker, B. and Brown, S. (eds), *The Origins of Music* (Cambridge, Mass.: MIT Press).

Miller, G. F. (submitted) 'Darwinian demographics of cultural production'.

Miller, G. F. and Todd, P. M. (1995) 'The role of mate choice in biocomputation: sexual selection as a process of search, optimization, and diversification', in Banzhaf, W. and Eeckman, F. H. (eds), *Evolution and Biocomputation: Computational Models of Evolution* (Berlin: Springer-Verlag), pp. 169–204.

Miller, G. F. and Todd, P. M. (1998) 'Mate choice turns cognitive', *Trends in Cognitive Sciences* 2(5): 190–8.

Moller, A. P. and Swaddle, J. P. (1997) *Developmental Stability and Evolution* (Oxford: Oxford University Press).

National Gallery Illustrated General Catalogue, 2nd edn (1986) (London: National Gallery).

Pinker, S. (1997) *How the Mind Works* (New York: Norton).

Plomin, R., DeFries, J., McClearn, G. and Rutter, M. (1997) *Behavioral Genetics* 3rd edn (New York: W. H. Freeman).

Pomiankowski, A. and Moller, A. (1995) 'A resolution of the lek paradox', *Proceedings of the Royal Society of London*, B 260 (1357): 21–9.

Ridley, M. (1993) *The Red Queen: Sex and the Evolution of Human Nature* (London: Viking).

Rowe, L. and Houle, D. (1996) 'The lek paradox and the capture of genetic variance by condition dependent traits', *Proceedings of the Royal Society of London*, B 263: 1415–21.

Russ, J. (1983) *How to Suppress Women's Writing* (Austin: University of Texas Press).

Ryan, M. J. and Keddy-Hector, A. (1992) 'Directional patterns of female mate choice and the role of sensory biases', *American Naturalist* 139: S4–S35.

Sadie, S. (ed.) (1993) *The Grove Concise Dictionary of Music* (London: Macmillan).

Simonton, D. K. (1988) 'Age and outstanding achievement: what do we know after a century of research?' *Psychological Bulletin* 104(2): 251–67.

Strong, M. C. (1993) *The Great Rock Discography* (Edinburgh: Canongate Press).

The Tate Gallery Collections, 8th edn (1984) (London: Tate Gallery).

Todd, P. M. and Miller, G. F. (1993) 'Parental guidance suggested: how parental imprinting evolves through sexual selection as an adaptive learning mechanism', *Adaptive Behavior* 2(1): 5–47.

Todd, P. M. and Miller, G. F. (1997) 'Biodiversity through sexual selection', in Langton, C. G. and Shimohara, K. (eds), *Artificial Life V: Proceedings of the Fifth International Workshop on the Synthesis and Simulation of Living Systems* (Cambridge, Mass.: MIT Press/Bradford Books), pp. 289–99.

Tooby, J. and Cosmides, L. (1990) 'On the universality of human nature and the uniqueness of the individual: the role of genetics and adaptation', *Journal of Personality* 58: 17–67.

Tooby, J. and Cosmides, L. (1992) 'The psychological foundations of culture', in Barkow, J. H., Cosmides, L. and Tooby, J. (eds), *The Adapted Mind: Evolutionary Psychology and the Generation of Culture* (Oxford: Oxford University Press), pp. 19–136.

Werner, G. M. and Todd, P. M. (1997) 'Too many love songs: sexual selection and the evolution of communication', in Husbands, P. and Harvey, I. (eds), *Fourth European Conference on Artificial Life* (Cambridge, Mass.: MIT Press/Bradford Books), pp. 434–43.

The Writers Directory 1992–1994, 10th edn (1992) (London: St James' Press).

Zahavi, A. and Zahavi, A. (1997) *The Handicap Principle: A Missing Piece of Darwin's Puzzle* (New York: Oxford University Press).

CHAPTER 6

'BEAUTY MAGIC':
THE ORIGINS OF ART

CAMILLA POWER

> No one would want to marry a girl who had not had her chisungu danced. She
> would not know what her fellow women knew. She would not be invited to other
> chisungu feasts. She would just be a piece of rubbish; an uncultivated weed; an
> unfired pot; a fool; or just 'not a woman'.
>
> Richards 1956: 120

This was the traditional view of men among the matrilineal, uxorilocal
Bemba on why the female puberty rite, *chisungu*, had to be performed.
Until the final stage when the bridegroom arrived, men were respectful
onlookers, averting their eyes as the *chisungu* procession passed their huts
(Richards 1956: 90). The celebrants were women, observing a strict,
ritually rehearsed hierarchy under the authority of the mistress of
ceremonies (*nacimbusa*) (Richards 1956: 64). Candidates were expected
to be humble at all times, even when subjected to torment and abuse
(Richards 1956: 67). An elderly woman, often of royal lineage, who was
proven as a midwife and had special ritual knowledge, the *nacimbusa*,
made the *chisungu* through her energy and charisma; she worked 'magic
of attraction' by attention to costly detail. Particularly important was a
series of pottery models – sacred emblems (*mbusa*) – which were time-
consuming and elaborate in construction, yet destroyed or discarded once
they had been used for specific ritual actions (Richards 1956: 82–3).
Throughout the ceremony, a three-week event in 1931, the primary cosmetic material was red camwood powder mixed with oil as a paint that
made vivid crimson splashes (Richards 1956: 96). On four climactic
occasions, the candidates and the main actors were daubed in this mixture
(Richards 1956: 124).

Among the Yombe of the Lower Congo, the ceremonial prior to
marriage formerly lasted up to a year (Jacobson-Widding 1979: 158–9).
A girl would enter 'seclusion' in a 'red house' (*kumbi*), painted as she was
with red pigment. She would be joined by girls from surrounding villages
and even some young men – but her fiancé would be excluded. All, girls
and boys, were daubed in red colour. Similar 'fattening seclusion' practices
prevailed in West Africa. At this time, according to Basden, the only

occupation of Ibo girls 'is the preparation of camwood dye wherewith to stain their bodies red' (1966: 223). Red camwood also marked the emergence of a girl from the lengthy ordeals and seclusion required for initiation into the *liengu* cult, a women's secret society prevalent in the Cameroon coastal area (Ardener 1975: 9). Among Middle Eastern and North African islamicized groups, the most frequent cosmetic is henna, which produces a deep red stain on the hands and feet. Exchange of gifts of henna was particularly important for Hausa women when they entered *kawa*, or bond friendship with other women (Smith 1954: 56–8, 191–2). Its most prominent ritual use was in the preparation of the bride; seven days prior to marriage, the bride's kinswomen catch her and rub her skin with henna, despite her efforts to resist (Smith 1954: 88).

In all these examples, primarily red cosmetics are being manipulated by coalitions of women, related and not related, in puberty and nubility ritual contexts. The red colour typically advertises imminent fertility of the initiate, but the cosmetics also provide mechanisms for marking reciprocal relations and obligations among the women. These costly, lengthy, often traumatic rituals appear to be critical in mate choice; girls who failed to undergo initiation were traditionally unmarriageable – 'fools' or 'weeds'. Much of the most elaborate art belonging to these cultures was produced either in the context of, or with reference to, female initiation. This includes the pottery models and designs characteristic of the Bemba (Richards 1956) and Venda (Nettleton 1992), and rock art of Khoisan peoples (Solomon 1992) and Bantu agriculturalists (Prins and Hall 1994).

Can these ethnographic illustrations of 'beauty magic' help shed light on the evolutionary origins of art?

WHY SEXUAL SELECTION?

'There is no reason to believe symbolic culture was ever essential for survival,' writes Chase (1994). *Homo heidelbergensis* appears to have weathered tough times in Middle Pleistocene Europe, yet has left no trace of a life and culture informed by symbolism (Pitts and Roberts 1997). If we lack compelling reasons for seeing natural selection at work in the emergence of art and symbolism, it is worth invoking sexual selection. By neglecting the influence of sexual selection in the evolution of language and art, we would 'rule out one of the most powerful, inventive and pervasive forces in nature' (Miller 1997). The extreme costliness and elaboration of art lead us to consider sexual selection theory. Selection for 'extravagance and waste' is identified by Zahavi (1991) as a central problem of sexual selection. Rather than being unique to sexual selection, this may be viewed as a problem of signal selection more generally (cf. Zahavi 1987; Zahavi and Zahavi 1997: 40).

Fisher's (1930) 'runaway process' provided the first coherent model for the evolution of secondary sex ornaments by mate choice. If females developed a heritable preference for a male trait, which was also heritable, then the two characteristics – female preference and male trait – could advance together with 'ever-increasing speed' until checked by severe counter-selection. The point here is that females need no more reason for choosing a particular trait than that other females choose it – arbitrary fashion (Ridley 1993: 134).

Opposed to Fisherian models in sexual (or signal) selection theory is the 'handicap principle' advanced by Zahavi (1975). Signals must have a cost in order to be reliable; the higher the cost, the more reliable the signal. So the evolution of signals differs fundamentally from the evolution of all other characters, which are selected for efficiency and ever lower investment. In certain interactions, the need for reliability justifies extra high investment that takes the form of extravagance and waste (Zahavi 1987). Just as the patterns evolved by animal species can be read as costly and reliable signals advertising individual quality, Zahavi (1978) suggests that a similar evolutionary function underlies human cultural production of decorative pattern.

Cross-cultural surveys by evolutionary ecologists Low (1979), Ludvico and Kurland (1995) and Singh and Bronstad (1997) have applied sexual selection hypotheses to specific forms of human body ornament. While intrasexual competition and intersexual mate choice may drive human cosmetic and symbolic display, some puzzling aspects remain to be explained. If we analyze the occasions for extremely costly 'artistic' display in various media including traumatic body mutilation, rock art production, masked dance or recital of myth, the contexts for the costliest signalling are ritual and religious. Participants regularly incur prohibitions on sexual activity – restrictions that may last for months or even years. Much of the 'display' may occur in strictest secrecy and cannot be directly signalled to members of the opposite sex, or even members of the same sex who are probable competitors. How would a sexual selection framework account for the centrality of ritual action and stringent taboos attached to human artistic traditions? Can sexual selection have anything to say about the evolution of monastic traditions of Gregorian chant, for example? The question may be clarified if we can develop a specific and testable model for the emergence of symbolism.

COSTLINESS OF SYMBOLIC BEHAVIOUR

Modern 'selfish gene' Darwinism has made its most crucial contribution to evolutionary biology through its focus on costs. From this standpoint, the salient feature of symbolic behaviour such as ritual and art is its high demands on time and energy. Clearly, if we do not pose questions about the relative costs and benefits of symbolic behaviour, we cannot begin to evaluate selection pressures that gave rise to symbolism. Humans regularly invest much time and energy in the production by ritual action of what might be termed 'collective fantasies' or 'deceptions' (Knight et al. 1995). This contrasts starkly with the imaginative life of non-human primates. The great apes, in particular, may display capacities to infer mental states from behavioural cues – mindreading (Byrne 1995: 144). But they put no time or energy into replicating one another's dreams, fantasies or illusions. While one primate in a group may fantasize or imagine events, no other individual will be motivated to share such imaginings.

Hunter-gatherer ritual activity has not been subject to rigorous time allocation studies comparable to optimal foraging analyses of subsistence behaviours. Yet from detailed fieldwork such as that on Ju/'hoan trance activity (Katz 1982), we can infer that people invest heavily in ritual. In the typical Kalahari case, this may occur all night long, normally continuing into the next night, more than once a month, with both women and men participating in highly energetic clapping and singing or dancing. They subject themselves to considerable stress in entering altered states of consciousness – having spent many years in developing the skills required. Around this activity they weave elaborate ideologies of experiencing death, changing into animals and roaming in that form across the desert to visit friends and relatives.

Hames (1992: 233) points to the conceptual problems of applying time allocation studies to ritual, political, social and 'non-economic' activities. Taking the common cross-cultural activity of ritual curing, in cases where a curer receives pay, this can reasonably be classed as somatic effort. But in numerous cases, a curer receives nothing 'even though he may chant to the spirits all day and night until exhausted and he may have consumed a considerable quantity of hallucinogenic drugs that took additional hours to gather from the forest and to process' (1992: 233). Perhaps, Hames suggests, the curer gains prestige, but what currency or proxy measure can be used to translate that prestige into reproductive fitness?

In the example of ritual curing, the expense falls on two sides. While the curer expends time and energy for no apparent gain, the patient and other attendants spend comparable levels of time and energy engaging in the curer's fictions – the chants to the spirits, addressing an unverifiable 'other' world. In this light, the human species appears not as the 'thinking' or 'tool-making ape' so much as the 'gullible ape'. To account for the evolutionary emergence of such costly engagement with the symbolic realm, we need convincing answers to the following questions. What selection pressures promoted an interest in sharing and propagating conspecifics' illusions? Why did it benefit individuals to share in the unverifiable fantasies of others, rather than develop resistance to what Dawkins (1993) would describe as 'parasitic' memes? Can we model a systematic process in which hominids were driven to expend increasing time and energy on things that did not exist – 'deceptions' entertained by groups of individuals?

THE COSTS OF REPRODUCTION: 'SEXUAL DIALECTICS'

In any sexually reproducing species, males and females get their genes into the next generation by different means. For mammals and especially primates, females undergo lengthy periods of gestation and lactation requiring the investment of considerable resources, while males are not necessarily committed to more than the energy needed to access and impregnate mates (Trivers 1972). There will be differential trade-offs between the sexes over investment of energy in current offspring (parental effort) as against energy expended for producing future offspring (mating effort). In the case of human evolution, these trade-offs are likely to have been critically affected by the extraordinary energetic costs imposed on hominid mothers by encephalization (Foley and Lee 1991; Martin 1990, 1996).

In terms of parental investment and sexual selection (Trivers 1972), human evolution, especially in the later stages of encephalization, presents a picture of radical change in the level of investment by males. Females necessarily continued to invest heavily in offspring, and as access to fertile females would limit male reproductive success we expect standard sexual selection factors of male–male competition and female choice to operate. However, we can infer that what really changed in the period leading to the emergence of modern humans was the level of investment by males in female partners – hence, the level of male discrimination in choosing which females to invest in – along with increased female–female competition for access to investing males. Therefore, atypical factors of male choice and female–female competition became increasingly prominent as determinants of variance in female reproductive success (Gowaty 1997; see also Harcourt 1996: 122; Andersson 1994: 161, 177).

As and when human mating systems tended towards 'social mono-gamy', selection on males became less intense relative to selection in more polygynous systems. Correspondingly, selection on females became more intense, as females competed for access to 'best quality' males. In these circumstances, where both sexes participate in extensive parental care and either sex stands to lose badly from defection by the other party, Møller suggests that sexual evolutionary conflict will generate elaborate signal evolution and adapted psychologies, a 'breeding ground for extreme abilities of mind-reading' (1997: 44–5). If 'sexual selection in socially monogamous species with challenging evolutionary conflicts of interests between the sexes' leads to co-evolutionary selection for larger and differently structured brains (Møller 1997: 45), then female hominids would have been caught in a feedback loop. As encephalization proceeded, female psychologies became increasingly adapted to test male quality, requiring increasing encephalization and renewed pressure on females. Such a feedback process may underlie the rapid phase of encephalization seen in archaic *Homo sapiens*.

Gowaty (1997) proposes that the evolution of mating systems is driven by 'sexual dialectics' – processes of male manipulation and control of female reproductive capacities co-evolve in an 'arms race' with female resistance to control. Where male manipulation-control operates via 'brokering' or trading of resources for access, female resistance strategies should lead to intersexual competition for control of resources (Gowaty 1997). These factors are likely to become increasingly important in the evolution of hominid mating systems as pressures of encephalization rendered high-quality food vital for female reproduction. It is argued here that symbolic culture emerged as a strategy of female resistance to male control through 'brokering' of high-energy resources.

SEXUAL SIGNALS AND BEHAVIOURAL CHANGE

Critical to the reproductive success of females as they came under selection pressure for larger-brained offspring was extracting energy from new sources. The first major increase in brain size occurs with the appearance of early *Homo* over two million years ago, culminating in *Homo ergaster*. The resulting costs could have been offset by shifts to high-quality diet, allowing reduction of gut size (Aiello and Wheeler 1995), increases in female body size (McHenry 1996; Aiello 1996); and changes in life history variables such as increased longevity, promoting grandmothering (Aiello, in press), and secondary altriciality, slowing down maturation rates of the larger-brained offspring (Foley and Lee 1991: 70). Investment by males may have been intermittent rather than systematic, and directed as mating effort towards cycling females, rather than pregnant/lactating females (Power and Aiello 1997; Aiello, in press). A period of over a million years, from the Lower to early Middle Pleistocene is characterized by stasis in relative brain size (Kappelman 1996; Ruff et al. 1997). The accelerated encephalization rates of the late Middle Pleistocene brought increased reproductive costs, particularly to mothers in early stages of lactation. These steeply increasing costs of reproduction are likely to have driven major social and sexual behavioural changes (see Foley and Lee 1996: 63–4; Power and Aiello 1997). Above all, those females who secured increased levels of investment from males would have enhanced their fitness.

For females, sexual signals are the primary mechanisms for eliciting behavioural changes in males. It is assumed here that by the stage of archaic grade *Homo sapiens*, overt signs of ovulation had already been lost and the modern pattern of 'loss of oestrus/continuous receptivity' established. These are effective mechanisms for forcing male attentiveness and promoting longer consortships (Alexander and Noonan 1979) which would have assisted early *Homo ergaster* females in gaining supplies of energy-rich food and meeting the costs of the earlier phase of brain expansion (*c.* 2 m.y.a.). However, concealment of ovulation can never guarantee more than mating effort, since once a female is pregnant/lactating the fact that she is *not* ovulating is not concealed. The most prominent remaining signal in the modern human female cycle is menstruation. In a natural fertility population, with most females of reproductive age pregnant or lactating, menstruation occurs relatively rarely and is a good indicator of *imminent* fertility (Strassmann 1997). Pleistocene males who were attentive to recently menstruating females in an effort to improve their mating prospects should therefore enhance their fitness. No male could afford to ignore this signal.

This implies that an archaic female who was menstruating could advertise her signal to males in the vicinity to promote mating effort. Menstrual blood, therefore, would have a material value translatable into energy in the form of male provisioning.

FEMALE COALITIONARY STRATEGIES: PROTORITUAL

For any pregnant/lactating female, a menstrual female is a potential threat capable of diverting male energy and investment away from her. One response to this problem, as archaic *Homo sapiens* females experienced increasing reproductive stress, would be to adopt a reciprocal altruistic coalitionary strategy of manipulating menstrual signals. Each female coalition needed to prevent any male from sequestering the imminently fertile female; they should surround her and restrict sexual access. Given the economic value of the signal, rather than hide the menstruant's condition, we would predict the opposite. Whenever a coalition member menstruated, the whole coalition joined in advertising this valuable signal as widely as possible to recruit available male energy to the coalition. The strategy succeeded as long as any mating effort generated by the menstruant's signal flowed into the whole coalition, benefiting both non-menstruants and menstruants. Non-menstruant coalition members would confuse matters by borrowing the menstruant's signal or mimicking it with other blood or blood substitutes. This strategy would effectively prevent males from discriminating in favour of cycling females and undermine attempts by would-be dominant males to monopolize imminently fertile females via brokering of energy-rich resources.

Such cosmetic manipulation of menstrual signals is termed 'sham menstruation'. Within any coalition, the strategy is well-designed for a reciprocal altruistic alliance, since any female must prove her commitment to the alliance when she is cycling before she can derive any benefits when she is not cycling. All fertile females alternate between being cyclic and non-cyclic. Between female coalitions, a competitive dynamic is expected as they strive to attract available male muscle power. This should drive an evolutionary 'arms race' of increasingly elaborate sham menstrual advertising, resulting in ritualistic amplification of displays. These could involve use of red pigment to amplify and broadcast the menstrual signal, with multimedia effects of movement, song and dance.

PREDICTIONS FROM THE 'SHAM MENSTRUATION' MODEL

The main prediction derived from the 'sham menstruation' model is that the earliest evidence of ritual traditions in the archaeological record will take the form of a cosmetics industry focused on red pigment.

Power and Watts (1996) argue for a two-tier process of the evolution of ritual, fundamentally determined by degree of reproductive stress on females. During earlier stages of the brain expansion of archaic *Homo sapiens*, they posit *context-dependent* sham menstruation displays, triggered by the incidence of menstruation in local populations. Female coalitions used these as opportunity arose to attract and retain male support, securing long-term bonds with mates. This strategy implies less planning depth in obtaining materials for cosmetic usage, with correspondingly greater reliance on biodegradable matter, and only occasional traces of utilized ochre. As late archaic to early anatomically modern females endured acute reproductive stress – roughly the period 160,000–130,000 BP, coincident with the Penultimate Glacial Maximum (Jouzel et al. 1993) – they posit the emergence of a habitual strategy of cosmetic ritual underpinning the sexual division of labour. Greater regularity, planning and organization of performances would lead us to expect abundant and regular use of ochre. The onset of this earliest ritual tradition would institutionalize an economic division of labour and forms of social co-operation both between the sexes and between kin groups. Therefore, it should permit relaxation of selection pressures for robusticity, especially in females, and reduce stress levels experienced by juveniles (see Kappelman 1996: 272; Brooks 1996: 146–8), possibly permitting earlier weaning. It should promote investment in campsites, with females and offspring able to stay 'home' while male hunters depart on logistic hunts.

The 'sham menstruation' strategy involves deceptive signals in that some females who are not imminently fertile pretend to be. Unlike primate tactical deception, which is always individualistic and egocentric (Whiten and Byrne 1988), the deception in this case is sociocentric, being maintained by a collective. As such, it represents a vital step towards sustaining an *imaginary construct* and sharing that construct with others – that is, establishing symbolism.

So long as such deceptive displays are staged only because a local female is menstruating, these signals, however amplified, are still embedded in perceptible reality: basically, they form loud advertisements of the presence of an imminently fertile female. But it is easy to see how a female coalition would be pushed into the signalling of imagined constructs which are impossibilities, corresponding to no perceptible reality – collective deceptions. Males who are attracted by cosmetic displays advertising imminently fertile females will be reluctant to leave the vicinity; they will instead be inclined to mate-guard. Some males may even be non-cooperative and attempt abduction of menstrual females. These circumstances would force the female coalition (with male kin support) to step up resistance by loudly signalling 'No access' to outgroup males. Knight et al. (1995: 84) argue that the way female coalitions would construct such a 'No' signal is by reversing the normal parameter settings of the species mate recognition system (cf. Paterson 1978, 1982). Where female animals in courtship normally display 'right species/right sex/right time', systematic reversal by a defiant female coalition would yield 'wrong species' – we are animals, not humans; 'wrong sex' – we are males, not females; and 'wrong time' – we are not fertile right now, but *soon* we will be. This is the predicted performance constructing the potency of the ritual domain and the inviolability, or 'taboo' state, of menstrual or body-painted females. Transmission of such signals counter to perceptible reality will involve energetically expensive, repetitive, iconographic pantomime – high-cost ritual signals sustaining fictitious 'gods'.

SEXUAL SELECTION AND SPECIATION

Besides sexual selection forces of female–female competition between body-painted coalitions, factors of male choice for cosmetically decorated females should also motor an explosive spread of ritual traditions. These processes of sexual selection could be implicated in speciation of anatomically modern humans with cultural, artificial secondary sexual signals marking divergence between modern and archaic forms (cf. Andersson 1994: 46–7, 223, 226).

Why should males be interested in choosing females who use cultural deceptive sexual signals, interfering with the genetic species mate recognition system? Although dishonest at one level, at another, ritual cosmetic display can be understood in 'handicap principle' terms as a costly signal which is honest about the quality of the signaller (Zahavi and Zahavi 1997). Suppose a young female reaches puberty. At the time of her first menstruation, a cosmetic ritual should be staged, involving immediate coalition members in costly preparations, gathering and processing pigment, followed by energetic performance. Not only does such ritual advertise a female of maximum reproductive value; it also demonstrates in ways that are 'hard to fake' and 'easy to judge' the extent of the female's kinship support network and its ability to organize coalitionary alliances.

Early modern human females are expected to be discriminating in their choice of mate. From the evidence of hunter-gatherer mating systems, the primary female criterion of choice is institutionalized in the form of bride-service. As a general rule, males do not gain access to mates unless they prove successful as hunters, either individually or as part of a team. To the extent that males must invest increasing levels of energy in gaining access to mates, they should be increasingly discriminating. But beyond a general requirement of high reproductive value, what were the criteria of male choice for long-term partner? The sham menstruation model suggests that female cosmetic display became an important selective criterion for choosy males.

In arguing that patterns evolve in the animal world as costly signals of individual quality, Zahavi (1978; Zahavi and Zahavi 1997: 53) suggests that the feature which will be elaborated through pattern or design will be critical for the reproductive success of the individual. For instance, length is a critical determinant of fitness in the anemone fish; its striped pattern draws attention precisely to this feature. In line with this argument, the species-specific adaptation which human cosmetic ritual advertises is the ability to form and deploy coalitionary alliances. The pubertal female whose kin coalition stages body-paint display is signalling to discriminating males: 'Invest in me, because I have extensive kinship support, and my children will have it.'

COSMETICS IN AFRICAN ETHNOGRAPHY

The model predicts periodic female inviolability as the focus of early human ritual traditions, signalled by real blood or cosmetic body paint, inverted sexual attributes and therianthropic metamorphoses. It expects taboos on access to 'menstruating' ritually potent females, these corresponding to taboos on sex for outgroup males prior to hunting (see Knight

1991: 389–91). Ingroup males should participate in signalling by mothers and sisters, becoming bloody and ambiguously sexed.

Watts (this volume) summarizes the archaeological record of pigment use by late archaic and early modern humans and its relationship to the onset of 'modern' behaviours. According to ethnohistorical accounts, Khoisan preparation and application of red ochre and haematite is primarily a women's occupation, occurring overwhelmingly in ritual contexts, and particularly during menarcheal observances (Watts, this volume). While she is in seclusion, stringent taboos are placed on a menarcheal girl, especially on any contact between her and male hunters. Power and Watts (1997) detail the 'wrong sex, wrong species' symbolic signalling involved in Khoisan and Hadza initiation ritual for both sexes.

The model also leads us to expect certain dynamics in the use of cosmetics in wider ethnography, not only among hunter-gatherer groups. Are cosmetics used chiefly in ritual contexts? Do those rituals establish and display extensive female reciprocal altruistic alliances? Do cosmetics advertise and amplify signals of imminent fertility – and is such signalling honest or dishonest? Is access to honest signallers of imminent fertility controlled by non-cycling females? Have we evidence of mechanisms of sexual selection for cosmetic display, including female–female competition and male choice? Is use of cosmetics sexually dimorphic or monomorphic, and does this vary with levels of parental investment by each sex?

Cosmetics usage appears virtually ubiquitous in African pubertal ritual for both sexes. Among peoples of the Lower Congo, red pigment formed the most general beauty preparation, mainly used by young women when going to dances, but also sometimes by young, unmarried men (Jacobson-Widding 1979: 157). In the Mpangu puberty ceremonial, boys after circumcision would apply red colouring during the healing and seclusion period, and paint themselves red all over for the feast on emergence. Girls followed almost identical procedure for their parallel rite involving tatooing (Jacobson-Widding 1979: 158–9). For both sexes, the red colour connotes beauty and sexual maturity. Close parallelism between girls' and boys' puberty rituals is broadly typical of African initiation, although many cultures stress and elaborate the rites for one sex more than the other. What can be said in general is that the signalling underlying these rituals mimicks *female* biology, revolving around bloodshed, and specifically genital bloodshed. In the course of circumcision rites, boys may be explicitly feminized, being made to wear the dress or ornaments of female relatives, or called by the names of women's body parts (for example Chagga, Raum 1940: 309; Fang, Stoll 1955: 159; Maasai, Hollis 1905: 298; Nandi, Hollis 1909: 53; Makonde, Harries 1944: 12; Ndembu, Turner 1967: 96, 223, 254; Wiko, Gluckman 1949: 153, 155). Dogon boys are explicitly described as 'having their periods' (Calame-Griaule

1965: 158). Girls or their female associates are correspondingly masculinized, dressed as hunters or warriors and/or treated as hunted animals (Nandi, Hollis 1909: 58; Hausa, Smith 1954: 93; Chagga, Dundas 1924: 214; Raum 1940: 353; Khoisan, Hadza, Power and Watts 1997; and see Bemba below).

The 1931 Bemba *chisungu* observed by Richards was truncated compared with the traditional performance owing to changing economic conditions (Richards 1956: 133). However, the mistress of ceremonies (*nacimbusa*) took great pains to show Richards how things should be done (1956: 61). An impressive display that drew large crowds and eminent visitors was a source of pride and political prestige for the *nacimbusa* herself, the village, the parents of the bride and the groom (Richards 1956: 133–4). The initiate entered into a special relationship with the *nacimbusa* who presided at her *chisungu* and effectively introduced her into the adult women's community. She was obliged to act as helper at subsequent *chisungu* ceremonies, while the *nacimbusa* was to act as midwife at her first birth (Richards 1956: 131). This placed the *nacimbusa* (often a senior woman of her patrikin) in a position of considerable power. Any trouble during the birth was taken as an indication of adultery, which the young woman would be made to confess to the *nacimbusa*. The young woman's moral character, as evidenced by her behaviour at the first birth, could 'be revealed or concealed by the *nacimbusa*' (Richards 1956: 132).

Red cosmetics punctuated the event. On the first day, the company was painted after the girls had passed a 'first test' of jumping over branches, the cosmetic treatment being the same as would be given to triumphant lion-killers (Richards 1956: 66); on the seventh day, red marked the appearance of the 'mock bridegrooms' – sisters of the bridegrooms – who swaggered around dressed as hunters with bows (Richards 1956: 73–4). On the fourteenth, red dye was used as part of the so-called 'whitening magic' associated with songs celebrating the end of menstruation, when the girls would emerge beautiful and 'white like egrets' (Richards 1956: 89–90, 124). Finally, after another trial by jumping, on the seventeenth day the girls and their entourage returned to the village in triumph as 'lion-killers' with a log as the 'dead lion', the entire company smeared with red paint 'so that we must have had an uncouth and eerie appearance' (Richards 1956: 96).

Besides the transvestite comic role-playing of the 'mock bridegrooms', the *nacimbusa* would adopt accoutrements of warriors or lion-killers such as an axe or plumed helmet (Richards 1956: 96, 101). The girls, too, had to perform 'male' tasks of ritual firelighting (Richards 1956: 77), while the entire company built, decorated and occupied a 'man's shelter' (*nsaka* – a place where soldiers would gather in the evening), just after the 'whitening magic' ceremony (Richards 1956: 90–1). Many obscure motifs in the rituals focus on reversal, such as the girls being made to climb backwards as 'tortoises' up a tree (Richards 1956: 70). The upside-down or counter-reality logic of these mimes was finally brought to an end by the coming of the bridegrooms, who sang 'I have tracked my game; now I have speared my meat', and shot arrows into marks on the wall over their brides' heads (Richards 1956: 106–7). Such ritual treatment of the female initiate as a hunted game animal is a feature of several *chisungu*-type ceremonies in matrilineal Central Africa, notably the Makonde ritual gazelle hunt (Richards 1956: 173, 182, 185, citing Harries 1944). In conjunction with these 'wrong species/sex' pantomimes, use of red pigment recurs. Among the Tonga, secluded girls 'passed the time grinding red ochre with which to anoint their bodies, blowing on a koodoo horn' (Colson 1958: 285). On emergence girls were ritually bathed and a feast held, when the women 'do a dance which represents the cattle killed for the occasion' (Richards 1956: 176, citing Colson). Structurally, this is reminiscent of the typical Khoisan menarcheal ritual, the Eland Bull dance, and as with the Khoisan, there is stress on the girl emerging 'fat'. The attitude of mission-educated Tonga to these practices is revealing: 'Seclusion is a bad thing as it advertises the fact that the girl is now mature, thus attracting the attention of men who might otherwise ignore her as a small girl' (Colson 1958: 283).

In documenting Venda girls' initiation from the 1950s, Blacking writes: 'A woman who has not graduated is not "a member of the club": she has no real say in women's affairs, nor any guarantee of assistance from other women in times of crisis' (1969: 4). The complex cycle of initiation schools, where girls would learn songs, dances and mimes, provided a framework for widespread reciprocity among Venda women. Throughout the cycle, initiates learned *milayo*, 'laws' or 'instructions', which functioned as shibboleths or passwords (cf. Nettle, this volume). These, says Blacking, 'supported a woman's claim to the benefits of an inter-district, inter-tribal, pan-Venda mutual aid society' (1969: 5).

Anointing with red ochre and fat occurred throughout the *vhusha* school, organized at the village level, and the centrally organized *tshikanda* and *domba* schools. The theme of menstruation and proper observance of menstrual taboos pervaded songs and recitations of *milayo* at all stages. Among numerous metaphors used to refer to menstruation was 'to abuse the old ladies', indicating tension between cycling and non-cycling women (Blacking 1969: 9). Ideally the cycle commenced after menarche with *vhusha*. Manipulation of red ochre marked specific relationships between the women involved. On the first day, the girl was rubbed with 'dirty' red ochre by her *mmane*, the woman to whom she first announced her onset of menses, a sister or co-wife of her mother (Blacking 1969: 13). The girl chose a ritual 'lover', actually a tiny boy whose mother had to supply the candidate with new clothes and red ochre with fat (Blacking 1969: 17).

After six days seclusion (eight for nobles), the candidate was taken for a ritual soaking in the river. The old ladies in charge inspected her virginity; then she was washed, covered in fat and red ochre, and dressed in a special goat-skin skirt with a bead necklace (Blacking 1969: 18). Nobles had even more elaborate costume, including the *thahu*, a ritual, tail-like object plastered with red ochre (Blacking 1969: 7; Stayt 1931: 109–10). The girl wore the ritual dress and red ochre for a week, adopting a ritually humble posture and exaggerated form of greeting for anyone she met. Women were supposed to give the girl a bangle when she greeted them (Blacking 1969: 18).

Descent and residence rules clearly affect the involvement of a mother in her daughter's initiation. Among the Venda, characterized by bilateral kinship, the mother of a girl was supposedly last to know about her daughter's menstrual onset. There was deliberate emphasis on a wider network of women making and publicizing the arrangements for a girl's initiation (Blacking 1969: 9–10). Yet, even among a patrilineal, patrilocal group such as the Chagga, the relationship might be strongly asserted through cosmetic signals. A Chagga girl would be installed in her mother-in-law's hut prior to menstruation, and spend at least three months in seclusion there before marriage. Ideally, she started to menstruate during this time. Evidence of her daughter's menstruation in the form of stained cloths would be sent back to her mother. Parading in the marketplace, the centre of the women's community, for the first time since her daughter left, the mother would wear these stained cloths, herself coated in red ochre (Dundas 1924: 238; Raum 1940: 103).

The 'sham menstruation' model argues that female coalition members will use cosmetic signals to confuse information about which female is at what reproductive stage, preventing male discrimination between attractive cycling females and relatively unattractive non-cycling females. We can expect that women at non-fertile reproductive stages will use red cosmetics to make themselves relatively more attractive to potential male investors. Here, sham menstruation acts as dishonest signalling, exploiting male sensory biases. During the Venda *vhusha* school, we find suggestions of deliberate confusion of cultural signals associated with menarcheal girls, pregnant women and new mothers. Noble girls are given 'pregnancy tonsures'; in the second stage of the school, the novices' special skin skirts are worn as cloaks, in a manner only otherwise seen on women just after confinement (Blacking 1969: 7). Before a Venda mother can leave her hut after a birth, her husband must visit her with a ceremonial preparation 'made from the blood of a menstruating woman, which he rubs on the palms of his hands and the soles of his feet.' (Stayt 1931: 87) His wife gives him a bracelet, the name of which means 'an intense desire'. Baba of Karo described a Hausa naming ceremony, held seven days after a birth when the mother is done up beautifully with henna by her kinswomen and *kawaye* (bond friends) (Smith 1954: 140). Before all the guests, the mother pantomimes persistent refusal to care for the child when it is brought to her. Publicly, the red signal is stressed while lactation is suppressed.

Among the Fang in Cameroon, a red powder called *baa* is used much in the same way as henna for both magical and aesthetic reasons, though lipstick is nowadays favoured by young women (Alexandre and Binet 1958: 88). Pregnant women anoint their breasts and stomachs with a mix of palm oil and *baa* (Alexandre and Binet 1958: 91). During lactation a Katab mother would 'cover her entire body and head with red ochre, to improve her supply of milk' (Gunn 1956: 76). In the Lower Congo, a Buissi woman was secluded for three months after giving birth while her mother looked after her. She would wash and smear herself with red pigment every day. For the feast held on her emergence from this seclusion, her mother would paint her body with red pomade (Jacobson-Widding 1979: 162–3). Pregnant women also painted their bodies red, and would take days off work to do so (Jacobson-Widding 1979: 163). Many of these practices are associated with taboos on sex during pregnancy and postpartum, with red cosmetics believed to afford magical protection. Body paint functions, in effect, as an anti-rape device, since any offender would, at least temporarily, be conspicuously marked with colour (cf. Knight 1991: 400–1). But the point here is that the signalling being used by both cycling, imminently fertile women and non-cycling women shows continuity and potential confusion.

By contrast, the Southeastern Nuba of Sudan clearly differentiate women at different reproductive stages in line with complex clan affiliations arising from a duolineal descent system (Faris 1972: 14). Girls prior to pregnancy wear either red or yellow ochre according to their patriclan section colour, covering themselves all over (Faris 1972: 32). Once pregnant, and subsequently until weaning, a woman wears oil and ochre on her head and shoulders of the colour of her infant's patriclan (Faris 1972: 30). The extremely elaborate traditions of Nuba personal art, particularly among men, appear to be driven by factors of sexual selection. For women it is ornate cicatrization which offers a costly means of demonstrating imminent fertility and sexual availability – a type of 'sham menstruation'. After an initial scarring early in puberty, a girl receives her second set of scars, all over her torso, at menarche (Faris 1972: 15, 32–3). The last, most elaborate set, all over the back of her body, is received by a woman when she has weaned her first child. Her husband is expected to pay for this, but if he fails to do so, another man may, and he will take the woman, wife theft being most common at this point of a woman's reproductive career (Faris 1972: 35–6). This form of ornamentation is traumatic; the operation itself takes two days and a woman may faint from lack of blood. She is isolated for several days, when she is treated as being in a state of blood pollution – in particular, she must not come into contact with weapons (Faris 1972: 33–4). All women (except haemophiliacs) are scarred, apparently under pressure of sexual selection, since the tradition is motivated by 'the demands of beauty' (Faris 1972: 36). Zahavi and Zahavi (1997: 213–14) suggest that menstruation is a reliable indicator of a woman's physical condition and readiness to bear offspring. In this light, Nuba scarification appears as a cultural 'handicap' signal, exaggerating the costs of biological menstruation (see Ludvico and Kurland 1995: 160). Singh and Bronstad (1997: 412) argue that stomach scarification such as that of the Nuba functions as a costly signal of pathogen resistance.

WHY NOT A MODEL OF MALE RITUAL ALLIANCES?

In arguing that female strategies drove the emergence of symbolism, this model of the origins of art challenges much received wisdom. Why not propose a model of male ritual coalitions? After all, the ethnographic record shows that most sacred ritual is performed by men, much of it excluding women in general and menstruating women in particular.

The model does not preclude the evolution of ritualistic displays by male coalitions. On Darwinian grounds, we can expect sexually selected male display of alliances among archaic *Homo* species, driven by male–male competition for access to or monopoly of fertile females. But there are several problems with understanding this activity as the root of modern human symbolism.

Firstly, there is the question of the energetics of encephalization. To the extent that males were putting their energy towards high-cost signalling of ritual alliances, they would not have been channelling high-energy foods to females burdened by encephalized offspring. The function of the ritual alliances would more likely be to attract cycling, non-pregnant females.

Secondly, the forms of signalling used by such male coalitions raise an even more fundamental objection. How do we explain the emergence of a symbolic domain of collective *deceptions*? We would expect male ritual coalitions to advertise their sexually selected qualities in 'hard to fake' terms, that is in ways that correspond to perceptible reality, visibly demonstrating size of coalition, strength, weaponry and so on. Singing and dancing might be media for such signalling, but there is no reason to suppose these songs or dances would access another world counter to perceptible reality. Why would males be interested in advertising themselves as 'female' or 'animal'? By contrast, a female coalition model straightforwardly yields deceptive sexual signals and habitual construction of 'counter-reality' in which males as kin participate.

Thirdly, a male ritual model fails to account for what we actually see in the ethnographic record. Why should ritual power celebrate celibacy? Surely, a male ritual model would predict the opposite, maximum access to females. Why should there be any taboos on menstruating women? Surely, male ritual coalitions would be especially anxious to mate-guard imminently fertile females. Strassmann (1992, 1996) has tracked the visits of Dogon women to menstrual huts, proving them to be honest signallers, and has argued that isolating women in menstrual huts is a male strategy of mate-guarding. But why should a Dogon husband wish to broadcast the information that his wife is imminently fertile to other men in the village? Why not keep her quietly at home where only he knows if she is menstruating? Calame-Griaule records the 'causerie des femmes en règles', when Dogon husbands would talk to their wives in the evenings from outside the menstrual hut; by neglecting to do so, a husband would show he did not love his wife (1965: 242–3). Rather as the Nuba woman makes her husband pay for her expensive scars at the time she returns to cycling, the Dogon woman is clearly testing her husband's ardour and affection. She is in a good situation to advertise her imminent fertility to other men, potentially inciting male–male competition.

Finally, why during their most sacred and esoteric rituals, should men display themselves as 'female', even to the point of 'menstruating'? A male-driven model offers no account for phenomena such as male 'menstruation', subincision and circumcision (Knight 1991). By contrast, once female coalitionary strategies have established the 'gods' as monstrous, gender-ambivalent, bleeding therianthropes, it is logical to expect male coalitionary counter-strategies to co-opt the pre-existing language of the 'gods'.

CONCLUSION

Symbolic culture arose as a response to increasing levels of reproductive stress experienced by females during the rapid phase of encephalization associated with archaic *Homo sapiens*. Once reliable fertility signals had been phased out, menstrual bleeding was left as the only cue offering males positive information on which females were imminently fertile. Because pronounced menstrual bleeding was valuable for extracting mating effort from males, even non-cycling females 'cheated' by joining in with menstruating coalition partners whenever blood was flowing, painting up with red pigments to signal 'imminent fertility'. Dance and body-painting constituted the earliest art media, long before the production of representational imagery on inanimate surfaces. Forces of sexual selection drove the elaboration of cosmetic body-paint traditions through factors of competition between female ritual coalitions and male mate choice for cosmetically decorated females. Ethnohistorical evidence of cosmetics usage in African initiation and other ritual contexts is elucidated in the light of this model.

ACKNOWLEDGEMENTS

I would like to thank Leslie Aiello, Robin Dunbar, Chris Knight, Dan Nettle and especially Ian Watts for their discussion of many ideas in this chapter.

REFERENCES

Aiello, L. C. (1996) 'Hominine preadaptations for language and cognition', in Mellars, P. and Gibson, K. (eds), *Modelling the Early Human Mind* (Cambridge: McDonald Institute Monographs), pp. 89–99.

Aiello, L. C. (in press) 'The expensive tissue hypothesis and the evolution of the human adaptive niche: a study in comparative anatomy', in *Proceedings of the Science in Archaeology Conference* (HBMC Archaeology Reports Series, English Heritage).

Aiello, L. C. and Wheeler, P. (1995) 'The expensive tissue hypothesis: the brain and the digestive system in human and primate evolution', *Current Anthropology* 36: 199–221.

Alexander, R. D. and Noonan, K. M. (1979) 'Concealment of ovulation, parental care, and human social evolution', in Chagnon, N. and Irons, W. (eds), *Evolutionary Biology and Human Social Behavior* (North Scituate, Mass.: Duxbury Press), pp. 436–53.

Alexandre, P. and Binet, J. (1958) *Le Groupe dit Pahouin* (Paris: Presses Universitaires de France).

Andersson, M. (1994) *Sexual Selection* (Princeton, NJ: Princeton University Press).

Ardener, E. (1975) 'Belief and the problem of women', in Ardener, S. (ed.), *Perceiving Women* (London: Dent), pp. 1–17.

Basden, G. T. (1966) *Niger Ibos* (London: Frank Cass).

Blacking, J. (1969) 'Songs, dances, mimes and symbolism of Venda girls' initiation schools. Part I: Vhusha', *African Studies* 28: 3–35.

Brooks, A. S. (1996) 'Behavior and human evolution', in Meikle, W. F., Howell, F. C. and Jablonski, N. G. (eds), *Contemporary Issues in Human Evolution* (San Francisco: California Academy of Sciences), pp. 135–66.

Byrne, R. (1995) *The Thinking Ape. Evolutionary Origins of Intelligence* (Oxford: Oxford University Press).

Calame-Griaule, G. (1965) *Ethnologie et Langage. La Parole chez les Dogon* (Paris: Gallimard).

Chase, P. G. (1994) 'On symbols and the palaeolithic', *Current Anthropology* 35: 627–9.

Colson, E. (1958) *Marriage and the Family among the Plateau Tonga on Northern Rhodesia* (Manchester: Manchester University Press).

Dawkins, R. (1993) 'Viruses of the mind', in Dahlbom, B. (ed.), *Dennett and His Critics* (Oxford: Blackwell), pp. 13–27.

Dundas, C. (1924) *Kilimanjaro and its People. A History of the Wachagga, their Laws, Customs, and Legends together with some Account of the Highest Mountain in Africa* (London: Witherby).

Faris, J. (1972) *Nuba Personal Art* (London: Duckworth).

Fisher, R. A. (1930) *The Genetical Theory of Natural Selection* (Oxford: Clarendon Press).

Foley, R. A. and Lee, P. C. (1991) 'Ecology and energetics of encephalization in hominid evolution', *Philosophical Transactions of the Royal Society of London* 334: 223–32.

Foley, R. A. and Lee, P. C. (1996) 'Finite social space and the evolution of human social behaviour', in Steele, J. and Shennan, S. (eds), *The Archaeology of Human Ancestry. Power, Sex and Tradition* (London: Routledge), pp. 47–66.

Gluckman, M. (1949) 'The role of the sexes in Wiko circumcision ceremonies', in Fortes, M. (ed.), *Social Structure* (London: Oxford University Press), pp. 145–67.

Gowaty, P. A. (1997) 'Sexual dialectics, sexual selection, and variation in mating behavior', in Gowaty, P. A. (ed.), *Feminism and Evolutionary Biology: Boundaries, Intersections, and Frontiers* (New York: Chapman & Hall), pp. 351–84.

Gunn, H. D. (1956) *Pagan Peoples of the Central Area of Northern Nigeria* (London: International African Institute).

Hames, R. (1992) 'Time allocation', in Smith, E. A. and Winterhalder, B. (eds), *Evolutionary Ecology and Human Behavior* (New York: Aldine de Gruyter), pp. 203–35.

Harcourt, A. H. (1996) 'Sexual selection and sperm competition in primates: what are male genitalia good for?' *Evolutionary Anthropology* 4: 121–9.

Harries, L. (1944). *The Initiation Rites of the Makonde Tribe* (Livingstone: Rhodes-Livingstone Institute).

Hollis, A. C. (1905) *Masai, Their Language and Folklore* (Oxford: Clarendon Press).

Hollis, A. C. (1909) *Nandi, Their Language and Folklore* (Oxford: Clarendon Press)

Jacobson-Widding, A. (1979) *Red-White-Black as a Mode of Thought. A Study of Triadic Classification by Colours in the Ritual Symbolism and Cognitive Thought of the Peoples of the Lower Congo* (Uppsala: Acta Universitatis Upsaliensis).

Jouzel, J., Barkov, N. I., Barnola, J. I., Bender, M., Chappellaz, J., Genthon, C., Kollyakov, V. M., Lipenkov, V., Lorius, C., Petit, J. R., Raynaud, D., Raisbeck, G., Ritz, C., Sowers, T., Stievenard, M., Yiou, F. and Yiou, P. (1993) 'Extending the Vostok ice-core record of palaeoclimate to the penultimate glacial period', *Nature* 364: 407–12.

Kappelman, J. (1996) 'The evolution of body mass and relative brain size in fossil hominids', *Journal of Human Evolution* 30: 243–76.

Katz, R. (1982) *Boiling Energy. Community Healing among the Kalahari Kung* (Cambridge, Mass.: Harvard University Press).

Knight, C. D. (1991) *Blood Relations. Menstruation and the Origins of Culture* (New Haven, Conn. and London: Yale University Press).

Knight, C. D., Power, C. and Watts, I. (1995) 'The human symbolic revolution: a Darwinian account', *Cambridge Archaeological Journal* 5: 75–114.

Low, B. S. (1979) 'Sexual selection and human ornamentation', in Chagnon, N. and Irons W. (eds), *Evolutionary Biology and Human Social Behavior* (North Scituate, Mass.: Duxbury Press), pp. 462–87.

Ludvico, L. R. and Kurland, J. A. (1995) 'Symbolic or not-so-symbolic wounds: the behavioral ecology of human scarification', *Ethology and Sociobiology* 16: 155–72.

McHenry, H. M. (1996) 'Sexual dimorphism in fossil hominids and its socio-ecological implications', in Steele, J. and Shennan, S. (eds), *The Archaeology of Human Ancestry. Power, Sex and Tradition* (London: Routledge), pp. 91–109.

Martin, R. D. (1990) *Primate Origins and Evolution. A Phylogenetic Reconstruction* (London: Chapman & Hall).

Martin, R. D. (1996) 'Scaling of the mammalian brain: the maternal energy hypothesis', *News in Physiological Sciences* 11: 149–56.

Miller, G. F. (1997) 'Mate choice: from sexual cues to cognitive adaptations', in Bock, G. R. and Cardew, G. (eds), *Characterizing Human Psychological Adaptations*, Ciba Foundation Symposium 208 (Chichester: Wiley), pp. 71–87.

Møller, A. P. (1997) 'Evolutionary conflicts and adapted psychologies', Bock, G. R. and Cardew, G. (eds), *Characterizing Human Psychological Adaptations*, Ciba Foundation Symposium 208 (Chichester: Wiley), pp. 39–50.

Nettleton, A. (1992) 'Ethnic and gender identities in Venda Domba statues', *African Studies* 51: 203–30.

Paterson, H. E. H. (1978) 'More evidence against speciation by reinforcement', *South African Journal of Science* 74: 369–71.

Paterson, H. E. H. (1982) 'Perspective on speciation by reinforcement', *South African Journal of Science* 78: 53–7.

Pitts, M. and Roberts, M. (1997) *Fairweather Eden. Life in Britain Half a Million Years Ago as Revealed by the Excavations at Boxgrove* (London: Century).

Power, C. and Aiello, L. C. (1997) 'Female proto-symbolic strategies', in Hager, L. D. (ed.), *Women in Human Evolution* (London and New York: Routledge), pp. 153–71.

Power, C. and Watts, I. (1996) 'Female strategies and collective behaviour. The archaeology of earliest *Homo sapiens sapiens*', in Steele, J. and Shennan, S. (eds), *The Archaeology of Human Ancestry. Power, Sex and Tradition* (London: Routledge), pp. 306–30.

Power, C. and Watts, I. (1997) 'The woman with the zebra's penis. Gender, mutability and performance', *Journal of the Royal Anthropological Institute* (n.s.) 3: 537–60.

Prins, F. E. and Hall, S. (1994) 'Expressions of fertility in the rock art of Bantu-speaking agriculturists', *African Archaeological Review* 12: 171–203.

Raum, O. F. (1940) *Chagga Childhood. A Description of Indigenous Education in an East African Tribe* (London: Oxford University Press).

Richards, A. I. (1956) *Chisungu. A Girls' Initiation Ceremony Among the Bemba of Northern Rhodesia* (London: Faber & Faber).

Ridley, M. (1993) *The Red Queen. Sex and the Evolution of Human Nature* (London: Viking).

Ruff, C. B., Trinkaus E. and Holliday T. W. (1997) 'Body mass and encephalization in Pleistocene *Homo*', *Nature* 387: 173–6.

Singh, D. and Bronstad, P. M. (1997) 'Sex differences in the anatomical locations of human body scarifications and tatooing as a function of pathogen prevalence', *Evolution and Human Behavior* 18: 403–16.

Smith, M. (1954) *Baba of Karo* (London: Faber).

Solomon, A. (1992) 'Gender, representation and power in San ethnography and rock art', *Journal of Anthropological Archaeology* 11: 291–329.

Stayt, H. A. (1931) *The Bavenda* (Oxford: Oxford University Press).

Stoll, R. P. A. (1955) *La Tonétique des Langues Bantu et Semi-Bantu du Cameroun* (Paris: Institut Français d'Afrique Noire).

Strassmann, B. I. (1992) 'The function of menstrual taboos among the Dogon: defense against cuckoldry', *Human Nature* 3: 89–131.

Strassmann, B. I. (1996) 'Menstrual hut visits by Dogon women: a hormonal test distinguishes deceit from honest signaling', *Behavioural Ecology* 7: 304–15.

Strassmann, B. I. (1997) 'Energy economy in the evolution of menstruation', *Evolutionary Anthropology* 5: 157–64.

Turner, V. (1967) *The Forest of Symbols. Aspects of Ndembu Ritual* (Ithaca, NY and London: Cornell University Press).

Trivers, R. L. (1972) 'Parental investment and sexual selection', in Campbell, B. (ed.), *Sexual Selection and the Descent of Man 1871–1971* (Chicago: Aldine), pp. 136–79.

Whiten, A. and Byrne, R. W. (1988) 'Tactical deception in primates', *Behavioral and Brain Sciences* 11: 233–44.

Zahavi, A. (1975) 'Mate selection: a selection for a handicap', *Journal of Theoretical Biology* 53: 205–14.

Zahavi, A. (1978) 'Decorative patterns and the evolution of art', *New Scientist* 80: 182–4.

Zahavi, A. (1987) 'The theory of signal selection and some of its implications', in Delfino, U. P. (ed.), *International Symposium of Biological Evolution* (Bari: Adriatic Editrice), pp. 305–27.

Zahavi, A. (1991) 'On the definition of sexual selection, Fisher's model, and the evolution of waste and of signals in general', *Animal Behaviour* 42: 501–3.

Zahavi, A. and Zahavi, A. (1997) *The Handicap Principle. A Missing Piece of Darwin's Puzzle* (New York and Oxford: Oxford University Press).

CHAPTER 7

THE ORIGIN OF SYMBOLIC CULTURE

IAN WATTS

AFRICA AND 'MODERN' HUMAN ORIGINS

Near unanimity exists that our species evolved recently in Africa, with several studies indicating a date close to 140,000 years ago (Stringer and McKie 1996). Initial migration beyond Africa is thought to have occurred sometime between *c.* 100,000 and 70,000 years ago, resulting in the replacement of archaic populations (Foley and Lahr 1997), although Klein (1995) has suggested that there was no significant migration until shortly after 50,000 years before present (BP). There is far less agreement about when we can identify symbolic behaviour (sometimes phrased less precisely as 'modern' human behaviour). Was symbolism already part of the behavioural repertoire of archaic populations (cf. Marshack 1990; Bednarik 1995; Hayden 1993)? Did symbolic culture first evolve with early *Homo sapiens sapiens* prior to initial migrations (Brooks 1996; Knight et al. 1995; Watts 1998)? Was it a later achievement by already dispersed populations (Stringer and Gamble 1993)? Following Klein (1995), was symbolic culture a consequence of a late 'macromutation' in the brain of African *H.s.s.*, which spread like wildfire after 50,000 BP? Or did symbolism mark a shift from modular (domain-specific) to generalized intelligence, a change which Mithen (this volume; 1996: 668) has variously placed between 100,000 and 30,000 BP? Both Stringer and McKie (1996) and Mithen seem to have converged on a view that while the earliest indications of symbolism may be in the order of 100,000 years old, it is only between 60,000 and 30,000 that this capacity becomes fully manifest in performance.

Evaluation of these different interpretations requires agreed criteria as to what constitutes evidence for symbolism and what is a viable (Darwinian) explanatory mechanism. I follow Chase and Dibble's (1987, 1992) criteria for identifying symbols in the archaeological record. We cannot confidently infer symbolism without evidence for repeated patterning and intentionality. This rules out most of the purported early symbolic data marshalled by Marshack and Bednarik. Until proponents of 'macromutations' can specify selection pressures in a cost/benefit

113

framework, such scenarios must be regarded as non-Darwinian. Similar criticisms might be raised of Mithen's scenario, although this at least has the merit of critically engaging with evolutionary psychology.

It is customary to distinguish between the African and Eurasian Pleistocene archaeological records, with the sequence in sub-Saharan Africa referred to as the (Early, Middle and Later) Stone Age and the Eurasian sequence as the (Lower, Middle and Upper) Palaeolithic. Palaeolithic archaeologists have traditionally interpreted the Middle Stone Age (MSA)/ Later Stone Age (LSA) transition in sub-Saharan Africa in much the same way as the Middle Palaeolithic (MP)/Upper Palaeolithic (UP) transition in Eurasia (e.g. Stringer and Gamble 1993; Klein 1992, 1995). Outside of the Levant and North Africa, the MP/UP transition is interpreted as a consequence of symboling modern humans replacing Neanderthals who, prior to such contact, left little if any trace of symbolic behaviour. Transposing this dichotomy onto sub-Saharan Africa ignores the continuity of population and discourages archaeologists from looking for any significant continuities in potentially symbolic behaviour across this technological transition. Over large parts of sub-Saharan Africa the transition does not occur until c. 25,000–20,000 BP (Phillipson 1993; Wadley 1993; Mitchell 1994), 20,000 years after the MP/UP transition. There is strong genetic evidence that some African 'hunter-gatherer' populations are descendants of some of the most ancient human lineages, extending back between 60,000 and 120,000 years (Vigilant et al. 1991; Soodyall and Jenkins 1992). Acceptance of the MSA/LSA transition as a behavioural Rubicon would imply that ancestral Khoisan (the aboriginal inhabitants of southern Africa) were among the last people to enter into the symbolic domain. Southern African archaeologists have long argued for continuities in material culture linking contemporary Khoisan populations with Pleistocene and Holocene Later Stone Age peoples. Some have ventured further, proposing continuities in social organization (e.g. Wadley 1987), or in relations of production and cosmology (e.g. Lewis-Williams 1984), although more recent work has focused on elucidating changes in economic and social organization (e.g. Mazel 1989; Hall 1990).

Advances in understanding our species' origin and in our knowledge about the Upper Pleistocene (post 128,000 BP) MSA (e.g. Barham 1995; Yellen et al.1995) suggest that it is time to discard the notion of a behavioural Rubicon between the MSA and LSA. However, the earliest MSA assemblages, in the order of 250,000 BP (Middle Pleistocene), provide very little to indicate symbolic culture or a 'campsite' organization (Watts 1998: 92–4), suggesting that the foundations for symbolic rule-governed behaviour were laid sometime in the course of the MSA.

TECHNOTYPOLOGICAL CHANGE
IN THE MSA

Volman (1981, 1984) proposed a chronological technotypological scheme, of predominantly informally characterized stages, for the development of the MSA south of the Limpopo. To date, this remains the only large-scale region where such a scheme has found widespread acceptance among archaeologists (Watts 1998: 65–6 with refs). The earliest MSA assemblages are quite variable (Watts 1998: 89–91 and App. 3a). It is not until Volman's MSA2a, correlated with the beginning of the Upper Pleistocene and probably extending back to the end of Oxygen Isotope stage 6, that flake-blade production became generalized throughout the region. Most subsequent technotypological change occurs at the same regional scale. From the MSA2a we can speak of a 'regional identity' (cf. Clark 1988). The periodization of the development of the MSA2b is imprecise but occurs sometime between 120,000 and 100,000 BP (Watts 1998: 95–9). Within-site patterns of long-term subtle drift in the attributes of flake blanks over the course of the MSA2 (Thackeray and Kelly 1988; Vogelsang 1993) reinforce the impression of regional identity. Recently, bladelet production, traditionally associated with microlithic LSA industries, has been added to the repertoire of blank production techniques available from the MSA2b onwards (Kaplan 1990; Harper 1994). Technologically, the MSA2b provides a package which, in terms of Clark's (1977) unilineal evolutionary model, embraces elements of Middle, Upper and Epipalaeolithic technologies ('Modes' 3 to 5). The MSA2b is followed by the Howieson's Poort, beginning c. 75,000 BP, characterized by backed geometrics (normally associated with Epipalaeolithic industries in Eurasia and some LSA industries in Africa). The duration of the Howieson's Poort is uncertain. Some sequences witness a reversion to a more orthodox MSA still beyond the range of C^{14} dating (c. 45,000 BP); others provide assemblages combining elements of an orthodox MSA, Howieson's Poort and LSA (Parkington 1990; Kaplan 1990; Harper 1994; Mitchell 1994). Following Volman, post-Howieson's Poort MSA assemblages are here termed MSA3, without implying that this term has any technotypological integrity.

While MSA technology is indisputably Middle Palaeolithic in overall character, of greater interest are the ways in which it differs from the Eurasian Mousterian. In southern Africa the differences repeatedly appear to be precocious:

1. A greater emphasis on flake-blades rather than points.
2. Arguably the use of an intermediate punch for some flake-blade production (whether this extends back to the early Upper Pleistocene as suggested by Volman (1981: 260), or is identified with the Howieson's Poort (Beaumont 1978: 137; Deacon in Shreeve 1995: 207)).

3. Some standardization of flake-blade attributes associated with the MSA2b and Howieson's Poort (Thackeray and Kelly 1988; Vogelsang 1993; Beaumont et al. 1978: Fig. 3; Ronen 1992).
4. Bladelet production at some sites from the MSA2b onwards (Kaplan 1990; Harper 1994; Mitchell and Steinberg 1992: 27).
5. Stillbay bifacial foliate points, sometimes compared to Solutrean (European Upper Palaeolithic) points in their refinement (Armstrong 1931: 248; Volman 1981: 147–8). The Stillbay is probably contemporary with the late MSA2b (Watts 1998: 137–8).
6. Although MSA backed geometrics are generally identified with the Howieson's Poort, they first appear in the MSA2b (Volman 1981; Kaplan 1990; Harper 1994).
7. Grindstones are extremely rare in MSA1 and MSA2a contexts; they become widely distributed from the MSA2b onwards (Watts 1998: 141–3), contradicting the assertion (Stiner 1993) that they were an Upper Palaeolithic/LSA development. They are not, contra Volman (1984: 211), restricted to the savanna biome (which would suggest a primary role in hard seed processing). At several sites, there is evidence for their use in the processing of pigments (Louw 1969: 47; Mason 1962: 273; Avery et al. 1997: 274, pers. obs. re Klasies and Apollo 11 – see Watts 1998: 141–3[1]).
8. The first appearance of worked bone in the MSA2b (Wendt 1974; Singer and Wymer 1982; see Watts 1998: 143–6 and 632–4[2]).

Given a recent African ancestry to modern humans, these developments can most appropriately be interpreted as indicating a common ancestry to different technological traditions developed by modern humans as they colonized the world over the last 100,000 years.

Regarding the technological transition to the LSA, several points need to be made. In southern Africa, the youngest MSA assemblages have been dated to c. 22,000 years BP (Opperman and Heydenrych 1990); the transition is generally placed between c. 25,000 and 20,000 BP (Mitchell 1994; Wadley 1993). In an overall characterization of the early LSA, Klein (1995: 182) contends that there is a marked increase in formal tools. This is not the case for the southern African early LSA, whether in its microlithic or non-microlithic variants (cf. Wadley 1993). Whether the transition appears pronounced or not is largely dependent on patterns of raw material use. In sequences where crypto-crystalline silicas (ccs) or quartz predominate, there is continuity in the predominant flaking technology – as seen in sequences where bladelet manufacture is a continuous feature

1. See also Watts (1998: Appendices 3i and 3j).
2. See also Watts (1998: Appendices 3k and 7t).

from the MSA2b through to the LSA. The transition appears most pronounced where there is a shift from hornfels or quartzite dominated
assemblages (an orthodox MSA) to ccs or quartz (e.g. Boomplaas).

I suggest that the significance of both the MSA2a and the MSA2b has been
underestimated, the MSA2a for its regional scale, the MSA2b for the package
it represents. If the transition to the LSA were treated in terms of changing
technical forces of production, it could be addressed in the same manner
as the Eurasian Epipalaeolithic (postdating *c.* 20,000 BP) to which in
technology it corresponds more closely than to the Upper Palaeolithic.

BEYOND TECHNOTYPOLOGY

Addressing wider aspects of behaviour, let me now stress some observations on the Upper Pleistocene MSA as a whole.

In terms of hearth structure and spatial patterning within shelters, no
qualitative difference can be demonstrated between Upper Pleistocene
MSA shelter occupations (Barham 1995; Opperman and Heydenrych
1990; Henderson 1992; Deacon 1993) and early LSA counterparts (e.g.
Parkington and Mills 1991; Deacon 1976; see also Watts 1998: 164–6[3]).

Klein's (1989, 1992, 1995) inference that significant behavioural
contrasts are discernible between MSA and LSA hunting abilities is an over-
interpretation of the data (see Deacon 1990: 181; Watts 1998: 179–80[4]).
The claim that suids were too dangerous for MSA hunters is contradicted
by data from pan-margin sites (Kuman 1989: App. IV; Brooks 1984:
48–9; Brown 1988; Wells et al. 1942) and by Klein's own data from
Border Cave (1977: Table 6). With respect to buffalo, the contrast
presented by Klein (1989: Fig. 27.2) rested on Holocene LSA samples, a
period characterized by economic intensification (cf. Hall 1990; Mazel
1989). If early LSA samples had been used, as in an earlier paper by Klein
(1978: 211), no MSA/LSA contrast would have been observed.

There are several significant behavioural developments which can be
associated with the MSA2b.

1. From the MSA2b onwards, there is some evidence for activity differences between shelters (Evans 1993; Watts 1998: 173–6), the best
   example being the apparent caching of large quantities of specularite at
   Olieboompoort.
2. Groundstone technology, which is far more widely distributed from
   the MSA2b onwards, is significant for several reasons. It is generally
   assumed to represent an important innovation in food-processing

3. See also Watts (1998: Appendices 4b, 4d, and 4e).
4. See also Watts (1998: Appendix 4g).

technology (e.g. Stiner 1993; Wendorf et al. 1993: 340). Cumbersome lower grindstones were probably cached and intensively curated, compatible with increased labour investment in sites as 'campsites'. While not refuting the assumption that grindstones played a role in food-processing, the evidence that some were used to process pigments suggests that this latter role was perhaps more significant in accounting for their expanded distribution (see also Wright 1992: 285–7). This coincides with an expanded distribution and dramatic increase in the relative frequency of pigment (see below).

3. There is some evidence for an expansion of habitat range into arid hinterlands with the MSA2b. This is the first time we have evidence of ostrich eggshell containers, coming from several MSA shelters in southwest Namibia (Vogelsang 1993: 419–23); previously only LSA examples were known. The full significance of Vogelsang's data emerges when contextualized with Corvinus's (1978: 88, 90) observation of a contrast in site distribution along the lower Orange River between the 'early' and 'late' MSA (the 'late' MSA being described as comparable to layers G and F at Apollo 11, i.e. MSA2b and Howieson's Poort). The distribution of the earlier material is similar to that in the Early Stone Age, restricted to migration routes along river terraces, while later MSA sites are also found well away from the river. This is the first indication of human settlement no longer being tethered to the local availability of surface water. It is also the first time we have evidence for 'exotic' lithic raw materials (Corvinus 1978: 90). The occupation of arid hinterlands implies significantly improved logistical mobility, giving this a qualitatively different significance from the earlier, still contentious, colonization of low-lying, possibly wooded, areas in central and eastern Africa associated with the Sangoan (cf. McBrearty et al. 1996).

Gamble (1996) has counterposed a model of a 'Local Hominid Network' to that of a 'Social Landscape' in an attempt to dichotomize the scale of regional organization between non-symbolic and symbolic hominids. He contends that evidence for 'Social Landscape' only emerges after *c.* 50,000 BP. To evaluate this in the southern African context, the very limited evidence regarding raw material transport distances needs to be summarized.

Lithic raw material procurement was almost exclusively local up to and including the MSA2a. A number of MSA2b assemblages (particularly in the Transvaal) witness a new interest in finer-grained raw materials which, in some cases at least, are considered to be exotic (Corvinus 1978; Evans 1993; cf. Watts 1998: 121–5, 184–9). Unfortunately, it is not presently possible to put figures on what constitutes local and exotic in a southern

African MSA context. Non-lithic items (pigments and marine shell) were sometimes transported considerable distances from at least the MSA2b onwards. Beaumont (1978: 37) suggested that among the varieties of 'pigment' encountered throughout the MSA sequence at Border Cave (extending back to the MSA2a), the high quality haematite and the specularite may have come from MSA workings on Ngwenya Ridge in western Swaziland, the location of the specularite mine of Lion Cavern – where initial workings predate 43,000 BP and probably extend back to the MSA2b (Dart and Beaumont 1971; Volman 1984; cf. Watts 1998).

Ngwenya Ridge lies about 130 km northwest of Border Cave. The ochre and micaceous rock present throughout the Boomplaas MSA sequence (Howieson's Poort and MSA3) are regarded as imports to the site (Deacon et al. 1983: 174). Deacon (pers. comm. 1993) considers the most likely source of the ochreous shales, the dominant pigment form (cf. Watts 1998), to be the Bokkerveld shales which outcrop about 70 km away towards the coast. Singer and Wymer (1982: 117) also regarded the 'haematite' (haematized shale) at Klasies to be exotic in origin. A few sea-mussel shell fragments are reported from Howieson's Poort units at Apollo 11 and Pockenbank (Vogelsang 1993: 102, 197), both sites being about 100 km from the coast. At Boomplaas, a few fragments of marine shell were recovered from the Howieson's Poort and a single worked piece from the MSA3 (Deacon et al. 1983: Fig. 40[5]). The site is presently c. 80 km from the coast. These rare occurences of marine shell are consistent with Levantine data associated with early H.s.s. (Bar-Yosef 1987).

Even on the scant evidence and inferences summarized above, distances of 70–130 km for the transport of high quality pigments and marine shell seem to be fairly well attested in the MSA2b and Howieson's Poort. Taken together with the observations on lithic raw materials, there appears to have been a significant increase in the maximum range of procurement distances in the MSA2b relative to preceding periods, consistent with the contemporary evidence from southwestern Namibia for greater logistical organization. There is nothing to suggest that the picture changed significantly until after the Last Glacial Maximum, and most of the evidence for change comes from the Holocene (cf. Mitchell 1996). The longest transport distance for any item reported from a Pleistocene LSA context is c. 200km for a marine shell from Sehonghong (Mitchell 1996: 48).

In a global context, Palaeolithic ochre and marine shell have been interpreted as the '"prestige goods" of a "non-prestige good" economy' (Gamble 1996: 262, citing Feblot-Augustins and Perles 1991), items which 'are not transported prior to 50,000 years ago' (Gamble 1996: 262).

5. See also Watts (1998: Appendix 7u). The possibility that these pieces derived from higher up the sequence cannot be ruled out – Deacon pers. comm.

The admittedly limited evidence presented above appears to refute this for the southern African MSA. It suggests that if Gamble's (1996) counterposed models were to be applied to southern Africa, the parameters would have to be changed. According to Gamble, Social Landscapes postdating c. 50,000 years are indicated by evidence for raw material transfers regularly exceeding 500 km (1996: 296). It is doubtful if this became the case in southern Africa until the last couple of millenia (cf. Wilmsen 1989). While southern African MSA procurement networks appear to be small scale in comparison to the European Upper Palaeolithic record, it is the precociousness of the appearance of exotic pigments and shell, combined with the vast regional scale at which early and mid-Upper Pleistocene technotypological changes have been identified, which distinguishes the southern African MSA from the Mousterian with respect to regional organization.

ARCHAEOLOGICAL OVERVIEW: CONCLUSION

In terms of subsistence strategies, organization of space in shelters, the basic technological template and, at several of the better known deep-sequence sites, patterns of lithic raw material use, there is little to differentiate the MSA2b from the MSA2a. As regards subsistence strategies and the organization of space, there seems to be little change up to and including the early LSA. While there is considerable continuity between the MSA2a and MSA2b, there are also significant developments associated with the latter stage. Of these, the first appearance of bladelet technology, the generalization of grindstones, the differential use of shelters, the indications of increased logistical organization and the procurement distances of potential 'prestige goods' are particularly notable. Contextualized with the technotypological changes previously outlined, I suggest that the MSA2b witnessed the most significant suite of behavioural changes seen in the course of the Upper Pleistocene.

Other than the final abandonment of MSA flaking techniques and the greatly expanded distribution of bladelet manufacture, the only other frequently cited changes associated with the early LSA are the greater likelihood of encountering ostrich eggshell beads and/or worked bone. However, it should be stressed that neither class of artifact makes its first appearance in the LSA; nor does either become common until considerably later (from c. 12,000 to 10,000 BP, Deacon 1984, 1990: 180; Wadley 1993). Interpreting the behavioural changes associated with the MSA2b will rest largely on the significance attached to the limited evidence for increased logistical organization, along with evidence to be presented concerning the ochre record. Nevertheless, I hope to have shown that it will no longer do to treat the Upper Palaeolithic and the LSA as comparable terms (*contra* Stringer and McKie 1996: 39; Lewin 1993: 164; Klein 1995).

UTILITARIAN HYPOTHESES CONCERNING OCHRE USE

Most archaeologists discussing the MSA have referred to the presence of pigment as a general phenomenon. Virtually all have interpreted it as a body paint (Volman 1984: 215; Deacon 1995: 128; Clark 1988: 299; Walker 1987: 142). However, little substantiation for this interpretation is ever provided, leaving it open for those who either wish to be more cautious (Wadley 1993: 276) or seek to refute symbolism in the MSA (Klein 1995: 189; Mithen, this volume) to cite utilitarian hypotheses as alternative explanations for its presence. The principal utilitarian hypothesis is that ochre may have been used as a hide preservative. Some arguments and observations weighing against such an interpretation of the early ochre record have been presented elsewhere (Knight et al. 1995: 88–9; Power and Watts 1996: 317–8; Watts 1998: 219–226[6]). Here I restrict myself to the following comments:

1. While laboratory experiments indicated that, at sufficient concentration, most metal ions will inhibit the breakdown of collagen by collagenases (Mandl 1961), experiments in the field with ochred and unochred hides (Audouin and Plisson 1982: 62) failed to support this expectation. Taxidermists have questioned whether ochre has any preservative effect (Philibert 1994: 449).
2. The hide preservation hypothesis has no implications for colour selection. Iron hydroxides (generally yellows) should be as acceptable as iron oxides (generally reds). Black minerals like manganese and magnetite (a black iron oxide) should be equally acceptable.
3. Ethnographic sources from diverse environments indicate that the threat from bacterial decay is less significant than sometimes assumed (Hayden 1990; Thomas 1960 [1959]: 91–2; Steyn 1971: 287).
4. The earliest evidence for the involvement of ochre in hide dressing comes from relatively late in the archaeological record (late Upper Palaeolithic and Epipalaeolithic). Recent studies indicate a connection with the production of 'prestige goods' (Hayden 1990; Philibert 1994; Bueller 1993).
5. Ethnographically reported use of ochre in hide-working overwhelmingly concerns decorative application in the finishing stages.

6. See also Watts (1998: Appendix 5c).

OVERVIEW OF MSA OCHRE RECORD

A global review of the earliest occurrences of potential earth pigments indicated that these first appear between 300,000 and 250,000 BP (Knight et al. 1995; Watts 1998: 197–202). Of the dozen or so Middle Pleistocene occurrences, all concern small assemblages (generally single pieces), and the materials are exclusively ochre or haematite producing red streaks. The timing, the irregular nature of the behaviour and the streaks of the materials are all consistent with predictions of the 'sham menstruation' hypothesis (Power and Aiello 1997). While the novelty of this behaviour is significant, its irregularity suggests that it was not tied to any habitual performance, as required of collective ritual. Irregular ochre use would be compatible with a context-dependent strategy in which the visual signalling was still indexical or iconic, referring to some feature/state that was present. In Eurasia, the few occurrences are clustered between *c.* 250,000 and 220,000 BP, followed by a find gap lasting until *c.* 100,000 BP (Wreschner 1985: 389; Watts 1998: 200–1). In Africa, Charama assemblages from a couple of cave sites in Zimbabwe and Zambia (Pomongwe, and possibly Mumbwa Cave) may provide evidence for continuous usage in the terminal Middle Pleistocene, linking earlier Fauresmith and earliest MSA occurences to the more extensive record from the early Upper Pleistocene. Pomongwe (Cooke 1963; Watts 1998: 201) presently provides the earliest *sequence* in the world for the regular use of ochre. Not only was ochre reported from all the Charama spits, but its relative frequency (as a percentage of the combined lithic and pigment assemblages) steadily increased, with further pronounced increases associated with the overlying 'Rhodesian Stillbay' (Bambata) assemblages. However, owing to excavation procedures and inconsistent reporting, the Pomongwe data is not very reliable; hopefully, the renewed excavations at Mumbwa Cave (Barham 1995) will throw further light on the issue.

To investigate the claimed artifactual status of archaeological 'pigments', selective criteria and temporal patterning, I focused on MSA sites south of the Limpopo. Three samples were constructed. The first, shown in Table 7.1, comprised 4,056 pieces of examined potential pigments drawn from seventeen sites – fifteen if the Klasies sites are treated as one (Watts 1998: Ch. 6).

The second was a comprehensive sample of sites spanning the period up until *c.* 20,000 BP where there was sufficient information to assess the presence or absence of pigment (Watts 1998: 79–86, 500–11). This sample is shown in Figure 7.1 and comprized seventy-four sites (279 excavation units), twenty-one open sites and fifty-three shelters (including the specularite mine of Lion Cavern).

Table 7.1 *The examined sample of potential pigment (excluding open sites, n = 4, potential pigment = 18)*

Site	Stages [a]	Mesh size (mm) [b]	Potential pigment (n)	Valid sample of potential pigment (n)	% modified (numerically)	Mass (kg)	% modified (by weight)
Sehonghong	6	1.5	99	99	1.0	0.07	9.8
Rose Cottage (Gail) [c]	6	2.0	295	295	5.4	0.24	20.0
Border Cave	1, 2	2.0 & 3.0	111	111	8.1	0.33	27.7
Apollo 11	1, 2, 4, 5	2.5 & 4.0	105	105	29.5	0.89	46.8
Hollow Rock Shelter	3	3.0	1,143	1,123	8.4	1.34	45.5
Umhlatuzana	2, 4, 5, 6, 7	3.0?	1,721	1,675	8.5	3.44	14.5
Bushman's Rock Shelter	1, 2, 5	3.0	58	41	39.0	0.91	30.7
Boomplaas	4, 5, 7	3.0	134	133	18.8	1.34	16.9
Klasies Shelter 1A	4	6.5	198	163	29.4	1.27	47.4
Klasies Cave 1	1, 2	13.0	37	32	81.2	1.42	56.0
Klasies Shelter 1B	1, 2	13.0	3	3	100.0	0.10	100.0
Rose Cottage (Malan)	2, 4, 5	n.k.	112	112	29.5	1.33	53.2
Mwulu's Cave	1, 2	n.k.	13	13	53.8	0.48	77.2
Olieboompoort	2	n.k.	304	304	13.2	11.95	18.2
Totals			4,038	3,914		24.87	

[a] Informal technotypological stages: 1 = MSA2a, 2 = MSA2b, 3 = Stillbay, 4 = Howieson's Poort, 5 = MSA3, 6 = Transitional MSA/LSA, 7 = early LSA.
[b] The 'not known' values for mesh size were all coarsely sieved excavations (>5 mm).
[c] Rose Cottage level 'Gail' was excluded from the main database because of uncertainties over the derivation of a small proportion of the material. It is included here for comparative purposes, but is excluded from column totals.

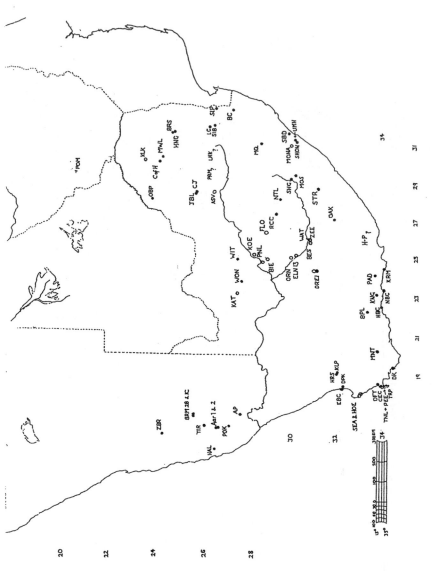

Fig. 7.1 *Map of sites used in the pigment presence/absence sample, spanning the period from the earliest* MSA *to c. 20,000* BP.

Key to site abbreviations used in Figure 7.1:

o = open site
● = shelter site
+ = site outside study region
? = no map available
Aar1&2 = Aar1 & Aar2
AP = Apollo 11
ASV = Aasvoelkop
BC = Border Cave
BES = Beskuitfontein 4
BIE = Biesiesput
BPL = Boomplaas Cave
BRM2B & 1C = Bremen
BRS = Bushman Rock Shelter
CEC = Cecilia State Forest Shelter
C of H = Cave of Hearths
CJ = Cave James
DFT = Duinefontein
DK = Die Kelders Cave
DPK = Diepkloof Shelter
DREI = Dreikoppen 1 & 2
EBC = Elands Bay Cave
ELN = Elandskloof 13
FLO = Florisbad
HAL = Haalenberg
HBC = Herrolds Bay Cave
HNG = Heuningsneskrans

HOE = Hoedjies Punt Shell Midden
H-P = Howieson's Poort
HRS = Hollow Rock Shelter
JBL = Jubilee Shelter
KAT = Kathu Pan
KLK = Kalkbank
KLP = Klipfonteinrand
KNG = Kangkara
KOE = Koedoesrand
KRM = Klasies River Mouth:
    Cave 1
    Shelter 1A
    Shelter 1B
    Cave 5
LC = Lion Cave
LNK = Linksfield
MNT = Montague Cave
Mona = Mona
MQ = Maqongo
MWL = Mwulu's Cave
NBC = Nelson Bay Cave
NTL = Ntloana Tsoana
OAK = Oakleigh Farm
OBP = Olieboompoort
ORN = Orangia 1
PAD = Paarderberg

PEE = Peers Cave
PNL = Pniel 6
POM = Pomongwe
PRM = Primrose Ridge
SBD = Sibudu
SEA = Sea Harvest Shell Maiden
SHG = Sehonghong
SHON = Shongweni
SIB = Sibebi
SIP = Siphiso
STR = Strathalan B
TIR = Tiras 5
TNL = Tunnel Cave
TRP = Trappieskop
UMH = Umhlatuzana
WAT = Waterval 16B
WTT = Witkrans
WON = Wonderwerk Cave
Zais = Zais
ZBR = Zebrarivier
ZEE = Zeekoegat 27a

Missing:
Garcia State Forest Shelter (a.k.a. Blombos)
Dale Rose Parlour

Open sites were fairly uninformative as associated lithic assemblages could rarely be placed with any confidence into Volman's informal scheme. The fifty-three shelter sites represent the majority of archaeologically investigated and reported shelters.[7] The third sample was a subset of the second, comprising excavation units with unselected lithic and pigment counts, allowing a measure of relative frequency to be derived (Watts 1998: 500–631).

The total mass of examined potential pigment was in excess of 25 kg, almost half of which was glittery specularite, overwhelmingly from Olieboompoort. A default category of ochre accounted for some 20 per cent, followed by shale (10.8 per cent), sandstones (6.5 per cent), and haematite (5.9 per cent) (Watts 1998: Table 6.5). Most assemblages were heterogenous in their composition, which weighs against a blanket autochthonous origin argument (Boyd et al. 1995; Butzer 1980). The distribution of the major forms by site was congruent with the broad outlines of ethnohistorical and contemporary commercial pigment exploitation data concerning regional differences in underlying geology. Haematites (including specularite) predominated in the Transvaal; they were also prominent at Rose Cottage and Border Cave. Shales predominated in all the southern Cape sites. Ochres of various forms other than shale were present in all assemblages and were the predominant form outside the Transvaal and southern Cape. A major determinant of the proportion of modified pieces (generally ground) in any particular assemblage was the size of mesh used for sieving, with far more small, unmodified debris coming from deposits passed through 3 mm or finer mesh. However, as shown in Table 7.1, there is considerable inter-site variation even where mesh sizes are identical. Forty per cent of the sample comprized pieces weighing less than 1 g. For the total sample, modification among pieces weighing less than 3 g was in the order of 6 per cent, rising to 30 per cent of pieces weighing between 3 g and 5 g, and nearly 50 per cent of pieces in the 10–20 g interval (Watts 1998: Table 6.13). Overall, 34 per cent of the haematite was modified, 14 per cent of shale and 8.4 per cent of default ochre. Making allowance for the biasing effects of the very large (finely sieved) assemblages from Umhlatuzana and Hollow Rock, 25 per cent of shale and 15 per cent of default ochre were modified. The modified proportion of specularite was reduced by the bias of the massive caching of this material at Olieboompoort; a less biased sample would probably have provided a modification rate at least as high as for haematite. A small subcategory of 'haematized shale' (largely restricted to Klasies and Apollo 11) also showed exceptionally high rates of modification. The different

---

7. There were a further twenty-four shelters with inadequate information to make presence/absence assessments. See Watts (1998: 'Preface' to Site Appendix 2).

rates of modification indicate a heirarchy of esteem comparable to ethno-historical data from the same region (see below).

Turning to streak values, only 3.6 per cent of the sample had yellow, orangey-brown or yellowey-brown streaks. Browns (including 'reddey-browns') accounted for 10.7 per cent, blacks, greys and whites accounted for less than 1 per cent, 'various colours' and pieces with no streak (pieces mistakenly curated as pigments) accounted for 2.4 per cent, while reds comprized 81.4 per cent. With the exception of light browns, all streak categories were modified in proportions approximating or slightly above their proportional contribution to the total sample. Light browns aside, unless there was human selection on the basis of streak among these otherwise very diverse raw materials, this patterning would be hard to explain. The relative insignificance of pieces producing yellow, yellowey-brown or orangey-brown streaks, and near absence of black pigments (despite their availability over large parts of the study region), counts against strictly utilitarian hypotheses.

In both the valid total sample (n = 3,978) and the sample where streaks were individually recorded (n = 2,024), 'light reds' (n = 679) and 'strong reds' (n = 721) comprise comparable proportions (17.1 per cent and 18.1 per cent in the former sample, 33.5 per cent and 35.5 per cent in the latter). However, while 36.6 per cent of 'strong reds' were modified, this applies to only 21.1 per cent of the 'light reds'. In choosing which pieces to modify, MSA people were clearly selecting the most saturated shades of red.[8] Focusing attention on 'definitely ground' specimens (n = 383, just under 10 per cent of the total sample), as distinct from the broader category of 'modified', 52 per cent were 'strong reds', 30.3 per cent were 'light reds' and 5 per cent were reddey-browns. I categorized forty-eight of the ground pieces as 'crayons' (e.g. Figures 7.2–7.4), intensively utilized pieces where ground facets tended to converge to a point.

This subgroup came from seven shelter sites, with examples from each of the informal stages from the MSA2a onwards. The colour selection was even more pronounced among these pieces, with 60.4 per cent having 'strong red' streaks. The form of these intensively utilized pieces permits the inference that MSA people were not solely concerned with the re-duction of lumps of pigment to powder. Abrasion resulting in honed points and much smaller facets than would be predicted by a powder reduction model suggests that some pieces were applied directly as pigment to rock and/or organic surfaces; more importantly, it also suggests that clearly defined areas of colour were sometimes required, indicating design or pattern.

8. The 'strong red' category primarily comprised streaks I perceived as 'poppy', 'blood red' and 'dark red'.

Fig. 7.2 *Specularite 'crayon' from Olieboompoort Bed 2, 18"–24", MSA2b. Four main facets, distal width c.3 mm, 33 g.*

The preoccupation with redness clearly indicates that ochre was primarily used for visual signalling. Among the potential range of widely available earth pigments, red ochre/haematite most readily meets the requirement for salience. These results are also consistent with and lend support to the findings of cognitive anthropology that red is the first colour to be linguistically encoded (Berlin and Kay 1969; D'Andrade 1995: 104–15). To the extent that the streaks I grouped within 'strong reds' can be characterized as saturated, MSA selective preferences are also consistent with MacLaury's (1992) refinement of the Berlin and Kay model, according to which terms designating degrees of 'brightness' (saturation) take evolutionary precedence over hue-orientated classification.

My subjective recording of streak, with no standardized measures of hue, brightness or saturation, represents a severe methodological limitation; nevertheless, an attempt was made to isolate a 'brilliant' sample. The criteria used (not mutually exclusive) were: (1) a streak close to focal yellow or red; (2) streaks described as 'rich' or 'bright'; (3) specimens described as 'metallic', 'sub-metallic', or 'lustrous' in appearance; (4) specimens with a high mica content (excluding Olieboompoort specularite because of the relatively low rate of modification of a highly esteemed material). In the resulting sample (n = 671), 40.8 per cent were modified. It appears that in addition to and overlapping with the preoccupation with 'redness', there was an interest in 'brilliant' qualities, also indicated by the

Fig.7.3 *Specularite 'crayon' from Olieboompoort Bed 2, no spit designation, MSA2b. 37.8 g. The bevelled edge is c. 2 mm wide.*

early mining of glittery specularite from Lion Cavern and the caching of specularite at Olieboompoort. This is consistent with Morphy's (1989) proposition that 'brilliance' is a cross-culturally effective sensory stimulus used as an 'aesthetic effect' in order to heighten the experiential impact of ritual (see also Bradshaw and Rogers 1993: 357–8).

Returning to the overall sample of potential pigment, based on evaluation of streak and texture assessments, the distribution of modification across geological forms and the forms of modification, I judged 90.1 per cent of the sample to be 'definite' or 'probable' pigments, 8.1 per cent to be 'possible' pigments and 1.8 per cent to be non-pigments. Most of the 'possible' pigments were pieces I judged to be pigment waste from Hollow Rock Shelter, less ferruginous expressions of the materials brought in as pigments. While the possibility that a small proportion of the ochre might be ceramicized deposit could not be conclusively ruled out, the suggestion that this might account for much of the purported MSA ochre record (Boyd et al. 1995; Butzer 1980) can be dismissed (Watts 1998: 228–9, 441–4). Most geological forms were clearly not a natural part of the shelter deposits, and a proportion of virtually all forms showed signs of utilization.

In the presence/absence sample, pigments were present in forty-three of the fifty-three shelter sites and seven of the twenty-one open sites. Most of the absences at shelter sites were either where only MSA1 units were used in the sample (Peers Cave and Elands Bay Cave) or where lithic assemblages were exceptionally small. At the level of excavation units, of

Fig. 7.4 *Haematized shale 'crayon' from Klasies River Mouth Cave 1, Layer 15. Plum colour with a blood-red streak. Four facets, 16.4 g, Cat. No. 12538.*

the twenty-nine MSA2a units (drawn from fourteen shelters), pigments were present in only fourteen (48.3 per cent); thereafter, the percentage never fell below 80 per cent (1998: Table 7.2).

Compared with the meagre ochre record for the terminal Early Stone Age and early MSA, there is clearly an increased frequency of ochre use with the MSA2a. However, only with the succeeding MSA2b did ochre use become virtually ubiquitous in shelter sites, remaining so for all subsequent stages.

Walker (1994), using data from LSA shelter occupations in the Matopos Hills of Zimbabwe spanning the last 13,000 years, has shown that pigment and lithic counts can be used to derive a relative frequency measure for ochre which can be treated as a reflection of past behaviour. His data showed pronounced peaks and troughs over time in the relative frequency of ochre. In the present study, the data came from far more diverse contexts (in terms of background geology, depositional histories and excavation procedures) and lacked chronological resolution. Nevertheless, clear temporal patterns were discernible; after investigating the effects of lagging (the removal of the fine component of the deposit), mesh size and excavated volume, the only assemblages that had to be excluded as unreliable were either from metre square test pits or some of the older, coarsely sieved excavations (Watts 1998: 514–613).

The resulting sample comprised 193 excavation units drawn from

Table 7.2 *Measures of central tendency for the relative frequency of pigment by informal stage, where relative frequency is pigment as a percentage of the combined lithic and pigment assemblages a*

Informal stage	Valid cases	Missing cases	Mean pigment %	s.d.	Median
MSA2a	28	0	0.05	0.11	0.00
MSA2b	33	8	0.53	1.45	0.11
Stillbay	5	3	8.73	1.67	9.28
Howieson's Poort	58	3	1.05	2.17	0.19
MSA3	48	4	1.45	1.98	0.42
Transitional and early LSA	18	2	0.98	0.97	0.76

[a] Excludes three MSA1 units, test-pit units where lithic counts are less than the respective stage cut-points, and suspect coarsely sieved units.

thirty-one sites. Mean percentages of pigment relative frequency were used to investigate temporal change (Table 7.2).

There was a tenfold increase between MSA2a and MSA2b means (Mann-Whitney test: p = 0.0002). The anomalously high Stillbay values are attributable to the single site derivation (Hollow Rock Shelter). Mean values double between the MSA2b and Howieson's Poort (p = 0.0413), followed by a further 50 per cent increase between the Howieson's Poort and MSA3 (p = 0.0405). Means for the MSA3 and collapsed 'Transitional/ early LSA' samples were statistically indistinguishable (p = 0.960).

The most pronounced temporal pattern is clearly the jump between MSA2a and MSA2b values. Given its magnitude relative to subsequent increases, this 'explosion' in the relative frequency of pigment indicates a qualitative change. If the Stillbay (a sub-regional industry restricted to the southwestern Cape) is incorporated into the MSA2b (Watts 1998: 134–8), the scale of increase between the MSA2a and MSA2b becomes even more pronounced (Figure 7.5), with no significant differences in mean values between the MSA2b and any subsequent stage.

From the MSA2b, both the range and the overall distribution of pigment relative frequencies is comparable to Walker's (1994: Fig. 4) LSA data. Walker interpreted his data in terms of differential site use and changing intensities of ritual activity (treating ochre primarily as a waste product of body painting). A *prima facie* case can be made for concluding that the kind of LSA variation seen in the Matopos extends back to the MSA2b. The present study's identification of selective criteria, focusing on bright red and brilliant/saturated qualities – perceptual qualities congruent with visual display – lend support to Walker's interpretation of the younger material.

The ubiquity and regularity of ochre use from the MSA2b onwards, combined with the selective criteria identified and the inferences made

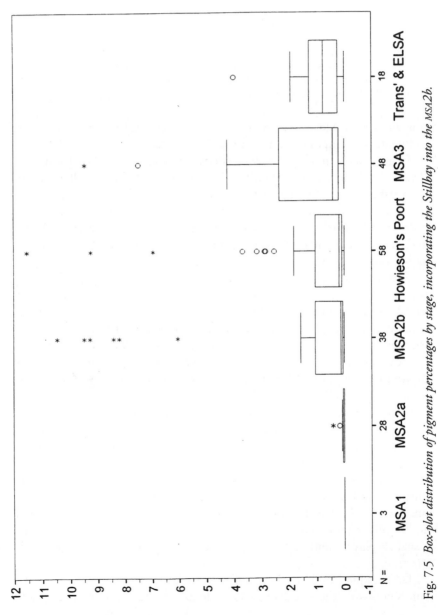

Fig. 7.5 *Box-plot distribution of pigment percentages by stage, incorporating the Stillbay into the MSA2b.*

regarding some of the more intensively utilized pieces, allows us to infer a continuous symbolic tradition linking most of the Upper Pleistocene MSA with the LSA down to the ethnographic present (see below). This would neither grant nor deny symbolic status to earlier ochre-using behaviours, but there should be no doubt remaining about such status applying to the rest of the Upper Pleistocene MSA pigment record. The onus is on those still wishing to defend utilitarian hypotheses to do so on a much more rigorous basis than hitherto.

KHOISAN USE OF REDNESS
AND BRILLIANCE

Below I address ethnohistorical material from the study region on the procurement and processing of pigments and the role of redness and brilliance in Khoisan cosmology.

The most highly esteemed pigments among the Khoisan were those with bright red or otherwise brilliant qualities (e.g. How 1970 [1962]: 34; Beaumont 1973; Bleek and Lloyd 1911: 377–9; Lewis-Williams and Biesele 1978; cf. Watts 1998: 250–6[9]), ideally haematite and specularite. In the sand-veldt, where earth pigments were scarce, red dye woods (particularly *Pterocarpus angolensis*) were held in similar esteem (Viegas Guerreiro 1968; Estermann 1976 [1956]; Wilmsen 1989: 75; Wilmsen and Denbow 1990: 492). Consequently these were the materials most likely to be transferred over considerable distances. The same selective criteria were identified in the MSA. Materials with these perceptual properties were those most likely to have been utilized.

Power (this volume) has suggested that female coalitions would demonstrate the quality of their alliances through high-cost cosmetic signalling. It is worth reviewing the southern African ethnohistorical and ethnographic literature on the procurement and processing of pigments in this light.

Cross-culturally in southern Africa, women seem to have played a major role in the quarrying of earth pigments (e.g. Arbousset and Daumas 1968 [1846]: 248; Engelbrecht 1936: 106). Most startling is an account from the 1820s claiming that 2000 Xhosa women were seen at one time quarrying the red clay near Bathurst (Beaumont 1973: 143 citing Butler 1969: 74). Beaumont (1973: 144) was also informed that up until the turn of the century, Bantu women would travel from as far as Zululand to the haematite workings at Malalene in the southeastern Transvaal, a distance of at least 200 km. Even where quarrying is not specifically

9. See also Watts (1998: Appendix 5g and Catalogue 5g).

mentioned, other accounts reinforce the impression that pigment procurement was primarily a female activity (e.g. Currle 1913: 114; Rudner 1982: 149; Jacobson 1990: 35). While men's involvement in pigment procurement is mentioned in some sources, the cumulative weight of evidence and its cross-cultural nature suggests that this was primarily a female activity of long standing. Cross-culturally within the study region, both the procurement and processing of pigments could occasion ritual injunctions (e.g. Bleek and Lloyd 1911: 379; Boshier 1965: 318, 1969: 26; How 1970 [1962]: 35; Köhler 1973: 235–6). In Ju/'hoan oral narratives, women's pounding of ochre serves as a metaphor of impending ritual action (Biesele 1993: 196). If the procurement of pigments was predominantly a female task, this was more emphatically the case when it came to their processing (e.g. Arbousset and Daumas 1968 [1846]: 248; Battiss 1948 cited in Rudner 1982: 223; Biesele 1993: 196; Burke and Farbman 1947: 43; Campbell 1822 (II): 301–2; Currle 1913: 114; How 1970 [1962]: 36; Gordon 1988 [1777–86]: 339–40; Jacobson 1990: 35; Köhler 1973: 235–6).

Leaving aside the decorative use of dyes and pigments during the finishing stages of hide-dressing (see Rudner 1982; Watts 1998), the contexts in which red pigments were used by Khoisan peoples were overwhelmingly ritual (Knight et al. 1995; Watts 1998). Even where they were used to make things or people 'beautiful' or 'attractive' (e.g. hide-finishing and cosmetics), the emotional response to redness and/or brilliance cannot be disentangled from the cultural ends to which these perceptual qualities were repeatedly used in constructing 'supernatural potency'. Elsewhere (Knight et al. 1995; Power and Watts 1996) I have concentrated on the role of red pigments in Khoisan menarcheal ritual. The red brilliance of the emergent Khoisan 'new maiden' is associated with the redness of the rain: her successful emergence should bring on the rains and help ensure the success of forthcoming hunting. Menarcheal ritual is the only context where red pigments are almost invariably present (see Knight et al.. 1995: 93–5; Watts 1998 for a comprehensive review and catalogue). Among Khoisan pastoralist groups, the use of red pigments to mark menstruation was, if anything, even more emphatic (e.g. Schinz 1891: 85; Fischer 1913: 259; Vedder 1928: 137). One reason for focusing on these rituals was that they provide a template for other rituals of transition (Knight et al. 1995: 95 with refs). No other ritual context is as concerned with human responsibility for ensuring the reproduction of the cosmos. It is not simply that menstruation is associated with future fertility; the performative force of correct menstrual observance is what mobilizes male labour in hunting, while the breach of such observances unleashes the most fearsome destructive powers. Menstrual observances, and menarcheal rituals in particular, are critical to the reproduction of society. This is consistent with a body of anthropological theory which holds that only communal ritual – particularly initiation ritual – is capable of implanting and replicating collective constructs such as 'supernatural potency' (Durkheim 1965 [1912]; Rappaport 1979; Gellner 1992: 36–7; cf. Knight et al. 1995).

Below I briefly consider the wider ritualized contexts in which redness and brilliance figure.

According to the Ju/'hoan, when god created the eland, his favourite animal (which serves as the archetypal *animal de passage* in Ju/'hoan and /Xam ritual), he used red mud (Lewis-Williams and Biesele 1978: 121). The red forelock of the animal was considered to be particularly potent (ibid.). The rain, which plays such a critical role in menarcheal observances, is identified with flowing blood and redness (Power and Watts 1997). In a Nama dance song, the lightning (daughter of the thunder cloud) is described as the one who paints herself red and does not drop the menses (Hahn 1881: 60). Red substances were widely used to attract the rain (Kaufmann 1910: 158; Lebzelter 1934: 53–4; Marshall 1986: 197–8); in Lebzelter's account, red ochre was used by the rain shaman when he ascended a magical thread to heaven and met the 'great captain' halfway up. Upon her emergence from seclusion the /Xam 'new maiden' would use powdered haematite to appease !Khwa (the Rain Animal) and ensure that the water supply would not dry out (Hewitt 1986: 281). In the Kxoe ritual for a special hunt (when the camp is starving), a brilliant red plant pigment powder (*kiaat*) is used to attract the attention of ancestors (Köhler 1973: 239). Human blood was widely used as a medicine to restore hunting luck (Bleek 1932: 248; Barnard 1980: 117; Estermann 1976 [1956]: 17; see also Schmidt 1986: 343); in all three examples it was the women who shed this blood (whether theirs or their husbands') and applied it to their husbands. For at least the last 10,000 years, red pigments were widely used in Khoisan mortuary rituals (Innskeep 1986), presumably mediating between worlds as in the previous contexts. In a few instances the ochre was particularly concentrated in the pelvic region (Innskeep 1986: 230–1), suggesting concepts of fertility. Such an interpretation is lent support by the historical Nama and Korana practice of coating red ochre on the pelvic bones of a goat ritually slaughtered during menarcheal ritual; this was believed to help ensure safe childbirth (Rudner 1982: 149; Engelbrecht 1936: 167).

No less important than the redness of the rain and new maiden is the brilliance associated with the potency of the emergent initiate and Rain Animal, in contradistinction to the soiled, unkempt state of seclusion.[10] If the medium for the representation of redness was typically red ochre or

10. See Watts (1998: Appendix 5h, Section 1.5).

haematite (itself made 'brilliant' and saturated by mixing with fat), that of brilliance (at least in the northern Cape and Transvaal) was specularite (also mixed with fat). Specularite was principally applied to the hair, particularly for initiates (both sexes) emerging from seclusion (for example Engelbrecht 1936: 160–1, 167). Brilliance is a recurrent feature in the description of G!kon//'amdina, the Python Girl – an archetypal new maiden in Ju/'hoan oral narratives (Biesele 1993: 121, 129, 134, 137). The /Xam term for specularite was //hara. Bleek and Lloyd's (1911) /Xam informant, Han//kasso, gave the following account of /Xam responses to its brilliant appearance: '//hara sparkles; therefore, our heads shimmer, on account of it; while they feel that they sparkle, they shimmer' (Bleek and Lloyd 1911: 377–9).

The Ju/'hoan use the same term, //hara, to describe the shining quality of the boy's face (rubbed with ash) during his first eland kill ritual. The boy's face will be the opposite of the dark ash, it will be light or shining, and consequently, in future eland hunts, the eland's face will split and it will die (Lewis-Williams 1981: 60). A similar power is indicated by a /Xam belief concerning the Rain and its manifestation as lightning (Bleek and Lloyd 1911: 397). Properties of brilliance were widely ascribed to the Rain Bull or the 'Big Snake' (Carstens 1975: 90; Schmidt 1979; Jolly 1986: 7).

In her study of 'Bushmen' pigment use, Rudner concluded that: 'Red ochre was the most widely used pigment, chiefly for cosmetic purposes' (1983: 18).

Rudner treated cosmetic use as distinct from ritual use (e.g. 1982: 116, 211), but the basis for such a distinction is not specified. From her sources (1982: Tables 15, 17, 40, 42) it appears that 'ritual' uses were those in which some ritual context was specified, while 'cosmetic' uses were any instances of face-painting not attributed to bodily protection (see also Watts 1998) and where no ritual context was mentioned. Several issues arise. Very few of the historical observers spoke a Khoisan language; without elucidation of the possible reasons for wearing face-paints, 'cosmetic' use necessarily becomes a default category. It seems probable that the most frequent occasion for cosmetic usage was the trance or healing dance (Watts 1998), generally held several times a month (Marshall 1969; Katz 1982). In Ju/'hoan society, the trance dance may be regarded as the central religious ritual (Biesele 1993: 74). There is, therefore, considerable overlap between the two supposedly distinct domains of cosmetic and ritual usage.

In summary, occasions for 'cosmetic' use of pigments tended also to be ritual occasions. The constructs strongly associated with red are interlinked – the anthropomorphic and therianthropic representations of deity, the menarcheal initiate, the rain and the rain animal (water-dwelling serpent or rain bull). Redness attracts potency and – in combination with brilliance – displays it. Redness and brilliance connote both beauty and danger, attracting and setting apart. In short, they signal supernatural potency. Neither redness nor brilliance can be divested of this original context of reference – even in actions as apparently 'non-ritual' as the decoration of hides or application of cosmetics for a healing dance.

CONCLUSION

I conclude that Khoisan menarcheal rituals provide us with the single most useful source of ethnographic information about the role of red pigments in the MSA, although this does not imply that MSA usage was restricted to such relatively rare events. The expectation of the sham menstruation/sex strike hypothesis is that while social contexts, meanings and behaviour should undergo historical change, the identification of ritual potency with periodic blood-flow should remain unchanging (Knight 1991, 1997; Knight et al. 1995; Power and Watts 1997). This implies that a focus on perceptual qualities such as redness and brilliance, used in giving performative force to constructs of ritual power, should also resist historical change.

The selective criteria evident in the MSA ochre record are consistent only with the use of red pigments in visual signalling. The habitual nature of such behaviour from the MSA2b onwards strongly suggests that the signalling was symbolic rather than solely indexical or iconic. The temporal span and fairly comprehensive coverage of MSA shelters in the study region allowed a strong case to be made that the quantitative change in the relative frequency of pigment associated with the MSA2b marked a qualitative transition. The case is all the more compelling in the context of the wide range of other behavioural changes identified in this informal stage. While most of the other developments are muted, considered as a whole and alongside the ochre record, they identify the MSA2b much more clearly with the onset of symbolic cultural behaviour.

The supposition that red ochre was initially and primarily used as a body paint in ritual performances accords not only with the 'sham menstruation' hypothesis, but also with a body of social anthropological theory on ritual. Bell (1992) regards the distinction between ritualization and other social strategies as lying in 'the unrecognized primacy of the body in a ritualized environment' (1992: 180). Turner (1980) proposed that the 'social skin' becomes the symbolic stage upon which the drama of socialization is enacted, seeing bodily adornment as the language through which socialization is expressed. Gell (1993), drawing upon Turner's work, inferred that techniques of 'skin-change' were functionally implicated in the maintenance and reproduction of encompassing social systems.

This line of argument implies that the first means through which people were ritualized – the most rudimentary of Mauss's (1979) 'technique du corps' – was body-painting. The 'sham menstruation' hypothesis specifies concrete selection pressures for the emergence of such strategies. Skin-changing performances, once they had become habitual, were sufficient to establish symbolic culture. Superimposed upon any residual indexical or iconic signalling, there was now symbolic reference to a collectively held construct of 'supernatural potency'.[11]

ACKNOWLEDGEMENTS

Financial support from the University of London Central Research Fund, the British Academy and the L. S. B. Leakey Trust is gratefully acknowledged. For access to archaeological collections I would like to thank: Aron Mazel of the Natal Museum; Lyn Wadley and Thomas Huffman, Department of Archaeology, University of Witwatersrand; Peter Beaumont, McGregor Museum, Kimberley; Graham Avery, South African Museum, Department of Archaeology; John Kinnahan, State Museum, Windhoek, and Eric Wendt (personal capacity); Hillary Deacon, Department of Archaeology, University of Stellenboesch; Royden Yates and Ursula Evans, Department of Archaeology, University of Cape Town; and Peter Mitchell.

REFERENCES

Arbousset, T. and Daumas, F. (1968 [1846]) *Narrative of an Exploratory Tour to the North-East of the Colony of the Cape of Good Hope* (Cape Town: C. Struik).

Armstrong, A. L. (1931) 'Rhodesian Archaeological Expedition (1929): Excavations in Bambata Cave and researches on prehistoric sites in southern Rhodesia', *Journal of the Royal Anthropological Institute* 61: 239–76.

Audouin, F. and Plisson, H. (1982) 'Les ocres et leurs témoins au Paléolithique en France: enquête et expériences sur leur validité archéologique', *Cahiers du Centre de Recherches Préhistoriques* 8: 33–80.

Avery, G., Cruz-Uribe, K., Goldberg, P., Grine, F. E., Klein, R. G., Lenardi, M. J,. Marean, C. W., Rink, W. J., Schwarcz, H. P., Thackeray, A. I. and Wilson, M. L. (1997) 'The 1992–1993 excavations at the Die Kelders Middle

11. To engage in ritual performance presupposes cognitive capacities no different from those involved in using inanimate surfaces or manufactured objects to give tangible form to collective representations. Mithen (this volume) argues that representations of intangibles cannot be stably transmitted unless they are materially embodied in artifacts. However – to take just one counter-example – the Ju/'hoan do not manufacture durable material symbols yet succeed in transmitting the concept of eland potency. They do this primarily through body-marking, pantomime performance, associative magic (using non-durable forms such as eland fat) and oral tradition (Power and Watts 1997; Knight, this volume).

and Later Stone Age cave site, South Africa', *Journal of Field Archaeology* 24: 263–91.

Barham, L. S. (1995) 'The Mumbwa Caves Project, Zambia, 1993–94', *Nyame Akuma* 43: 66–72.

Barnard, A. (1980) 'Sex roles among the Nharo Bushmen of Botswana', *Africa* 50: 115–24.

Bar-Yosef, D. (1987) 'The prehistoric use of shells as jewellery', *Mitekufat Haeven* 20: 182–4.

Battiss, E. (1948) *The Artists of the Rocks* (Pretoria: Red Fawn Press).

Beaumont, P. (1973) 'The ancient pigment mines of Southern Africa', *South African Journal of Science* 69: 140–6.

Beaumont, P. (1978) 'Border Cave' (unpublished MSc thesis, University of Cape Town).

Beaumont, P. B., de Villiers, H. and Vogel, J. C. (1978) 'Modern man in Sub-Saharan Africa prior to 49,000 BP: a review and evaluation with particular reference to Border Cave', *South African Journal of Sciences* 74: 409–19.

Bednarik, R. G. (1995) 'Concept-mediated marking in the Lower Palaeolithic', *Current Anthropology* 36: 605–34.

Bell, C. (1992) *Ritual Theory, Ritual Practice* (New York and Oxford: Oxford University Press).

Berlin, B. and Kay, P. (1969) *Basic Color Terms: Their Universality and Evolution* (Berkeley, Calif.: University of California Press).

Biesele, M. (1993) *Women Like Meat. The Folklore and Foraging Ideology of the Kalahari Ju/'hoan* (Johannesburg: Witwatersrand University Press).

Bleek, D. (ed.) (1932) 'Customs and beliefs of the Xam Bushmen (from material collected by Dr. W. H. I. Bleek and Miss L. C. Lloyd between 1870 and 1880). Part III: game animals', *Bantu Studies* 6: 233–49.

Bleek, W. H. I. and Lloyd, L. C. (1911) *Specimens of Bushman Folklore* (London: Allen).

Boshier, A. K. (1965) 'Ancient mining of Bomvu Ridge', *Scientific South Africa* 2: 317–20.

Boshier, A. K. (1969) 'Mining genesis', *Mining Survey* 64: 21–8.

Boyd, B., Pettitt, P. and White, M. (1995) 'Response to "The human symbolic revolution: a Darwinian account', *Cambridge Archaeological Journal* 5: 75–114.

Bradshaw, J. and Rogers, L. (1993) *The Evolution of Lateral Asymmetries, Language, Tool Use, and Intellect* (San Diego, Calif.: Academic Press).

Brooks, A. (1984) 'San land-use strategies, past and present: implications for southern African prehistory', in Hall, M. et al. (eds), *Frontiers: Southern African Archaeology Today*, Cambridge Monographs in African Archaeology No. 10, BAR International Series 207.

Brooks, A. (1996) 'Behaviour and human evolution', in Meikle, W. E., Howell, F. C. and Jablonski, N. G. (eds), *Contemporary Issues in Human Evolution* (San Francisco: California Academy of Sciences, Memoir 21).

Brown, A. J. V. (1988) 'The faunal remains from Kalkbank', in Mason, R. (ed.), *Cave of Hearths, Makapansgat, Transvaal* (Johannesburg: University of the Witwatersrand), pp. 658–63.

Bueller, J. (1993) 'The methodology to establish the types of microwear on sampled blades from Urkan e-Rub IIa and Netiv Hagdud', *Journal of the Israel Prehistoric Society* 25: 163–88.

Burke, D. and Farbman, N. R. (1947) 'The Bushmen: an ancient race struggles to survive in the South African deserts', *Life* II(4): 40–8.

Butzer, K. W. (1980) 'Comment on Wreschner: Red ochre and human evolution', *Current Anthropology* 21: 635.

Campbell, J. (1822) *Travels in South Africa, undertaken at the request of the London Missionary Society*, 2 vols (London: Francis Westley).

Carstens, P. (1975) 'Some implications of change in Khoikhoi supernatural beliefs', in Whisson, M. G. and West, M. (eds), *Religion and Social Change in Southern Africa* (Cape Town: David Philip; London: Rex Collings).

Chase, P. G. and Dibble, H. L. (1987) 'Middle Palaeolithic symbolism: a review of current evidence and interpretations', *Journal of Anthropological Archaeology* 6: 263–96.

Chase, P. G. and Dibble, H. L. (1992) 'Scientific archaeology and the origins of symbolism: a reply to Bednarik', *Cambridge Archaeological Journal* 2(1): 43–51.

Clark, J. D. (1977) *World Prehistory: A New Perspective* (Cambridge: Cambridge University Press).

Clark, J. D. (1988) 'The Middle Stone Age of East Africa and the beginnings of regional identity', *Journal of World Prehistory* 2(3): 235–305.

Cooke, C. K. (1963) 'Report on excavations at Pomongwe and Tshangula Caves, Matopo hills, southern Rhodesia', *South African Archaeological Bulletin* 18: 75–151.

Corvinus, G. (1978) 'Palaeontological and archaeological investigations in the Lower Orange valley from Arrisdrift to Obib', *Palaeoecology of Africa* 10: 75–91.

Currle, L. (1913) 'Notes on Namaqualand Bushmen', *Transactions of the Royal Society of South Africa* 3: 113–20.

D'Andrade, R. (1995) *The Development of Cognitive Anthropology* (Cambridge, New York and Melbourne: Cambridge University Press).

Dart, R. A. and Beaumont, P. B. (1971) 'On a further radiocarbon date for ancient mining in Southern Africa', *South African Journal of Science* 67: 10–11.

Deacon, H. J. (1976) 'Where hunters gathered: a study of Holocene stone age people in the eastern Cape', *South African Archaeological Society Monograph Series* 1.

Deacon, H. J. (1993) 'Planting an idea: an archaeology of stone age gatherers in South Africa', *South African Archaeological Bulletin* 48: 86–93.

Deacon, H. J. (1995) 'Two late Pleistocene-Holocene archaeological depositories from the Southern Cape, South Africa', *South African Archaeological Bulletin* 50: 121–31.

Deacon, H., Deacon, J., Geleijnse, V. B., Thackeray, F., Scholtz, A. and Brink, J. S. (1983) *Late Quaternary environment and culture relationships in the southern Cape. Final Report to the National Monuments Council on excavations in the Oudshoom, Heidelberg, Wittomore and Joubertina Districts* (unpublished report, Department of Archaeology, University of Stellenboesch, RSA).

Deacon, J. (1984) 'Later Stone Age people and their descendants in Southern Africa', in Klein, R. G. (ed.), *Southern African Prehistory and Palaeoenvironments* (Rotterdam: Balkema).

Deacon, J. (1990) 'Changes in the archaeological record in South Africa at 18,000 BP', in Gamble, C. and Soffer, O. (eds), *The World at 18,000 BP, Vol. 2: Low Latitudes* (London: Unwin Hyman).

Durkheim, E. (1965 [1912]) *The Elementary Forms of the Religious Life* (New York: Free Press).

Engelbrecht, J. A. (1936) *The Koranna* (Cape Town: Maskew Miller).

Estermann, C. (1976 [1956]) *The Ethnography of Southwestern Angola. Volume I: The Non-Bantu Peoples; The Ambo Ethnic Group*, Gibson, G. D. (ed.) (New York: African Publishing Company).

Evans, U. (1993) 'Hollow Rock Shelter (Sevilla 48)' (unpublished Honours project for BA degree in archaeology, University of Cape Town).

Fischer, E. (1913) *Die Rehobother Bastards* (Jena: Gustav Fischer).

Foley, R. and Lahr, M. (1997) 'Mode 3 technologies and the evolution of modern humans', *Cambridge Archaeological Journal* 7(1): 3–36.

Gamble, C. (1996) 'Making tracks: hominid networks and the evolution of the social landscape', in Steele, J. and Shennan, S. (eds), *The Archaeology of Human Ancestry: Power, Sex and Tradition* (London, and New York: Routledge).

Gell, A. (1993) *Wrapping in Images: Tattooing in Polynesi.* (Oxford: Clarendon Press).

Gellner, E. (1992). *Reason and Culture* (Oxford: Blackwell).

Gordon, R. J. (1988) *Cape Travels 1777 to 1786*, Raper, P. E. and Boucher, M. (eds) (South Africa: Brenthurst Press).

Hahn, T. (1881) *Tsuni!-Goam. The Supreme Being of the Khoi-Khoi* (London: Trübner).

Hall, S. L. (1990) *Hunter-Gatherer-Fishers of the Fish River Basin: a contribution to the Holocene Prehistory of the Eastern Cape* (PhD thesis, University of Stellenboesch, RSA).

Harper, P. (1994) 'The Middle Stone Age sequences at Rose Cottage Cave: a search for continuity and discontinuity' (unpublished Masters' Degree thesis, Department of Archaeology, University of Witwatersrand, RSA).

Hayden, B. (1990) 'The right rub: Hide working in high ranking households', in Knutson, K. (ed.), *Proceedings of the Ninth Conference on Use-Wear, Uppsala*, AUN Special Issue (Uppsala, Sweden).

Hayden, B. (1993) 'The cultural capacities of Neaderthals: a review and re-evaluation', *Journal of Human Evolution* 24: 113–46.

Henderson, Z. (1992) 'The context of some Middle Stone Age hearths at Klasies River Shelter 1B: implications for understanding human behaviour', *South African Field Archaeology* 1: 14–26.

Hewitt, R. L. (1986) *Structure, Meaning and Ritual in the Narratives of the Southern San* (Quellen zur Khoisan-forschung 2) (Hamburg: Helmut Buske Verlag).

How, M. W. (1970 [1962]) *The Mountain Bushmen of Basutoland* (Pretoria: J. L. van Schaik).

Inskeep, R. (1986) 'A preliminary survey of burial practices in the Later Stone Age, from the Orange River to the Cape coast', in Singer, R. and Lundy, J. K. (eds), *Variation, Culture and Evolution in African Populations* (Johannesburg: University of Witwaterstrand Press).

Jacobson, M. (1990) *Himba: Nomads of Namibia* (Cape Town: Struik).

Jolly, P. (1986) 'A first-generation descendant of the Transkei San', *South African Archaeological Bulletin* 41: 6–9.

Kaplan, J. (1990) 'The Umhlatuzana Rock Shelter sequence: 100,000 years of Stone Age history', *Natal Museum Journal of Humanities* 2: 1–94.

Katz, R. (1982) *Boiling Energy. Community Healing Among the Kalahari !Kung* (Cambridge, Mass.: Harvard University Press).

Kaufmann, H. (1910) 'Die =Auin. Ein Beitrag zur Buschmannforschung', *Mitteilungen aus den deutschen Schutzgebeiten* 23: 135–60.

Klein, R. (1977) 'The mammalian fauna from the Middle and Later Stone Age (Later Pleistocene) levels of Border Cave, Natal Province, South Africa', *South African Archaeological Bulletin* 32: 14–27.

Klein, R. (1978) 'Stone Age predation on large African bovids', *Journal of Archaeological Science* 5: 195–217.

Klein, R. (1989) 'Biological and behavioural perspectives on modern human origins in southern Africa', in Mellars, P. and Stringer, C. (eds), *The Human Revolution* (Edinburgh: Edinburgh University Press).

Klein, R. (1992) 'The archaeology of modern human origins', *Evolutionary Anthropology* 2: 5–14.

Klein, R. (1995) 'Anatomy, behaviour and modern human origins', *Journal of World Prehistory* 9: 167–98.

Knight, C. D. (1991) *Blood Relations. Menstruation and the Origins of Culture* (New Haven, Conn. and London: Yale University Press).

Knight, C. D. (1997) 'The wives of the sun and moon', *Journal of the Royal Anthropological Institute* (n.s.) 3: 133–53.

Knight, C. D., Power, C. and Watts, I (1995) 'The human symbolic revolution: a Darwinian account', *Cambridge Archaeological Journal* 5: 75–114.

Köhler, O. (1973) 'Die rituelle jagd bei den Kxoe-Buschmännern von Mutsiku', in Tauchmann, K. (ed.), *Festschrift zum 65 geburtstag von Helmut. Petri* (Cologne and Vienna: Bohlau Verlag), pp. 215–57.

Kuman, K. A. (1989) *Florisbad and ≠Gi: The Contribution of Open-air Sites to Study of the Middle Stone Age in Southern Africa* (PhD dissertation, Department of Anthropology, University of Pennsylvania).

Lebzelter, V. (1934) *Die Vorgeschichte von Sud und Sudwest-afrika … Band II. Eingeborenenkultruen in Sudwest- und Sudafrika* (Leipzig: Hiersemann).

Lewin, R. (1993) *Human Evolution: An Illustrated Introduction*, 3rd edn (Oxford: Blackwell Scientific).

Lewis-Williams, J. D. (1981) *Believing and Seeing. Symbolic Meanings in Southern San Rock Paintings* (London: Academic Press).

Lewis-Williams, J. D. (1984) 'Ideological continuities in prehistoric southern Africa: the evidence of the rock art', in Schrire, C. (ed.), *Past and Present in Hunter-Gatherer Studies* (Orlando, Fla. and London: Academic Press), pp. 225–52.

Lewis-Williams, J. D. and Besiele, M. (1978) 'Eland hunting rituals among the northern and southern San groups: striking similarities', *Africa* 48: 117–34.

Louw, A. W. (1969) 'Bushman Rock Shelter, Ohrigstad, Eastern Transvaal: a preliminary investigation, 1965', *South African Archaeological Bulletin* 24: 39–51.

McBrearty, S., Bishop, L. and Kingston, J. (1996) 'Variability in traces of Middle Pleistocene hominid behaviour in the Kapthurin Formation, Baringo, Kenya', *Journal of Human Evolution* 30: 563–80.

MacLaury, R. E. (1992) 'From brightness to hue. An explanatory model of color-category evolution', *Current Anthropology* 33: 137–86.

Mandl, I. (1961) 'Collagenases and elastases', *Advances in Enzymology* 23: 164–264.

Marshack, A. (1990) 'Early hominid symbol and evolution of the human capacity', in Mellars, P. (ed.), *The Emergence of Modern Humans* (Edinburgh: Edinburgh University Press).

Marshall, L. (1969) 'The medicine dance of the !Kung Bushmen', *Africa* 39: 347–81.

Marshall, L. (1986) 'Some Bushmen star lore', in Vossen, R. and Keuthmann, K. (eds), *Contemporary Studies on Khoisan* (Hamburg: Buske).

Mason, R. (1962) *Prehistory of the Transvaal* (Johannesburg: University of Witwatersrand Press).

Mauss, M. (1979) 'Body Techniques', in Mauss, M., *Sociology and Psychology*, trans. B. Brewster (London: Routledge & Kegan Paul), pp. 95–123.

Mazel, A. D. (1989) 'People making history: the last ten thousand years of hunter-gatherer communities in the Tukela Basin', *Natal Museum Journal of Humanities*, vol. 1 (Pietermaritzburg: Natal Museum).

Mitchell, P. J. (1994) 'Understanding the MSA/LSA transition: The pre-20,000 BP assemblages from new excavations at Sehonghong rock-shelter, Lesotho', *South African Field Archaeology* 3: 15–25.

Mitchell, P. J. (1996) 'Prehistoric exchange and interaction in southeastern Southern Africa: marine shells and ostrich eggshell', *African Archaeological Review* 13: 35–76.

Mitchell, P. J. and Steinberg, J. M. (1992) 'Ntloana Tsoana: a Middle Stone Age sequence from western Lesotho', *South African Archaeological Bulletin.* 47: 26–33.

Mithen, S. (1996) 'On Early Palaeolithic "concept-mediated marks", mental modularity, and the origins of art', *Current Anthropology* 37: 666–9.

Morphy, H. (1989) 'From dull to brilliant: the aesthetics of spiritual power among the Yolngu', *Man* 24: 21–40.

Opperman, H. and Heydenrych, B. (1990) 'A 22,000 year-old Middle Stone Age camp site with plant food remains from the north-eastern Cape', *South African Archaeological Bulletin* 45: 93–9.

Parkington, J. (1990) 'A critique of the consensus view on the age of Howieson's Poort assemblages in South Africa', in Mellars, P. (ed.), *The Emergence of Modern Humans* (Edinburgh: Edinburgh University Press).

Parkington, J. and Mills, G. (1991) 'From space to place: the architecture and social organization of Southern African mobile communities', in Gamble,

C. S. and Boismier, W. A. (eds), *Ethnoarchaeological Approaches to Mobile Campsites* (Ann Arbor, Mich.: International Monographs in Prehistory).

Philibert, S. (1994) 'L'ocre et le traitement des peaux: révision d'une conception traditionelle par l'analyse fonctionelle des grattoirs ocrés de la Balma Margineda (Andorre)', *L'Anthropologie* 98(2–3): 447–53.

Phillipson, D. W. (1993) *African Archaeology*, 2nd edn (Cambridge: Cambridge University Press).

Power, C. and Aiello, L. (1997) 'Female proto-symbolic strategies', in Hager, L. D. (ed.), *Women In Human Evolution* (London and New York: Routledge).

Power, C. and Watts, I. (1996) 'Female strategies and collective behaviour: the archaeology of earliest *Homo sapiens sapien*', in Steele, J. and Shennan, S. (eds), *The Archaeology of Human Ancestry: Power, Sex and Tradition* (London: Routledge), pp. 306–30.

Power, C. and Watts, I. (1997) 'The woman with the zebra's penis: gender, mutability and performance', *Journal of the Royal Anthropological Institute* 3: 1–24.

Rappaport, R. A. (1979) *Ecology, Meaning, and Religion* (Berkeley, Calif.: North Atlantic Books).

Ronen, A. (1992) 'The emergence of blade technology: cultural affinities', in Akazawa, T., Aoki, K. and Kimura, T. (eds), *The Evolution and Dispersal of Modern Humans* (Tokyo: Hokusen-sha).

Rudner, I. (1982) 'Khoisan pigments and paints and their relationship to rock paintings', *Annals of the South African Museum* 87: 1–280.

Rudner, I. (1983) 'Paints of the Khoisan rock artists', *South African Archaeological Society Goodwin Series* 4: 14–20.

Schinz, H. (1891) *Deutsch Sudwest Afrika* (Oldenburg and Leipzig: Schulz).

Schmidt, S. (1979) 'The rain bull of the South African Bushmen', *African Studies* 38: 201–24.

Schmidt, S. (1986) 'The relations of Nama and Dama women to hunting', *Sprache und Geschichte in Afrika* 7: 329–49.

Shreeve, J. (1995) *The Neaderthal Enigma: Solving the Mystery of Modern Human Origins* (Harmondsworth: Penguin).

Singer, R. and Wymer, J. (1982) *The Middle Stone Age at Klasies River Mouth in South Africa* (Chicago: University of Chicago Press).

Soodyall, H. and Jenkins, T. (1992) 'Mitochondrial DNA polymorphisms in Khoisan populations from Southern Africa', *Annals of Human Genetics* 56: 315–24.

Steyn, H. P. (1971) 'Aspects of the economic life of some nomadic Bushman groups', *Annals of the South African Museum* 56: 275–322.

Stiner, M. (1993) 'Modern human origins – faunal perspectives', *Annual Review of Anthropology* 22: 55–82.

Stringer, C. and Gamble, C. (1993) *In Search of the Neanderthals: Solving the Puzzle of Human Origins* (London: Thames & Hudson).

Stringer, C. and McKie, R. (1996) *African Exodus: The Origins of Modern Humanity* (London: Cape).

Thackeray, A. I. and Kelly, A. J. (1988) 'A technological and typological analysis of Middle Stone Age assemblages antecedent to the Howieson's Poort at Klaises River main site', *South African Archaeological Bulletin* 43: 15–26.

Thomas, E. M. (1960 [1959]) *The Harmless People* (London: Secker & Warburg).

Turner, T. S. (1980) 'The social skin', in Cherfas, J. and Lewin, R. (eds), *Not Work Alone: A Cross Cultural View of Activities Superfluous to Survival* (London: Temple Smith).

Vedder, H. (1928) 'The Nama', in *The Native Tribes of South West Africa* (Cape Town: Cape Times).

Viegas Guerreiro, M. (1968) *Bochimanes [!khũ] de Angola; estudo ethnográfico* (Lisbon: Instituto de Investigação Científica de Angola, Hunta de Investigações do Ultramar).

Vigilant, L., Stoneking, M., Harpending, H., Hawkes, K. and Wilson, A. C. (1991) 'African populations and the evolution of mitochondrial DNA', *Science* 253: 1503–7.

Vogelsang, R. (1993) 'Middle-Stone-Age-Fundstellen im Südwestern Namibias' (unpublished PhD thesis, University of Cologne).

Volman, T. (1981) 'The Middle Stone Age in the southern Cape' (unpublished PhD thesis, University of Chicago).

Volman, T. (1984) 'Early prehistory of Southern Africa', in Klein, R. G. (ed.), *Southern African Prehistory and Paleoenvironments* (Rotterdam: Balkema), pp. 169–220.

Wadley, L. (1987) *Later Stone Age Hunters and Gatherers of the Southern Transvaal: Social and Ecological Interpretation* (Oxford: British Archaeological Reports International Series 380).

Wadley, L. (1993) 'The Pleistocene Later Stone Age south of the Limpopo River', *Journal of World Prehistory* 7: 243–96.

Walker, N. (1994) 'Painting and ceremonial activity in the Late Stone Age of the Matopos, Zimbabwe', in Dowson, T. A. and Lewis-Williams, D. (eds), *Contested Images. Diversity in Southern African Rock Art Research* (Johannesburg: Witwaterstrand University Press).

Walker, N. J. (1987) 'The dating of Zimbabwean rock art', *Rock Art Research* 4(2): 137–49.

Watts, I. (1998) 'The origin of symbolic culture: the Middle Stone Age of southern Africa and Khoisan ethnography' (unpublished PhD thesis, University of London).

Wells, L. H., Cooke, H. B. S. and Malan, B. D. (1942) 'The associated fauna and culture of the Vlakkraal thermal springs, O.F.S.', *Transactions of the Royal Society of South Africa* 29: 203–33.

Wendorf, F., Schild, R., Close, A. and associates (1993) *Egypt during the Last Interglacial: The Middle Palaeolithic of Bir Tarfawi and Bir Sahara East* (New York and London: Plenum Press).

Wendt, W. E. (1974) '"Art mobilier" aus der Apollo 11-Grotte in Sudwest-Afrika: die ältesten datierten Kunstwerke Afrikas', *Acta Praehistorica et Archaeologica* 5: 1–42.

Wilmsen, E. N. (1989) *Land Filled with Flies: A Political Economy of the Kalahari* (London: University of Chicago Press).

Wilmsen, E. N. and Denbow, J. R. (1990) 'Paradigmatic history of San-speaking peoples and current attempts at revision', *Current Anthropology* 31: 489–24.

Wreschner, E. E. (1985) 'Evidence and interpretation of red ochre in the early prehistoric sequences', in Tobias, P. V. (ed.), *Hominid Evolution: Past, Present and Future* (New York: Alan R. Liss), pp. 387–94.

Wright, K. I. (1992) 'Ground stone assemblage variations and subsistence strategies in the Levant, 22,000 to 5,000 BP. Volume 1' (unpublished PhD thesis, Yale University).

Yellen, J. E., Brooks, A. S., Cornelissen, E., Mehlman, M. J. and Stewart, K. (1995) 'A Middle Stone Age worked bone industry from Upper Semliki Valley, Zaire', *Science* 268: 553–6.

CHAPTER 8

SYMBOLISM AND THE SUPERNATURAL

STEVEN MITHEN

INTRODUCTION

During the last thirty years many of the bastions that were once thought to divide humans from other animals have been severely challenged, if not crushed: tool-making and using are now recognized as present in many animal species (Beck 1980), as are advanced systems of vocal communication (e.g. Cheney and Seyfarth 1990) that some may wish to label as linguistic in nature (Parker and Gibson 1990). Primate social behaviour is now appreciated as being complex and flexible, involving Machiavellian like tactics that have a striking resemblance to the political manoeuvrings of humans (e.g. de Waal 1982; Byrne and Whiten 1988). Few would argue that the great apes lack a theory of mind and self-awareness, although these may not be as well developed as in humans (Byrne 1996). But some bastions still remain, one of which is the belief in supernatural beings. We cannot, of course, ask a chimpanzee whether he or she believes in a deity, but behavioural observations suggest that it is quite unnecessary to invoke such beliefs to explain chimpanzee behaviour – or indeed that of any non-human animal.

Humans are quite different. In both the past and the present a great deal of time and effort has been spent in worshipping gods and spirits. Fortunately, this effort has not been wasted as it has led to some of the most impressive cultural achievements of humankind including great architecture, art, music and literature; unfortunately, however, it has also resulted in some of the most appalling episodes of violence and suffering due to the intolerance that people have for those with different religious beliefs to their own.

The material symbols involved in religious behaviour, especially those that represent supernatural beings, appear to capture the epitome of the human symbolic capacity. Not only does an image of a deity represent something that is not present in time and space; it represents something that *could not* be present. Hard, tangible objects, such as carvings in stone, are used to symbolize intangible ideas and concepts: people appear to have no difficulty in understanding such symbolic links.

As the propensity to have religious ideas appears to be both pervasive among human beings, and quite unique to our species, this type of thinking provides a clear challenge to those who believe that viewing the human mind as a product of biological evolution can throw light on the nature of human thought and behaviour. Other aspects of the mind are much more readily understood as products of evolution. Consider, for instance, thoughts about food choice and sexual partners. Few would challenge the notion that these have been influenced by our evolutionary past as they have direct and immediate consequences for reproduction and survival. When examining these types of behaviour precisely the same methods that are used to study food choice and mating patterns in non-human animals can be applied. This has indeed thrown considerable light on human behaviour. Perhaps the best example is the study of foraging behaviour by modern hunter-gatherers which has been tackled by using the theoretical and methodological approaches of foraging theory originally developed for non-human animals (i.e. Stephens and Krebs 1986; e.g. O'Connell and Hawkes 1984; Winterhalder 1986; Mithen 1990). In this regard a robust methodology exists for examining the food choice behaviour of human beings from an evolutionary perspective. But no such methodology exists for human religious behaviour.

When this problem is considered from the perspective of an archaeologist attempting to explain the patterning and variability in the archaeological record, it can be characterized by the absence of any theoretical approaches to explain the appearance in that record of items that most probably relate to religious belief, such as images of unreal creatures, or burials with evidence for complex ritual and items placed within graves as offering. In this chapter I will suggest some possible directions for research on the evolution of symbols which relate to belief in supernatural beings. I will consider how we might conceive of 'protosymbolic' activity by Early Humans, and how this may have a different cognitive basis to the symbolic capacities of modern humans. I will also address the role of material artifacts in the conception and transmission of religious ideas, especially those concerned with the supernatural. My argument will be that material artifacts function as anchors for these ideas in the mind, and without them the development of religious institutions and thought about the supernatural are severely constrained. My first step is to clarify the problem that religious thought poses to the evolutionary anthropologist.

THE PERVASIVENESS OF RELIGIOUS BELIEF

Belief in the existence of supernatural beings is pervasive among living human communities, and has been among those documented throughout historical times. The prehistoric archaeological record with its tombs and effigies suggests that many of those people who lived before the time of writing had also believed in supernatural beings. Indeed, it could be argued that belief in the supernatural is universal among human groups – or at least has been until the emergence of atheism in the very recent past. As I have already noted, this widespread belief in the supernatural poses major problems to those who believe that many of the critical features of being human can be explained by recourse to evolutionary theory. An evolutionary approach has been characterized as assuming that our thought processes have been honed by natural selection to match the realities of the world – those individuals for whom this was the case would have benefited from increased reproductive success (Cosmides and Tooby 1994). From this perspective, those who prayed to Gods for rain, rather than who spent their time building irrigation channels, would hardly have managed to spread their genes in the next generation when under competition from those who set to work with the spade; those who believed that celibacy was a required part of their religious devotion would have had even greater difficulty.

What is particularly perplexing from an evolutionary perspective is not just that apparently maladaptive ideas and ways of behaviour have existed, but that they appear to have been so pervasive throughout human populations. The potential to believe in the supernatural appears to be a universal feature of the human mind; in the vast majority of individuals this potential has become realized. How can this be?

DEFINITIONS AND THE ROLE OF MATERIAL CULTURE

I have as yet made no attempt to offer any definitions of religious behaviour; this is, of course, fraught with difficulty. At most one can perhaps highlight four beliefs which are of greatest significance to that way of thinking which we call religious: (1) the belief in non-physical beings; (2) the belief that a non-physical component of a person may survive after death; (3) the belief that certain people within a society are likely to receive direct inspiration or messages from supernatural agencies, such as gods or spirits; (4) the belief that performing certain rituals in an exact way can bring about change in the natural world (see Boyer 1994; Guthrie 1993; Park 1994: 32–9 for discussion of attempts to define religion and identify universals).

We might add another common element to religious thought and practice: the use of material symbols. Although a few exceptions might be found, it is common practice for religious practices to involve the creation of images of supernatural beings, or symbols of those beings and the ideas about the world that they represent. Indeed Durkheim (1915: 381) suggested that 'the principle forms of art seem to have been born out of religious ideas'. As the earliest representational art appears to include images of supernatural beings (i.e. the Hohlenstein-Stadel lion man, and the bison/man figure from Chauvet cave – Mithen 1996a), the evidence from the archaeological record supports Durkheim's assertion. Leach (1976: 37) argued that we convert religious ideas into material objects to give them relative permanence so that they can be subjected to operations which are beyond the capacity of the mind. But this appears to beg the question of why this should be necessary at all.

Although we may not understand why there is such an intimate relationship between religious behaviour and material objects, that such a relationship exists is fortunate for archaeologists. If we have an archaeological record that lacks material symbols, and if we can be confident that this is not due to the lack of preservation, discovery and our ability at recognizing symbols when present, then we might be confident that religious beliefs are unlikely to have existed. Now, such thinking might be challenged. It could be argued that the role of material symbols in religious practices function for cultural transmission alone; that their absence would simply mean that this was absent or inefficient and that religious institutions did not exist. Yet individuals may still have had their own religious belief systems. As I will explain below, I think that this is an erroneous argument: material symbols are critical not just to the sharing of religious beliefs but in their conceptualization within the mind of an individual. As such, the archaeological record of material symbols (assuming that it is not biased by preservation and discovery) should provide a true record for the emergence not just of shared religious ideologies, but for the first emergence of religious ideas themselves. To support this assertion we need to consider the evolution of the human mind, with specific regard to how religious ideas may arise. But first, it is appropriate to briefly review the archaeological and fossil evidence for the belief in the supernatural and related symbolic behaviour.

ARCHAEOLOGICAL EVIDENCE

Colin Renfrew (1985) has discussed the formidable problems that archaeologists face when attempting to identify past religious activity and when trying to draw inferences regarding religious ideas. He quite rightly warns against being either unduly pessimistic or immodestly optimistic about our abilities at these tasks. With regard to early prehistory (i.e. prior to farming) the last decade has seen a rigorous re-examination of the evidence for ritual resulting in the rejection of much of the claimed evidence. The development of our understanding of taphonomy has led to the dismissal of Neanderthal bear cults, cannibalism and grave ritual involving the placement of flowers at Shanidar (Gargett 1989; Gamble 1989; White and Toth 1991).

In contrast to the view that 'primitive thought' was originally religious in nature, the archaeological evidence suggests that religious ideas and ritual activities appeared relatively recently in human prehistory. Although the first members of *Homo* are present in the fossil record 2.5 million years ago, the first unambiguous evidence for religious ritual is only associated with the appearance of anatomically modern humans not more than 100,000 years ago in terms of what appear to be ritualized burials in the caves of Skhūl and Qafzeh in the East. In Qafzeh a child was found buried with the skull and antlers of a deer (Vandermeersch 1970), while in Skhūl one of the burials had been laid on its back and the jaws of a wild boar placed within its hands (McCown 1937). Two things should be noted about these burials. First the associations between these animal parts and human bodies have been critically examined in recent years following claims that they are fortuitous – the mere result of post-depositional processes (Lindly and Clark 1990). Such claims have been rejected and there seems little doubt that parts of animals were intentionally placed within these graves. Secondly, artificially made symbols appear to be absent from these societies, neither placed within the graves nor worn on the bodies themselves. As much as 60,000 years elapsed before any symbols appear to have been manufactured. The first of these appears just 30,000 years ago at the cave of Chauvet in France, and Hohlenstein-Stadel in Germany. Both of these sites have produced images of half-man/half-animal figures which are likely to be representations of supernatural beings from an ice age mythology (Mithen 1996a). Before we consider those images, some of the more ambiguous evidence for religious and/or symbolic behaviour by pre-modern humans should be examined. There are three types of evidence to consider: material objects that have been claimed to have symbolic meanings or to have been used in creating them; Neanderthal burials; and the remarkable 'pit of bones' from Atapuerca.

EARLY PALAEOLITHIC SYMBOLIC ARTIFACTS

There has been a vigorous debate within the archaeological literature concerning artifacts from the Lower and Middle Palaeolithic periods that some claim to carry intentional marks which have symbolic importance. These artifacts have two champions in the form of Alexander Marshack (1990, 1997) and Robert Bednarik (1992, 1995) both of whom have made a major contribution by bringing the existence of such objects to the attention of the academic community. But few archaeologists have been convinced that these artifacts are symbolic in nature (Chase and Dibble 1987, 1992; Davidson 1992; Mithen 1996b). Bednarik has collated descriptions of pieces of bone or stone which carry incised marks and which have no apparent utilitarian explanation. It is likely that many of these could be explained as the unintentional by-product of activities such as cutting plant material on bone supports. None of them is representational, and there are no repeated motifs which would be expected if we were dealing with the remnants of a symbolic code. Unfortunately there has been a marked absence of methodologically rigorous microscopic study of these artifacts, comparable to that undertaken on incised artifacts of the Upper Palaeolithic by D'Errico (e.g. 1991, 1995). Until such work is undertaken, it is most unwise to attribute any significance to these Early Palaeolithic objects.

While Marshack (1990) has also promoted these incised stones and bones as evidence for Early Human symbolic activity, the most important artifact he has described is the Berekhat Ram 'figurine' (Marshack 1997). This is a 35 mm 'scoria', a pebble that had once been ejected from a volcano. It was found at Berekhat Ram on the Golan Heights in 1980 in a context dating to 250,000–280,000 BP. The stone has been claimed to have been intentionally modified to represent a female figurine. That this is the case has yet to be adequately argued, for although Marshack published some impressive photographs of the piece they certainly do not demonstrate that the lines are indeed intentional, and that if they were that they were intended to create a female form. It is most unfortunate that Marshack did not follow the recommendation of Pelcin (1994), who favoured a geological explanation for the 'figure' and argued that it is necessary to examine scoria which are found in non-archaeological contexts to see whether they too carry incisions that might be confused with those made by stone tools. All that can be said at present is that the Berekhat Ram 'figure' remains highly contentious.

Falling in the same category as these pieces of incised bone and odd shaped stones is the presence of ochre in Early Palaeolithic deposits. Although many claims have been made, it is only in South Africa that the presence of ochre in the Early Palaeolithic has been studied in detail (see Watts, this volume). Knight et al. (1995) argued that during the Middle Palaeolithic period, people made 'regular and copious' use of red ochre, at least from 110,000 BP and possibly as far back at 140,000 BP. Ochre was used, they argue, to paint bodies and, they claimed, this should be considered as the earliest symbolic tradition. As with Marshack's interpretation of the Berekhat Ram figurine they may be correct; but I think it wise to be more cautious and the evidence remains to be adequately presented. It remains unclear, for instance, from Knight et al.'s study precisely what quantities of ochre we are dealing with. Utilitarian explanations for ochre usage can be offered – as indeed Knight et al. acknowledge – which cannot as yet be confidently rejected. Nevertheless, the ochre deposits in the Middle Stone Age of South Africa appear to be the most persuasive at present for non-utilitarian behaviour prior to the start of the Late Stone Age/Upper Palaeolithic. This may not, of course, be surprising as it is also in South Africa that the first traces of anatomically modern humans are found.

Other than these ambiguous pieces of scratched bone, incised stones and ochre the archaeological record prior to 50,000 years lacks artifacts of a symbolic nature. We must always entertain the possibility, of course, that a considerable amount of symbolic behaviour was being undertaken in the form of dance, song and artifacts made from organic materials. As such, there would be no trace of these left in the archaeological record. As is so frequently stated: the absence of evidence is not evidence of absence. So what can we do about this as archaeologists? My own position is simply to argue that it is inconceivable that such symbolic activities could have been present, but not have also been expressed in ways that did indeed leave an archaeological trace. It is, I think, most prudent to adopt a cautious and conservative interpretation of the archaeological record for symbolic activity. Otherwise there seems no constraint on attributing symbolic dances, songs and feather headdresses not only to Neanderthals and archaic *H. sapiens*, but also to *H. ergaster* and the Australopithecines.

PROTO-SYMBOLISM?

To summarize, my own feeling is that we should be very cautious about interpreting the scratched bones, the Berekhat Ram figurine or the presence of ochre as evidence of symbolism. But even if we are generous with our interpretations, what is striking about these artifacts is their immense simplicity and rarity. If they do indeed reflect a capacity for symbolism, that capacity appears quite different from that which underlies the production of art as seen from the start of the Upper Palaeolithic. This is not to deny that the Upper Palaeolithic of Europe is an oddity and the symbolic explosion that it represents is largely explained by particular ecological and historical conditions. Nevertheless, 60–30,000 years ago does appear to mark some form of threshold in human cognitive development in light of the changes in the archaeological record at that time which are apparent throughout the world, including the colonization of arid regions, technological developments as well as the first representational art.

It appears to me profitable to treat the Early Palaeolithic artifacts I have described as evidence for a 'protosymbolic' capacity, in the same manner as one might refer to chimpanzee language use in laboratory conditions as evidence for a 'protolanguage' (Mithen 1996b). Just as chimpanzee 'language' has some similarities to human language but appears to be far too simple to be placed into the same category, so too do the symbolic artifacts of Lower and Middle Palaeolithic Early Humans appear far too simple to be placed into the same category as the symbols of modern humans. Chimpanzee language most probably derives from quite different cognitive capacities than human language – possibly no more than a capacity for associative learning (Mithen 1996a). I suspect that Early Human symbolic behaviour also derives from associative learning and the fact that it never went beyond body marking with ochre, or non-repeated incised lines, reflects the constraints on symbolic behaviour that arise when it has such a cognitive basis (Mithen 1996b). The symbolic behaviour of modern humans, like their linguistic abilities, most likely derive from quite different cognitive abilities.

Early Palaeolithic body painting is a particularly good example of something that might be characterized as protosymbolic behaviour. Although a symbol is notoriously difficult to define, one essential feature is a degree of displacement between the signifier and the signified in terms of space and/or time. It is for this reason that we do not refer to facial expressions as symbolic in nature: although the muscular contractions of my face to produce a smile signify that I have a bodily sensation of happiness, there is no displacement between the smile and my body and consequently the smile is not truly symbolic. So if Early Palaeolithic body painting was used to exaggerate or draw attention to various bodily characteristics – such as the size of breasts or muscles, or the redness of lips – such body painting should not be described as truly symbolic as there is no displacement between the signifier and signified. Using the same ochre pigment for painting images on cave walls is quite different.

NEANDERTHAL BURIAL AND THE 'PIT OF BONES' AT ATAPUERCA

A second body of contentious evidence regarding symbolic behaviour by pre-modern humans is that of Neanderthal burial. Although several examples of claimed Neanderthal burials can be confidently rejected (Gargett 1989), others remain ambiguous, such as that of Tesik Tash (Stringer and Gamble 1993), while further examples seem to be irrefutable cases in which a Neanderthal body was placed into a pit, notably those at La Ferrassie (Mellars 1996) and Kebara (Bar-Yosef et al. 1992). There is only one example where strong evidence for grave goods is present, the Neanderthal infant from Amud (Rak et al. 1994; Hovers et al. 1995). Known as Amud 7, the degree of preservation of this infant implies that it was a burial. A red deer maxilla was found lying on the pelvis. Currently undated, its location in the cave suggests a relatively recent date, i.e. younger than 60,000 BP.

This date does indeed appear to mark a boundary only after which all good examples of Neanderthal burials are found. Whether this is due to preservation or does indeed reflect a change in Neanderthal behaviour is unclear. It is evident that the Middle Palaeolithic archaeological record after this date shows other signs of change, such as the appearance of the Mousterian of Acheulian Tradition in sw France (Mellars 1996), and evidence for hunting rather than scavenging in west central Italy (Stiner and Kuhn 1992). So a case could be made that later Neanderthals were cognitively different from those of earlier periods. But again, if a symbolic capacity is present, it appears to be quite minimal.

The most intriguing context for hominid fossils of pre-modern humans is not the few Neanderthal burials but the remarkable collection at the Sima de los Huesos site, at Atapuerca, Spain dating to *c.* 300,000 BP (Arsuaga et al. 1997). Otherwise known as the 'pit of bones', this chamber contains the remains of at least thirty-two human individuals, which were most likely deposited as complete bodies rather than skeletal elements. The remains of many bears, wolves and other carnivores were also found within the chamber. These animals are likely to have entered the chamber by accident, falling in and becoming trapped. Some of the carnivores may have been attracted to rotting human bodies. But the chamber itself does not appear to be a carnivore den, and the absence of herbivores and stone tools indicates that it was not an occupation site. So quite how and why the human bodies entered the chamber remains unexplained. The excavators favour an anthropogenic explanation and suggest mortuary behaviour. If so, could this reflect the possession of religious ideas and belief in supernatural beings? One must recall that there are no artifacts from this period which are symbolic in nature, and no traces of any ritual activity other than this collection of bodies.

In this regard, the pit of bones poses archaeologists with a similar dilemma as the Neanderthal burials: can religious ideas exist without material symbols that represent supernatural beings or are used in burial ritual? I believe not. Even if we conclude that Neanderthal burials and the Sima de los Huesos accumulation should be described as mortuary behaviour, it appears to me that the absence of material symbols indicates that it should not be described as religious behaviour. I would argue that without material symbols, there is a significant constraint on the extent to which religious ideas and conceptualizations of supernatural beings can be shared. To explain this, we need to consider the role of material objects in both the formation and the transmission of religious ideas. But let us first briefly consider the appearance and character of objects in the archaeological record which undoubtedly undertook this function.

THE FIRST UNAMBIGUOUS SYMBOLS AND SIGNS OF RELIGIOUS BEHAVIOUR

The very first art we possess appears to be intimately associated with religious ideas by containing images of what are likely to be supernatural beings. The earliest piece is a 28.1 cm high carving in mammoth ivory of a figure half man and half lion from Hohlenstein Stadel and dating to *c.* 33,000 years ago (Marshack 1990). Contemporary with this are the paintings in Chauvet Cave which include a half-human/half-bison figure (Chauvet et al. 1996). Such anthropomorphic figures persist in Palaeolithic art even as the major animal themes change from carnivorous/dangerous animals to herbivores (Clottes 1996). In Trois Frères, for instance, there is the famous sorcerer figure probably 15,000–12,000 years old, which appears to have the posture, legs and hands of a human, the antlers of a reindeer, the tail of a horse and the phallus positioned as that of a feline. As we move beyond the Palaeolithic, anthropomorphic figures continue as a critical part of the archaeological record, such as the human/fish images from Lipinski Vir (Srejovic 1972). During later prehistory figurative images pervade prehistoric art and are most readily interpreted as images of supernatural beings (Gimbutas 1974).

It is also likely that many of the non-figurative images from prehistory relate to supernatural beings and religious ideas in light of the use of geometric forms to represent religious ideas by ethnographically documented groups. For instance, Howard Morphy (1989) has described Yolngu art in which, although Ancestral beings may be figuratively depicted, their transformational aspects (the manner in which they can exist in different states such as human, animal, feature of the landscape) are principally depicted in a geometric fashion. The multivalency of these designs enable the paintings to encode the transformational aspect of Ancestral Beings and events.

A more familiar example of a multivalent abstract image encoding ideas about supernatural beings is the Christian cross used as a symbol of the crucifixion and consequently the resurrection of Jesus. It is a distinct possibility, or even probability, that the abstract images from prehistory, such as those cut into limestone blocks 30,000 years ago in France (Delluc and Delluc 1978), and much later in prehistory such as on the stones at New Grange (O'Kelley 1982), are also encoding information about supernatural beings, a mythological world and religious ideas.

In summary, there can be little doubt that after 30,000 years ago religious ideas, ritual activity and material symbols pervade all human societies. This date is, of course, somewhat arbitrary but is a time when anatomically modern humans would have been dispersed throughout most of the Old World and entered Australia, and unambiguous evidence for symbolic behaviour exists in Africa, Asia, Europe and Australasia. Even though the meanings associated with the figurative or abstract images that are found cannot be inferred, there can be little doubt that the majority of this art related to religious ideas. Why should there be such a compulsion to represent religious ideas in material form? And could religious ideas have been held by those pre-modern hominids who were responsible for the pit of bones and the Middle Palaeolithic burials at a time when material symbols appear absent? To answer such questions we must consider the cognitive origins of religious thought.

THE COGNITIVE EVOLUTION OF RELIGIOUS IDEAS

IS IT ADAPTIVE TO HAVE RELIGIOUS IDEAS?

In my introduction to this chapter I have asserted that religious ideas have no adaptive value: indeed they often appear to be quite maladaptive, which poses a considerable evolutionary problem in light of their pervasiveness in human minds. Let me briefly question that assertion, for it could be wrong. One might argue that having strong beliefs in something, whether it is a single benign God, a whole panoply of deities some of whom are good and some bad or whatever, is in fact of considerable benefit to an individual. Having strong beliefs may remove uncertainty in decision-making, prevent worry about why the world is the way it is, and provide one with a degree of confidence in one's actions that would otherwise be absent. The possession of religious beliefs may be the solution *par excellence* to the problems of decision-making in highly uncertain environments: we simply follow the rules of appropriate behaviour, or use divination and waste no time on information processing when the value of different behavioural options is inherently unpredictable. Indeed some would argue that the major function of divination in hunter-gatherer societies is to ensure that behavioural choices are randomized (Tanner 1978).

RELIGIOUS BELIEFS AS A MENTAL SPANDREL

The alternative to this adaptive interpretation of religious beliefs is that these are no more than a mental spandrel – a by-product of other cognitive features which are of adaptive value but which contribute nothing in themselves, and do not incur costs of sufficient magnitude to cause a loss of reproductive fitness. I think this is a more likely possibility.

Here we must be careful to distinguish between, say, the idea of a supernatural being and the ends to which that idea are put. It is being able to have the original idea that may be no more than a mental spandrel. Once such ideas exist in people's minds, and especially if they can be shared as I will discuss below, these can act as a powerful medium for certain individuals to manipulate and control the behaviour of other individuals – and hence enhance their inclusive fitness. Religious ideologies are the pre-eminent means to legitimize political power. So, just as individuals exploit the physical bodies of others to achieve their ends (as in harnessing labourers, soldiers or reproductive partners) so too can the ideas existing in other minds be exploited. It is how those ideas could arise in the first place that might be explained in terms of an evolutionary spandrel.

Elsewhere (Mithen 1996a) I have presented one possible evolutionary scenario, which has significant similarities with the ideas of Boyer (1993, 1994, 1996) and Guthrie (1993). In our work the critical feature of super-natural beings is that they possess features which cross-cut the 'natural' categories of entities in the world. For instance a supernatural being may be able to transform itself into many different species although species in the natural world are immutable. In this sense it is like an artifact, which can be easily transformed into different types – a stone tool can be flaked again and again changing what artifact category it should be placed in. Supernatural beings may have a body like a human, but be invisible, just as an idea is invisible. Supernatural beings may need to eat in the manner that humans need to eat, but do not undergo the normal processes of birth and death. In that respect they are more like inert physical and seemingly timeless objects, such as a piece of stone.

It is, therefore, the human propensity to bring together knowledge that 'naturally' resides in quite separate cognitive domains – cognitive domains about material objects, living things, the human social world – that under-lies the ability to create ideas about supernatural beings. When I say 'nat-urally' resides, I am referring to the notion that for the majority of human evolution, thought was of a domain-specific character, with limited, if any, integration of knowledge and ideas from different cognitive domains (Mithen 1996a). That notion suggests that Early Human ancestors and relatives had at least three specialized cognitive domains, which I have referred to as 'social', 'technical' and 'natural history' intelligence. These are characterized as bundles of interacting mental models resulting in complex activity in each of those behavioural domains. As such it was an excellent cognitive adaptation for living in complex natural and social environments which is testified by the success of Early Humans in colon-izing such large parts of the Old World for almost two million years of the Pleistocene.

I have laid out the evidence for this model of Early Human mentality in detail elsewhere (Mithen 1996a). In essence it is constituted by the strange character of the Palaeolithic archaeological record that indicates Early Humans were extremely modern-like in some ways, and very archaic in others. Consider the tool-making of Neanderthals, for instance. Recent studies on the manufacture of levallois flakes and points has emphasized the complexity of this process, one that required considerable technical skill such that Upper Palaeolithic blade technology might be characterized as quite simple in comparison (Van Peer 1992; Dibble and Bar-Yosef 1996). Once hafted, a levallois point would make an effective, but simple, hunting weapon, as would spears such as those recently found at Schöningen (Thieme 1997) and most probably associated with *H. heidelbergensis*. Neanderthals, however, did not design complex, specialized hunting weapons, which would have been putting their technical skills to use in the domain of foraging; neither did they make material objects to wear as body decoration – putting their technical skills to use in the social domain (for reviews of Neanderthal technology see Mithen 1996a; Mellars 1996; Stringer and Gamble 1993). The explanation I favour for this curious lack of technical application is that their thoughts about the social, natural and technical worlds were quite isolated from each other.

We should not view this from our own mental perspective, concluding that domain-specific Early Human mentality was primitive or even an evolutionary failure. Quite the reverse. We should recognize that this domain-specific mentality allowed *Homo* to become one of, if not the, most successful genus of large terrestrial mammals during the Pleistocene, successfully occupying both low- and high-latitude environments.

THE ADAPTIVE VALUE OF COGNITIVE FLUIDITY

In comparison to modern humans, however, this domain-specific mentality was indeed quite limiting. While it allowed complex behaviour within each cognitive domain, that at the boundaries remained quite simple as the knowledge and ways of thought of each cognitive domain could not be integrated together. Modern humans acquired the ability to do just that, which can be described as having cognitive fluidity. This evolutionary transition to a cognitively fluid mind is similar to a transition that occurs during cognitive development within an individual that has been described in various ways, including that of 'mapping across domains' (Carey and Spelke 1994) and the emergence of 'representational redescription' (Karmiloff-Smith 1992).

With regard to cognitive evolution, cognitive fluidity was of immense adaptive value. It allowed, for instance, technical and natural history intelligence to be integrated so that specialized hunting weapons could be designed. By combining elements of social and technical intelligence items could be manufactured which conveyed social messages, such as beads and necklaces. This capacity for cognitive fluidity, the emergence of which is likely to be closely tied up with that of language and consciousness (Mithen 1996a: 185–94), gave *Homo sapiens sapiens* considerable adaptive advantage over other species of *Homo* who maintained a domain-specific mentality.

Quite why *H. sapiens sapiens* alone evolved this cognitive fluidity remains unclear; it may be accounted for purely on the basis of historical contingency – a mutation that happened by chance in one member of

H. sapiens sapiens rather than another hominid species. Alternatively, cognitive fluidity may indeed have been emerging in other hominid species. This is a possibility I have discussed elsewhere (Mithen 1996a: 209–10) with regard to the late Neanderthals (those after 60,000 BP). They appear to be showing traces of behaviour which may have depended upon some degree of cognitive fluidity, such as intentional burial and making artifacts with social meanings, which is just one possible interpretation of the hand-axes of the Mousterian and Acheulian Tradition (Mellars 1996). They were replaced simply because the *H. sapiens sapiens* dispersing from Africa possessed cognitive fluidity to a much higher degree.

My argument is, therefore, that the capacity for cognitive fluidity was of substantial adaptive value. Those who possessed it gained considerable reproductive benefit by improving their foraging efficiency, such as by using well-designed hunting weapons and plant processing equipment. Anthropomorphizing animal behaviour would also have been of significant value. As shown by Blurton-Jones and Konner (1976) this can lead to very effective predictions about animal behaviour – as effective as those achieved by behavioural ecology. As such, thinking that animals have human-like minds would have been of considerable adaptive benefit for those with cognitively fluid minds (Mithen 1996c).

RELIGIOUS IDEAS AS A PRODUCT OF COGNITIVE FLUIDITY

If, as I described above, the essence of religious ideas is indeed the combination of elements from different natural categories, then this appears to be another product of cognitive fluidity – but one that does not need any adaptive value. In other words it is a spandrel of those ways of thinking that allow the development of more efficient foraging and social communication. If religious thinking and behaviour does involve costs, if it is maladaptive, these are more than compensated for by the benefits of cognitive fluidity gained from other types of thinking.

It is important to note here that cognitive fluidity may not have evolved in one go (Figure 8.1); my own argument has been that it was a two-stage process with an initial integration of social and natural history intelligence, followed by one of technical intelligence (Mithen 1996a). Only with this latter integration did the substantial cultural developments occur which are often referred to as the cultural explosion of the Upper Palaeolithic. Prior to that anatomically modern humans maintained a Middle Palaeolithic material culture, even though they appear to have been behaving in markedly different ways to Early Humans, as evident from their burial and hunting patterns in the Near East (Lieberman and Shea 1994) and the functional aspects of their anatomy (Trinkaus 1992). Those behavioural changes derived, I believe, from the first stage of the cognitive

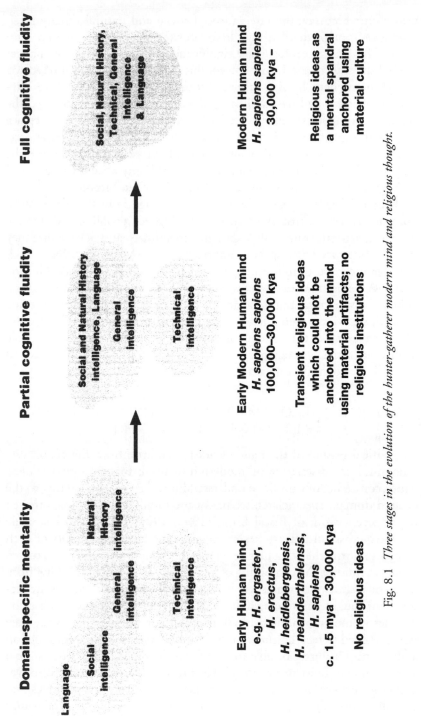

Fig. 8.1 *Three stages in the evolution of the hunter-gatherer modern mind and religious thought.*

transition which saw the integration of social and natural history intelligence. Although this left few direct archaeological traces, it may have been of far greater evolutionary significance than any cognitive changes around the start of the Upper Palaeolithic. If we follow the 'out of Africa' model for modern human origins (Stringer and McKie 1996) an integration of social and natural history intelligence may have provided the cognitive competitive edge which allowed modern humans to replace existing species of Early Humans in Africa, Asia and Europe. In some parts of the world this occurred many thousands of years before we see the widespread cultural developments which could only arise once technical intelligence was also integrated into a cognitively fluid mind.

By being able to integrate ideas and knowledge from the two evolved domains of natural history and social intelligence people could, for the first time, attribute human-like thoughts to animals, and believe that they shared ancestors with specific animal species (Mithen 1996c). Such anthropomorphic thinking lies at the heart of religious ideas (Guthrie 1993). A mapping could be created of the social world onto the natural world, and vice versa. But if the domain of technical intelligence remained isolated, such ideas were unable to find material expression. To consider the consequence of this for religious thought, we need to consider the role of material artifacts as 'anchors' for ideas which are not firmly embedded into a single cognitive domain.

THE ROLE OF MATERIAL ARTIFACTS IN RELIGIOUS THOUGHT

The critical feature of the religious ideas that arise from the cognitively fluid mind, as possessed by all modern humans, is that they involve ideas which contradict our intuitive understanding of the world, relating to the evolved domain-specific architecture of the mind. This has been stressed in the recent work of Pascal Boyer (1993, 1994, 1996) who has made extensive cross-cultural studies of religious thought. The results of such studies confirm the idea that religious thinking is intimately linked to cognitive fluidity, the combining of knowledge and ways of thinking from different cognitive domains. As he explains, supernatural beings are frequently thought of as being able to defy the laws of physics such as by effortlessly moving through physical objects or walking on water; they may not need to feed or undergo the 'normal cycle of birth, reproduction and death'. They may be able to transform themselves into other animal species, or into humans or into physical features of the landscape. Boyer provides a host of no less bizarre examples from other religions: trees that can talk, mountains that can breathe. Such features of supernatural beings arise from cognitive fluidity – the bringing together knowledge and ideas from different cognitive domains. If Neanderthal minds, and indeed those of all Early Humans, had a domain-specific mentality, then the ability to imagine talking trees or invisible people would have been simply beyond them.

THE CULTURAL TRANSMISSION OF RELIGIOUS IDEAS

Boyer argues that such violations to an evolved understanding of the world draw our attention to religious ideas; but it also make such ideas transient, and difficult to comprehend and to transmit. This is because they do not relate to an evolved feature of mental architecture. In an evolutionary context they do not 'fit' into the domain-specific cognitive domains, and in a developmental context they do not 'fit' into domains of intuitive knowledge found within children's minds (for discussion of intuitive physics, psychology and biology during child development see Mithen 1996a). As such, religious ideas contrast with other types of ideas. For instance, transmitting knowledge about material artifacts is relatively easy, as all human minds appear to have an intuitive physics – concepts of inertia, momentum, gravity appear to be deeply embedded within human minds (Spelke 1991; Spelke et al. 1992). The remarkable stability in technological traditions during early prehistory, such as the Acheulian or Levallois Mousterian, demonstrates very high levels of cultural transmission, much of which may have occurred among pre-linguistic hominids. That such tool-making traditions could be transmitted with such high degrees of fidelity is a reflection of an evolved understanding of technology – that which I have referred to as technical intelligence. In other words, Early Humans could have readily assumed that other individuals would have shared a substantial amount of intuitive knowledge about tool-making which made communication within that domain relatively easy.

Few people in the modern world develop specialized knowledge concerning artifacts; but consider how easy it is to transmit ideas about the social world. We all routinely explain complex social relationships to each other, perhaps about third parties. This is done effortless as we 'tap into' an evolved understanding of social relationships, an intuitive psychology that derives from the social intelligence of our early ancestors: we all share a set of basic concepts without these needing to be transmitted themselves.

Religious ideas are in total contrast to this. If my evolutionary scenario for the mind is correct, and as Boyer has argued, there is no domain-specific basis to religious ideas. Such ideas are subject to immense diversity and there can be no assumptions that other individuals will be able to grasp the ideas that one possesses. As a consequence the cultural transmission of religious knowledge is fundamentally different – fundamentally more difficult – to that of technical and social knowledge. Rather than being informal, it is often undertaken in the context of ritual: ordered sequences of action, rigidly adhered to which serve to maintain the fidelity of the ideas during cultural transmission. Without this, religious ideas would too readily become corrupted and dissipated. But even with the bulwark of ritual, religious ideas are 'winnowed' by the process of cultural transmission; those which survive are those which can most easily find an 'anchor' in the human mind.

Pascal Boyer has drawn on this inevitable winnowing of religious ideas to explain certain recurrent features of supernatural beings. He argues that the religious ideas which are most likely to survive cultural transmission are those anchored into one of the domains of intuitive knowledge within the mind. So while they need to violate some aspects of our intuitive knowledge of the world to have salience, they also need to conform to some aspects of this to have survival value. This has been recognized by both Guthrie (1993) and Boyer (1994). Boyer stresses how supernatural beings very frequently possess a belief-desire psychology, one that we intuitively understand, while Guthrie stresses that supernatural beings are often very human like: 'For most people, gods and humans are very similar … In various cultures gods eat, drink, make war and love, have offspring, fall sick, grow old and die, very much as humans do' (1993: 178).

MATERIAL CULTURE AS ANCHORS FOR RELIGIOUS IDEAS

By attributing religious ideas with such features they are anchored into the human mind: if everything about a supernatural being violated what we understood about the natural world, people would have immense problems in grasping religious concepts. Such concepts would be impossible to communicate and share. But there is a second, and perhaps a far more significant, way in which religious ideas are anchored: they are represented in material form. Religious ideas that are represented in material form gain survival value for the process of cultural transmission. When translated into material symbols they become easier to communicate and comprehend as their material form provides a second anchor into the human mind. Representation in physical form provides a means whereby those features of supernatural beings that violate intuitive knowledge may themselves be anchored into the mind, rather than having to ride upon the back of the human-like features of the supernatural beings. In other words, we should expect that representations of supernatural beings stress the intuitive knowledge violations (rather than conformities) of those beings. By doing this, anchors are provided for those religious ideas in the human mind that would otherwise rapidly become dissipated because they violate an evolved understanding of the world. Such anchors allow the ideas to be acquired, recalled, understood and transmitted, supplementing the manner in which this is achieved by the ideas having other features which conform to intuitive knowledge.

Faulstich (1992: 22), summarizing the role of art among the Walpiri of the central Australian desert, expresses this most clearly:

> Among the Walpiri, the natural world is visualized in terms of totemic features and mythological histories. The art makes those unseen realities tangible and reminds the people of their tribal origins and religious obligations ... When a people's relationship with the spiritual is made tangible, pertinent concepts can be transmitted easily and easily appreciated. The Walpiri excel in employing symbols to communicate and comprehend an intricate belief system.

One aspect of this communication has to be communication to oneself: material symbols allow one to continually grasp the difficult concepts of religious ideas; the need is for these to be continually reaffirmed within a mind that is not 'designed' by evolution to have such ideas.

CONCLUSION: MATERIAL SYMBOLS AND RELIGIOUS IDEAS

As I noted above, Durkheim (1915: 381) argued that the 'the principle forms of art seem to have been born out of religious ideas'. I think that this should be reversed: that religious ideas, or at least those which are shared, are born out of art, for without material symbols they cannot be sufficiently anchored into human minds. It is on this basis, therefore, that I feel we can be confident that ideas about supernatural beings did not exist within people's minds before material symbols were made. Whatever Neanderthals were doing when they placed individuals in pits, or whatever *H. heidelbergensis* was doing at Atapuerca that led to the accumulation of bodies at Sima de los Huesos, it could not have involved shared beliefs in supernatural beings. For that to arise, material symbols which anchor those ideas into human minds are of immense value, if not an actual requirement. Indeed, I would question whether those early anatomically modern humans at Qafzeh and Skhul who placed animal parts into graves with their dead also had religious ideas that we would recognize as such today. Of course, we must always be aware that material symbols may have been made from organic materials and simply did not survive in the archaeological record. But at present, we have no evidence that prior to 30,000 years ago material symbols did indeed exist. And without them, nor could shared ideas about supernatural beings.

REFERENCES

Arsuaga, J. L., Martinez, I., Gracia, A., Carretero, J. M., Lorenze, C. and Garcia, N. (1997) 'Sima de los Huesos (Sierra de Atapuerca, Spain). The site', *Journal of Human Evolution* 33: 109–27.

Bar-Yosef, O., Vandermeersch, B., Arensburg, B., Belfer-Cohen, A., Goldberg, P., Laville, H., Meignen, L., Rak, Y., Speth, J. D., Tchernov, E., Tillier, A.-M. and Weiner, S. (1992) 'The excavations in Kebara Cave, Mt. Carmel', *Current Anthropology* 33: 497–551.

Beck, B. (1980) *Animal Tool Behaviour* (New York: Garland STPM Press).

Bednarick, R. G. (1992) 'Palaeoart and archaeological myths', *Cambridge Archaeological Journal* 2: 27–57.

Bednarik, R. G. (1995) 'Concept mediated marking in the Lower Palaeolithic', *Current Anthropology* 36: 605–34.

Blurton-Jones, H. and Konner, M. J. (1976) '!Kung knowledge of animal behaviour', in Lee, R. and DeVore, I. (eds), *Kalahari Hunter-Gatherers* (Cambridge, Mass.: Harvard University Press), pp. 326–48.

Boyer, P. (1993) *The Naturalness of Religious Ideas: A Cognitive Theory of Religion* (Berkeley: University of California Press).

Boyer, P. (1994) 'Cognitive constraints on cultural representations: natural ontologies and religious ideas', in Hirschfeld, L. A. and. Gelman, S. A. (eds), *Mapping the Mind: Domain Specificity in Cognition and Culture* (Cambridge: Cambridge University Press), pp. 391–411.

Boyer, P. (1996) 'What makes anthropomorphism natural: intuitive ontology and cultural representation', *Journal of the Anthropological Institute* 2: 83–97.

Byrne, R. W. (1996) *The Thinking Ape: Evolutionary Origins of Intelligence* (Oxford: Oxford University Press).

Byrne, R. W. and Whiten, A. (eds) (1988) *Machiavellian Intelligence: Social Expertise and the Evolution of Intellect in Monkeys, Apes and Humans* (Oxford: Clarendon Press).

Carey, S. and Spelke, E. (1994) 'Domain-specific knowledge and conceptual change', in Hirschfeld, L. A. and. Gelman, S. A. (eds), *Mapping the Mind: Domain Specificity in Cognition and Culture* (Cambridge: Cambridge University Press), pp. 169–200.

Chase, P. and Dibble, H. (1987) 'Middle Palaeolithic symbolism: a review of current evidence and interpretations', *Journal of Anthropological Archaeology* 6: 263–93.

Chase, P. and Dibble, H. (1992) 'Palaeoart and archaeological myths (a reply to Bednarik, R.)', *Cambridge Archaeological Journal* 2: 43–51.

Chauvet, J-M., Deschamps, E. B., and Hillaire, C. (1996) *Grotte Chauvet: The Discovery of the World's Oldest Paintings* (London: Thames & Hudson).

Cheney, D. and Seyfarth, R. (1990) *How Monkeys see the World* (Chicago: Chicago University Press).

Clottes, J. (1996) 'Thematic changes in Upper Palaeolithic art: a view from the Grotte Chauvet', *Antiquity* 70: 276–88.

Cosmides, L. and Tooby, J. (1994) 'Origins of domain specificity: the evolution of functional organization', in Hirschfeld, L. A. and. Gelman, S. A. (eds),

Mapping the Mind: Domain Specificity in Cognition and Culture (Cambridge: Cambridge University Press), pp. 85–116.

Davidson, I. (1992) 'Palaeoart and archaeological myths (a reply to Bednarik, R.)', *Cambridge Archaeological Journal* 2: 52–7.

Delluc, B. and Delluc, G. (1978) 'Les manifestations graphiques aurignaciennes sur support rocheux des environs des Eyzies (Dordogne)', *Gallia Préhistoire* 21: 213–438.

Dibble, H. and Bar-Yosef, O. (eds) (1996) *The Definition and Interpretation of Levallois Technology* (Madison, Wis.: Prehistory Press).

D'Errico, F. (1991) 'Microscopic and statistical criteria for the identification of prehistoric systems of notation', *Rock Art Research* 9: 59–64.

D'Errico, F. (1995) 'A new model and its implications for the origin of writing: the La Marche antler revisited', *Cambridge Archaeological Journal* 5: 163–206.

Durkheim, E. (1915) *The Elementary Forms of Religious Life* (London: Allen & Unwin).

Faulstich, P. (1992) 'Of earth and dreaming: abstraction and naturalism in Warlpiri art', in Morwood, M. J. and Hobbs, D. R. (eds), *Rock Art and Ethnography* (Melbourne: Occasional AURA Publication No. 5), pp. 19–23.

Gamble, C. (1989) 'Comment on "Grave shortcomings: the evidence for Neanderthal burial by R. Gargett"', *Current Anthropology* 30: 181–2.

Gargett, R. (1989) 'Grave shortcomings: the evidence for Neanderthal burial', *Current Anthropology* 30: 157–90.

Gimbutas, M. (1974) *The Goddesses and Gods of Old Europe* (London: Thames & Hudson).

Guthrie, S. (1993) *Faces in the Clouds: A New Theory of Religion* (Oxford: Oxford University Press).

Hovers, E., Rak, Y., Lavi, R. and Kimbel, W. H. (1995) 'Hominid remains from Amud cave in the context of the Levantine Middle Palaeoliothic', *Paléorient* 21: 47–61.

Karmiloff-Smith, A. (1992) *Beyond Modularity: A Development Perspective on Cognitive Science* (Cambridge, Mass.: MIT Press).

Knight, C., Power, C. and Watts, I. (1995) 'The human symbolic revolution: a Darwinian account', *Cambridge Archaeological Journal* 5: 75–114.

Leach, E. (1976) *Culture and Communication* (Cambridge: Cambridge University Press).

Lieberman, D. E. and Shea, J. J. (1994) 'Behavioural differences between Archaic and Modern Humans in the Levantine Mousterian', *American Anthropologist* 96: 330–2.

Lindly, J. and Clark, G. (1990) 'Symbolism and modern human origins', *Current Anthropology* 31: 233–61.

McCown, T. (1937) 'Mugharet-es-Skhul: description and excavation', in Garrod, D. and Bate, D. (eds), *The Stone Age of Mount Carmel* (Oxford: Clarendon Press), pp. 91–107.

Marshack, A. (1990) 'Early hominid symbol and the evolution of human capacity', in Mellars, P. (ed.), *The Emergence of Modern Humans* (Edinburgh: Edinburgh University Press), pp. 457–98.

Marshack, A. (1997) 'The Berekhat Ram figurine: a late Acheulian carving from the Middle East', *Antiquity* 71: 327–37.

Mellars, P. (1996) *The Neanderthal Legacy* (Princton, NJ: Princton University Press).

Mithen, S. (1990) *Thoughtful Foragers: A Study of Prehistoric Decision Making* (Cambridge: Cambridge University Press).

Mithen, S. (1996a) *The Prehistory of the Mind: A Search for the Origins of Art, Science and Religion* (London: Thames & Hudson).

Mithen, S. (1996b) 'On early Palaeolithic "concept mediated marks", mental modularity and the origins of art', *Current Anthropology* 37(4): 666–70.

Mithen, S. (1996c) 'Putting anthropomorphism into evolutionary context' (a comment on Boyer 1996), *Journal of the Royal Anthropological Institute* (n.s.) 2: 717–21.

Morphy, H. (1989) 'On representing Ancestral Beings', in Morphy, H. (ed.), *Animals Into Art* (London: Unwin Hyman), pp. 144–60.

O'Connell, J. and Hawkes, K. (1984) 'Food choice and foraging sites among the Alyawara', *Journal of Anthropological Research* 40: 504–35.

O'Kelley, M. J. (1982) *Newgrange: Archaeology, Art and Legend* (London: Thames & Hudson).

Park, C. C. (1994) *Sacred Worlds: An Introduction to Geography and Religion* (London: Routledge).

Parker, S. and Gibson, K. R. (eds) (1990) *'Language' and Intelligence in Monkeys and Apes* (Cambridge: Cambridge University Press).

Pelcin, A. (1994) 'A geological interpretation for the Berekhat Ram figurine', *Current Anthropology* 35: 674–5.

Rak, Y., Kimbel, W. H. and Hovers, E. (1994) 'A neanderthal infant from Amud Cave, Israel', *Journal of Human Evolution* 26: 313–24.

Renfrew, C. (1985) *The Archaeology of Cult: The Sanctury at Phylakopi* (London: British School of Archaeology at Athens).

Spelke, E. S. (1991) 'Physical knowledge in infancy: reflections on Piaget's theory', in Carey, S. and Gelman, R. (ed.), *Epigenesis of Mind: Studies in Biology and Culture* (Hillsdale, NJ: Erlbaum).

Spelke, E. S., Breinlinger, K., Macomber, J. and Jacobsen, K. (1992) 'Origins of knowledge', *Psychological Review* 99: 605–32.

Srejovic, D. (1972) *Lepenski Vir* (London: Thames & Hudson).

Stephens, D. and Krebs, J. (1986) *Foraging Theory* (Princeton, NJ: Princeton University Press).

Stiner, N. and Kuhn, S. (1992) 'Subsistence, technology and adaptive variation in Middle Palaeolithic Italy', *American Anthropologist* 94: 12–46.

Stringer, C. and Gamble, C. (1993) *In Search of the Neandertals: Solving the Puzzle of Human Origins* (London: Thames & Hudson).

Stringer, C. and McKie, R. (1996). *African Exodus: The Origins of Modern Humanity* (London: Pimlico).

Tanner, A. (1978) 'Divinations and decisions: multiple explanations for Algonkin scapulimancy', in Schwimmer, E. (ed.), *The Yearbook of Symbolic Anthropology 1* (Montreal: McGill University Press), pp. 89–101.

Thieme, H. (1997) 'Lower Palaeolithic hunting spears from Germany', *Nature* 385: 807–10.

Trinkaus, E. (1992) 'Morphological contrasts between the Near Eastern Qafzeh-Skhul and Late Archaic humans samples: grounds for a behavioural difference', in Akazawa, T. Aoki, K. and Kimura, T. (eds), *The Evolution and Dispersal of Humans in Asia* (Tokyo: Hokusen-sha), pp. 277–94.

Van Peer, P. (1992) *The Levallois Reduction Strategy* (Madison, Wis.: Prehistory Press).

Vandermeersch, B. (1970) 'Une sépulture moustérienne avec offrandes découvertre dans la grotte de Qafzeh', *Comptes Rendus Hebdomadares des Séances de l'Académie des Sciences* 270: 298–301.

de Waal, F. (1982) *Chimpanzee Politics: Power and Sex among Apes* (London: Jonathon Cape).

White, T. D. and Toth, N. (1991) 'The question of ritual cannibalism at Grotta Guattari', *Current Anthropology* 32: 118–38.

Winterhalder, B. (1986) 'Diet choice, risk and food sharing in a stochastic environment', *Journal of Anthropological Archaeology* 5: 369–92.

PART III

THE EVOLUTION OF LANGUAGE

CHAPTER 9

THE EVOLUTION OF
LANGUAGE AND LANGUAGES

JAMES R. HURFORD

LANGUAGES AND THE HUMAN
LANGUAGE FACULTY

Human languages, such as French, Cantonese or American Sign Language, are socio-cultural entities. Knowledge of them ('competence') is acquired by exposure to the appropriate environment. Languages are maintained and transmitted by acts of speaking and writing; and this is also the means by which languages evolve. The utterances of one generation are processed by their children to form mental grammars, which in some sense summarize, or generalize over, the children's linguistic experiences. These grammars are the basis for the production of a new avalanche of utterances to which the next generation in its turn is subjected. (This picture is simplified, of course, as generations overlap.)

Languages inhabit two distinct modes of existence, which have been called (by Chomsky 1986) 'E-Language' and 'I-Language'. E-language is the external observable behaviour – utterances and inscriptions and manifestations of their meanings. E-Language is regarded by some as so chaotic and subject to the vicissitudes of everyday human life as to be a poor candidate for systematic study. (E-Language corresponds to what Chomsky, in earlier terminology, called 'performance'.) Out of this blooming buzzing confusion the individual child distils an order internal to the mind; the child constructs a coherent systematic set of rules mapping meanings onto forms. This set of rules is the child's I-Language (where 'I' is for 'internal'). No two individuals' I-Languages have to be the same, although those of people living in the same community will overlap very significantly. But there will usually be at least some slight difference between the I-language features prevalent in one generation and those prevalent in the next. This is the stuff of language evolution, in the sense of the historical development of individual languages, such as Swedish, Navaho or Zulu.

The evolution of languages in the sense just sketched is patently not biological, but socio-cultural. This kind of language evolution is the stock in trade of historical linguistics. Historical linguistics is a relatively mature discipline. It has accumulated vast amounts of theory and fact concerning how languages have changed over the last few thousand years. It has reconstructed in detail many of the protolanguages from which modern languages are descended. Examples are Proto-Indo-European, presumed to have been spoken somewhere in Eastern Europe about five thousand years ago, and Proto-Iroquoian, the ancestor language from which the modern American languages of the Iroquoian family, such as Mohawk, are descended. Historical linguists have catalogued many types of change that can occur in the evolution of individual languages, changes such as weakening and strengthening of the meanings of words, change of basic word order, loss of inflections, grammaticalization of lexical words (nouns, verbs, adjectives) into grammatical function words (articles, pronouns, auxiliaries), merger of phonemes, the emergence of novel phonemic distinctions, lowering, raising, fronting, backing and rounding of vowels, palatalization, glottalization, and so on. (See MacMahon 1994, and Aitchison 1991 for recent introductions.)

Typically, historical linguistics has subscribed to the doctrine of uniformitarianism. This is the principle that any reconstructed protolanguage has to be recognizably of the same general type as observable modern languages. This principle was an important element of the discipline, acting as a methodological constraint on possible reconstructions. Clearly, any reconstruction, from modern evidence, of a language spoken thousands of years ago, is a speculative venture (as any science is), and the need for such a constraint is understandable. 'If it were true that language structure universally requires more than one vowel in a phonemic system, the fact that older Indo-European seems to reconstruct with only one vowel would be highly suspicious' (Hoenigswald 1960: 137). But the constraint of uniformitarianism, while probably well-motivated for events within the last ten thousand years, is clearly, for speculation about the evolution of forms of human communication over hundreds of millennia, both false and an obstacle to research.

The prefix *proto-* is viciously ambiguous. It is used, by historical linguists, to designate reconstructed ancestral languages which are cut from the same pattern as modern languages. The protolanguages reconstructed by historical linguists are not simpler than their modern counterparts. They are recognizably modern in all aspects except the date at which they happen to have been spoken. On the other hand, the term *protolanguage* has been used, influentially, by Bickerton (1990) to designate a different type of language from modern languages. Protolanguage, for Bickerton, was not blessed with the syntactic intricacies of modern languages, but only had very simple devices for stringing words together.

We presume that, to a first approximation, all modern humans have the same biologically given aptitude for language acquisition. All the developments discussed by historical linguists, therefore, have taken place within constraints imposed by the modern genome. To be a possible modern language (such as modern German, Classical Latin or ancient Egyptian), a system has to be acquirable by a biologically modern human. Modern humans were preceded by various (sub)species for whom different, more limited, classes of systems were acquirable as their 'languages'. Bickerton's term *protolanguage* is a useful attention-focusing device, postulating that the class of 'languages' biologically available to *Homo erectus* was the class of protolanguages, defined quite roughly as systems for concatenating vocabulary with none of the complex syntactic dependencies, constituencies, command and control relations characterizing modern languages. A *Homo erectus* individual, even if somehow presented with modern linguistic experience, could not make of it what a modern child makes of it due to innate limitations. Bickerton likens this type of 'language' to that which intensively trained chimpanzees are capable of.

In the sense in which Bickertonian protolanguage has evolved into modern human language, we are speaking of evolution of the human language faculty, of 'Language with a capital L'. The transmission of information relevant to the evolution of the language faculty is through an entirely different mechanism from the evolution of individual languages. The language faculty has evolved as other genetically determined traits have evolved, via selection over the millions of alleles that contribute to the human genome. The phylogenetic evolution of the language faculty must have been slower by several orders of magnitude (assuming one could even quantify such things) than the sociocultural evolution of individual languages.

It is instructive to compare the mechanisms of sociocultural evolution of languages with those of phylogenetic evolution of the language faculty. For biological evolution, we have a relatively well understood distinction between genotype and phenotype. In the case of Language, the genotype is the features of the genome relevant to language acquisition and use, while the phenotype is the brain, vocal tract and behaviour involved in actual processes of language acquisition and use during the lifetimes of individuals. One might be tempted to seek analogues of genotype and phenotype in the mechanism of sociocultural evolution of languages, in the constant cycle, over the generations, through E-Language and I-Language. But no analogy will hold satisfactorily. The E-Language of one generation is a necessary link in the chain of language transmission across generations, a necessary input for a child in the next generation to construct an I-Language. If a whole community became Trappists for a generation, the historical continuity of their language would be broken.

Competence in a particular language is an acquired characteristic of an individual. Biological heredity, as of an innate language faculty, does not provide for the inheritance of acquired characteristics. In theory, a modern human language faculty could pass intact through thousands of years in a totally silent community (assuming the community itself could somehow survive); with the lifting of the vow of silence, the children of the new generation would be as ready as any others to acquire any language they were exposed to. This last point assumes, perhaps too strongly, that there would be no significant decay in the language faculty due to lack of any pressure of natural selection through linguistic behaviour. I will return in a later section to the question of the contribution that linguistic performance makes to fitness.

Organisms survive and reproduce in antecedently given environments, which are the outcomes of factors and forces external to the organisms. But, to varying degrees, lineages of organisms also create parts of their environment. So it is with languages. A significant aspect of the environment into which a human child is born is the language of the community. The particular syntax, phonology and lexicon of the language is a historical creation of the child's cultural forebears. If the child is to prosper, he or she must be able to acquire this particular syntax, phonology and lexicon. But here we see an apparent paradox for the evolution of languages. Evolution means change, but it would seem that the requirement to acquire the language of one's community is a prescription for stasis rather than change. The paradox can be resolved by invoking the ideas of tolerance and intelligibility. A child does not need to learn to speak exactly like (one of) his or her parents; if the child acquires a syntax, phonology and lexicon permitting tolerable mutual intelligibility with the community he or she is born into, that child will prosper tolerably well. Fitting this picture, languages do indeed change very slowly, as we have seen, and stay well within the constraints of intergenerational intelligibility.

Although languages change historically, they do so within the bounds of universal constraints on the forms of syntactic and phonological systems. So a child acquiring a language slightly different from that of the previous generation in the community still will not acquire a language that is different in type from that of the community. The capacity to acquire a modern human language is genetically transmitted. So, barring mutations and new recombinations, a child cannot acquire a language of a formal type that the parents were incapable of acquiring. To the extent that they share the same relevant genes, the qualitative language acquisition capacity of the child is identical to that of the parents. We assume that there were relevant mutations and recombinations in the evolution of the modern human language faculty. Accordingly, there must have been children who were born capable of acquiring a class of languages different from the class of languages acquirable by their parents. These 'transitional' children would have been presented with data (spoken utterances) produced from grammars of the old type, and internalized grammars of a new type, while still maintaining tolerable mutual intelligibility with the previous generation.

Something like this actually happens in the process of creolization. Take the extreme cases of plantation pidgins, which, according to Bickerton (1981), develop into creoles in just one generation. Here, the adult slaves share no common language, but make shift with a crude set of conventions for stringing together words mainly borrowed from the slavemaster's language. The adult slaves, though they have internal grammars of their native languages, have been forced into a situation where their native languages are of no use to them or they are prevented from using them. Being adults, and therefore beyond the critical period for full grammar acquisition, the pidgin language they make do with is in fact of a different formal type from the creole language spontaneously created by their children. Bickerton's story of evolution from crude pidgins to fully modern human creoles in one generation may be an exaggeration and has been contested (see Alleyne 1980, 1986). But clearly there are in the pidgin/creole literature cases of new language creation within the space of a few generations. Perhaps the most compelling evidence is from Senghas (1997), who describes the formation of a new sign language creole in a single generation in a deaf school in Nicaragua.

Such pidgin-to-creole cases are presumably a kind of microcosm of what happened millennia ago, perhaps many times over, in many ancestral campsites. But the crucial intergenerational differences from those early times that are of interest to us are not the artificial differences such as are created by slavery, but biologically based differences in what classes of languages the earlier and later individuals were capable of acquiring. At some point an individual must have arisen who was capable of internalizing a grammar of a type that none of his or her ancestors (no matter what data they were exposed to) could possibly have internalized.

The focus of the rest of this chapter will be on the evolution of the human language faculty, and not on the evolution of particular languages.

EXPLAINING A UNIQUE PHENOMENON

The human language faculty is unique. This poses problems for explanation. We like scientific explanations to be general, to account for wide ranges of data. Darwinian accounts of the evolution of the eye are convincing because they apply to many different convergent instances, from mammals to molluscs. If a professor throws a pile of essays down a flight of stairs, we can invoke an elegant general explanation of why they all fall – gravity, but any attempted explanation of why the one particular essay that lodged furthest down the stairs should have done so is, *ipso facto*, less general. Biological adaptationist accounts of the human language faculty face the difficulty that the initial conditions providing the platform for the adaptation must be presumed to contain some unique factor or combination of factors. Otherwise, why should we only find language in one species? The focus of explanation shifts away from the general pervasive tendency of species to adapt to their environments towards some specific one-off circumstance that has occurred only once in history.

Adaptation is still part of the picture, however. Selective pressure for individuals (or groups) to be better adapted to their environments undoubtedly played a part in the evolution of the language faculty, just as the force of gravity affects all the essays thrown down the professor's stairs.

Let us stay with the essays-and-stairs analogy a little longer and say a breeze blows through the house, so that essays sporadically get shifted from higher to lower stairs (as gravity always applies). After a while, there will be several, perhaps many, essays on or beyond the stair which was originally the furthest reached by any essay. We modern humans are the first species, but we may not be the last, to acquire a language faculty. In retrospect, for each of the major transitions in evolution, there must have been a unique standard-bearer at one time. Only after each new phase became widely represented could any scientist (if one had existed!) propose explanatory mechanisms for it accounting for a wide range of data.

Scientists of our era are stuck, then, with the inevitability of less-than-general explanations for the evolution of the human language faculty. But there are still serious constraints on what can count as a satisfactory particular explanation. Any circumstances invoked as explaining the emergence of Language have to be argued to be true. Where special brain structures are proposed as the crucial *explanans*, for example, one has to be able to verify that humans, and no other species, have just such structures. Or where special social arrangements of humans are invoked as the crucial significant factor, one has to be able to argue that these social arrangements did apply to humans at the relevant time, and not to other species. And in general, more realistically and more eclectically, for any set of circumstances proposed as individually necessary and collectively sufficient to explain the emergence of Language, one has to show that this combination of circumstances applies (or applied) to humans and to no other species. We have a long way to go.

SOME SUGGESTED PREADAPTATIONS OR CRUCIAL STEPS

For a purposeful agent, assembling any set of individually necessary and collectively sufficient elements for some task poses the problem of keeping all the accumulating and yet still insufficient subsets together until the last key member is put in place, finally rendering the whole set sufficient. How much more unlikely it must be for blind, non-teleological evolution to keep subsets of circumstances together until the final key circumstance arises that makes the whole collection sufficient to give rise to some evolutionary development. This is why the term 'preadaptation' may at first seem to have a contradictory, or teleological, ring to it; the term might almost seem to suggest that evolution anticipates the adaptations it will have to make in future. In fact, however, the notion of preadaptation is not so problematic.

The idea of preadaptation is clearly envisaged and defended in Darwin's *Origin*, especially in the 6th edition:

> I have now considered enough, perhaps more than enough, of the cases, selected with care by a skilful naturalist, to prove that natural selection is incompetent to account for the incipient stages of useful structures; and I have shown, as I hope, that there is no great difficulty on this head. A good opportunity has thus been afforded for enlarging a little on gradations of structure, often associated with changed functions.
>
> Darwin 1872: 204

In any environment there is scope for variation which has little or no effect on fitness. And genomes and cultures can wander randomly through the possibility space so that many different neutral possibilities are represented. These possibilities may be genetic, or neural, or other physiological, or individual behavioural, or social. An account of how preadaptations can accumulate in a system with multiple layers of organization – DNA, neural nets, behaviour, fitness – is given in Miglino et al. (1996). These authors also show how the accumulation of such preadaptations can lead to apparent discontinuities or phase-changes in evolution.

I give below a brief survey of some traits which have been suggested as preadaptations for language. The ideas briefly reviewed below are a small selection from many found in the literature (see Richards 1987: 246–73 for a good concise survey). For each of these, it has been suggested that its presence was a necessary precondition for the emergence of Language. There is seldom, if ever, any serious consideration of the relative chronology of the various proposed preadaptations. Thus, each of the 'preadaptations' reviewed below might be seen as the last and crucial step that gave us Language, or it might be one of an accumulation of necessary characteristics preceding that final step.

One must further always be aware that such talk of 'steps', whether 'final', 'crucial' or otherwise, involves idealization. Evolutionary steps are instances of normally continuous and gradual processes suddenly accelerating or precipitating qualitative phase changes. In reality, evolutionary steps may take thousands, even millions, of years to complete. This should be taken into account when considering the relative chronology of any proposed preadaptations for Language. Many of the various necessary steps were certainly being taken simultaneously.

COGNITIVE PREADAPTATIONS

THEORY OF MIND

A capacity to attribute to other individuals versions of one's own beliefs and desires is evident in much modern linguistic behaviour. There could conceivably be quite elaborate communication systems whose use does not require a theory of mind on the part of its users, but human languages, and especially the pragmatic systems of inference used with them, are not such systems. The acquisition and use of human languages requires substantial inferential machinery about the likely intentions of others (see Sperber and Wilson 1986 for the tip of this iceberg). Control of complex grammatical structures *per se* does not presuppose a Theory of Mind. Heyes (in press) reviews the evidence for whether apes have any such theory of mind, and concludes that there is as yet no convincing evidence that they do, although she does not rule out the possibility of such evidence being found. (Heyes' article is a good introduction to the large literature on ape theory of mind.) My own reading leads me to suspect that it is a matter of degree, with normal adult humans having the strongest capacity for reading the minds of others, followed, in order, by normal human children, chimpanzees, autistic people, orang utans, gorillas and monkeys. It is noteworthy that children's growing ability to make inferences about others' intentions lags behind their acquisition of quite complex grammatical structures. Literature on Theory of Mind is heavily interwoven with discussion of closely related concepts under the headings of 'social intelligence' (Worden 1998) and 'Machiavellian intelligence' (Byrne and Whiten 1988). See also Sperber (1994) on human 'meta-representational capacity'.

BICKERTON'S PHONETICS-TO-THETA-ROLE LINK

Bickerton (1998) has proposed a single catastrophic event precipitating the emergence of the modern language capacity. This is the appearance of a connection in the brain between the (hypothetical) component that processes understanding of complex social relations between individuals (who-did-what-to-whom) and the symbol-processing machinery that can already handle isolated words but not syntax. This proposal is one of the more extreme 'Big Bang' style proposals for the emergence of the language faculty.

MIMESIS

This is an idea first put forward by Merlin Donald (1991), who sums it up as follows.

> Mimesis is a non-verbal representational skill rooted in kinematic imagination, that is, in an ability to model the whole body, including all its voluntary action-systems, in three-dimensional space. This ability underlies a variety of distinctively human capabilities, including imitation, pantomime, iconic gesture, imaginative play, and the rehearsal of skills. My hypothesis is that mimesis led to the first fully intentional representations early in hominid evolution, and set the stage for the later evolution of language.
>
> Donald 1998

Evidence for such intentional and imaginative capabilities can also be gleaned from Palaeolithic tools (see Wynn 1991).

'SYMBOLIC REFERENCE'

It is all too tempting to think of a language as consisting of a set (infinite, of course) of independent meaning–form pairs. This way of thinking has become habitual in modern linguistics, although there is also much in the subject which reminds one of its artificiality. Deacon (1997) emphasizes that in human language any concept which is the sense of some linguistic item (such as a word) is also enmeshed in a net of relationships with the senses of other words. This network of senses embodies a complex constructed world-picture in the mind of the speaker. The complexity and combinatorial productivity of modern languages arise from humans' unique facility for relating signals to coordinates in such complex abstract conceptual networks.

SOCIAL PREADAPTATIONS

ALTRUISM, COOPERATION

Communication may arise, as Dawkins and Krebs (1984) claim, from an arms-race between mind-reading and manipulation. A view (with versions which may be either complementary or opposed to this 'Machiavellian' view) is that a certain degree of altruism and mutual cooperation is a prerequisite for the rise of complex communication systems, in particular where these can be used by one individual to convey factual information to another. It would seem that there is usually little immediate benefit to a speaker in 'giving' declarative information to another. Classic references on the evolution of altruism, though with no reference to language, are Trivers (1971) and Hamilton (1964).

GROUP SIZE

Robin Dunbar (1993, 1996) has argued that the typical size of human clans and networks of intimates hovers significantly around the number

150. Briefly, language evolved as a response to the necessity of servicing the enormous number of relationships with other individuals that a group of 150 presents. Bonding by physical grooming with so many other people is not practical. But words are cheap, and having a language capable of expressing quick gossipy messages enables humans to keep up their social networks. The argument does not say anything about the intricate grammatical structures of human languages.

PHYSIOLOGICAL PREADAPTATIONS

BRAIN SIZE

Everybody agrees that there is some connection between humans' abnormally large brains and their capacity for language, but nobody has been able to specify very precisely what this connection is. Deacon (1992) points out that in the two-million-year period in which brains have doubled in size, no clearly new structures have been added, although there has been warping of the proportions of the parts, with the frontal areas of cortex becoming more prominent. It is these parts which handle 'verbal short-term memory, combinatorial analysis, and sequential behavioral ability' (Deacon 1992: 64). For other accounts, see also Eccles (1989) and Wilkins and Wakefield (1995).

SERIAL MOTOR CONTROL

The complex gesture of, say, throwing a stone, can be likened to a phrase; it consists of a series of subgestures which must be carefully coordinated with each other. One school of thought sees in the evolution of such complex gestures a basis for the mental organization of grammatical phrases and sentences. Such proposals do not go beyond such simple grammatical relationships as serial ordering of elements. Representative works in this vein are Calvin (1983), Kimura (1979) and Lieberman (1984). Interestingly, Chomsky's (1959) influential review of Skinner's *Verbal Behavior* also pointed to the relevance of serial order in behaviour, specifically to Lashley's (1951) work.

VOCAL TRACTS

Human vocal tracts differ significantly in shape from those of chimpanzees, allowing us to produce a range of distinct sounds that chimpanzees are not capable of. Lieberman (1992, 1984, 1975) is the most prominent exponent of this topic. Lieberman's work also argues that the Neanderthal vocal tract was incapable of articulating the range of modern human speech sounds. This view has recently been challenged by Arensburg and co-workers (1989, 1990) and Duchlin (1990). Aiello (1998) briefly surveys some evidence that the human vocal tract was an early preadaptation, motivated by dietary changes in early hominids. Although the range of sounds available to modern humans is, by definition, characteristic of human language, it can be argued that this is a less crucial characteristic than some others (e.g. syntax). If we were capable of articulating fewer phonemes, we would have to use longer words. Perhaps there is some ideal trade-off between the capacity to make fine articulatory distinctions and the size of short-term memory buffers.

FITNESS AND LANGUAGE

Preadaptations, such as those just discussed, are enabling rather than forcing. Having a particular preadaptive trait simply makes certain later steps possible; preadaptations for language are not in themselves selected for by any measure of fitness involving language. By contrast, (neo-)Darwinian accounts tend to stress adaptations, which, by definition, are selected for.

One must, of course, avoid the 'strict adaptationist' fallacy of assuming that every trait is adaptive; there are spandrels, accidental, non-functional aspects of morphology or behaviour (Gould 1987; Gould and Lewontin 1979). Lightfoot's (1991) position is that the formally interesting features of the language faculty, which give human languages their characteristic features (e.g. the syntactic principle of subjacency – see exposition below), are not particularly fitness-enhancing; the human language capacity is more complex than it needs to be, and even in places dysfunctionally complex. Such features as subjacency may indeed be, Lightfoot argues, just accidents (spandrels); but scientific methodology abhors accidents, and a powerful theory predicting the occurrence of such features would be preferable, if one could be found. One cannot be happy with a general stance of classifying any interesting phenomenon as a spandrel. Lieberman has put it very well:

> Gould's (1987) 'spandrel theory' paper on the origins of language is nothing more than a restatement of Darwinian preadaptation with the added dubious claim that *no subsequent natural selection occurred*. This is most unlikely, all specialized organs appear to involve both preadaptation and natural selection.
> Lieberman 1991: 63–4 [emphasis in original]

In this section I briefly explore questions which arise when trying to see in what ways aspects of the human language faculty could be adaptive, and might have been privileged by natural selection. I will also mention the alternative possibility that the search for adaptedness in humans is misplaced; this is the idea that it is not we humans who are adapted, but that languages, as sociocultural constructs, have evolved and adapted to us.

The massive expressive power of human languages (not a topic centrally addressed by syntactic theorists) is, of course, fitness-enhancing. Fitness is not an absolute matter but always relative to an environment. What is fit in one environment is unfit in another. Language was undoubtedly instrumental in conferring on humans fitness across an unprecedentedly wide range of environments. Many environments are still no-go areas for humans, but we can survive and reproduce in a range greater than that of any other species. Our ability to communicate precise and complex messages to each other must have helped. This much is a broad truism; we can explore the matter of fitness in relation to Language, and languages, in more subtle ways.

If we assume that the innate human language faculty, in all its specific detail, arose by natural selection, the central puzzle is the relation between intricate universal principles of grammatical structure and fitness. Clearly, the space between fitness and principles of grammar had to be bridged by some intermediate theoretical construct, such as expressive power. To take a specific example, a relatively robust principle, under modern grammatical theory, is subjacency. Putting it informally:

> Subjacency, in effect, keeps rules from relating elements that are 'too far apart from each other', where distance apart is defined in terms of the number of designated nodes that there are between them.

> Subjacency accounts for the violations of grammaticality in the English sentences (4a–b):

> 4. a. *What$_i$ do you wonder where John put _____$_i$?
>   b. *What$_i$ do you believe the claim that John ate _____$_i$?

> In these sentences, two bounding nodes intervene between the gap and the word *what*.
>
> Newmeyer 1991: 12

Given the assumption under consideration, we have to explain how a creature innately disposed to internalize a grammar conforming to the principle of subjacency has a reproductive advantage over one that doesn't. Newmeyer's (1991) paper makes a brave and worthwhile start at such an account. He cites the widely accepted conclusion that the subjacency principle is a helpful constraint on the assignment of an understood grammatical role for displaced elements such as question words and relative pronouns (e.g. *what*), because a sentence not conforming to subjacency is likely to put a heavy strain on working memory (Berwick and Weinberg 1984). Then Newmeyer builds this and arguments relating to other grammatical principles into the following general conclusion:

> In sum, the innate principles of UG can be motivated functionally. As the language faculty evolved, pressure for more successful communication (and with it the reproductive advantage that this would bestow) conferred an evolutionary advantage on those whose grammars incorporated them.
>
> Newmeyer 1991: 20

There is a difficulty with this explanation (unnoticed by any of the commentators on Newmeyer's paper). Recall from discussion above that the environment in which an alleged mutant must succeed is partly a linguistic environment. Imagine a stage in human evolution which we will call *Homo pre-subjacentia*, 'pre-subjacency humans'. Now, a mutant child, who (*ex hypothesi*) is disposed to acquire a grammar containing the subjacency constraint, is born into a community producing utterances that do not conform to this constraint. The pre-subjacentian linguistic environment would be full of utterances depending for their successful interpretation on assignment of co-indexing relations (as between *what* and its 'gap') which violate the mutant's innate principle. Surely the child would be at a disadvantage rather than at an advantage. To put it concretely, the child's pre-subjacentian parent might say to it something along the lines of *What do you wonder where John put?*, intending to convey *I know you are wondering where John put something – what was that something?* This interpretation would be barred for the child, who, at worst, would have to conclude that its parent was talking gibberish. (The situation would be asymmetric, as anyone in the population would understand utterances produced by the mutant. The child's grammar would generate a proper subset of the structures generated by the grammars of the rest of the population.) Only if the mutant child somehow survived his confusing childhood and procreated a brood of little post-subjacentians, who would be able to understand their parent perfectly, could the subjacency mutation get a foothold in the population. It is not impossible, I suppose, but this is certainly a difficulty for Newmeyer's proposed adaptationist/nativist explanation of such grammatical principles.[1] The problem just noted is completely general; it will be hard for constraints, which *limit* the sets of structures that grammars will generate, to evolve.

Beside this objection, there is a more common one, expressed by several commentators on Newmeyer's paper, of which Fouts' version is typical:

> It seems critical to me that he [Newmeyer] demonstrate how a human male or female who uses Chomskian perfect grammar has a better chance of breeding than one who failed English 101 and is noted for ungrammatical monosyllabic utterances yet has bedroom eyes and drives a BMW.
>
> Fouts 1991: 42

We should, however, remember that conditions for *Homo erectus* or archaic *Homo sapiens* were very different from modern conditions with BMWs and English 101. Perhaps, way back then, better communicators really did have an advantage.

Two broad strands are apparent in arguments that effective communication enhances the reproductive chances of individuals. One strand

---

1. See Kirby and Hurford (1997) for further arguments along these lines.

emphasizes the successful receipt of informative messages by the hearer, such as 'Watch out for that falling rock.' This leaves any possible advantage to the speaker to be accounted for in terms of altruism – a plausible move, in my view. The other strand emphasizes the successful use of a code by speakers to enhance their positions in a social group. Better talkers get more prestige and therefore more mates. This view places less emphasis on the informative content of messages and more on the function of utterances to forge and maintain social relationships. While undoubtedly language is used for social 'grooming' purposes, this emphasis fails to account for the impressive and subtle referential power of language. Unfortunately, although it seems to be a truism that effective communication is likely to have been advantageous, when we get down to the level of individuals reaping that advantage on particular occasions, all stories that we can tell seem oddly inept. Perhaps this is just a measure of the temporal and cultural gap between us and the relevant ancestors.

Bickerton (1990, 1991) is among those who emphasize the role of (internal) representation over that of communication in any adaptive account of human language. 'In any account of the functional motivation of language, the question of whether it was the communicative or the representational aspects that contributed most to the adaptedness of language surely bulks too large to be ignored' (Bickerton 1991: 37). Superior mental representational power has been listed as a necessary precondition to language. If communication is envisaged in Saussurean terms of a meaning in one head (speaker) being recreated in another head (hearer), the two heads involved clearly must have the power to represent these meanings. I cannot convey an idea to you that I am unable to grasp myself. Powerful mental representational capacity, without there necessarily being any means to externalize it in utterances, is very probably adaptive in itself.

But Bickerton's view that we can apparently compare the contribution of representation with that of communication is mistaken, because (internal) representation and communication achieve different goals in different circumstances. Human languages are all public languages, elaborate systems for externalizing complex mental representations as essentially linear signals. The representation task just doesn't face some of the problems that the expression task faces. Take for instance the proposition represented by a reflexive sentence in English, a sentence such as *Kim hit herself*. The decision having been 'made' (presumably for purposes of regularity) that the verb *hit* requires an object, there arises the expression task of conveying that this object denotes the same individual as does the subject of the sentence. This task, indeed any task involving control over a relation between form and meaning, is something that a mental capacity for internally representing complex concepts never has to face. A creature (non-linguistically) entertaining the thought corresponding to *Kim hit herself* need only have a single entity, Kim, in mind, not two – 'subject-Kim' and 'object-Kim'. When managing internal mental representations alone, there is never any issue of denotation; denotation is only an issue that arises when the externalization of concepts in public utterances arises.

Note that the examples of subjacency given above involve an antecedent (*What*) and a subsequent 'gap' in the sentence. This anaphoric relation between antecedent and gap is no part of any plausible mental representation of the meaning of *What do you wonder where John put*? (unless you believe that one thinks in English). The movement rules that generative grammarians have concentrated on are motivated by apparent discrepancies between the needs of internal representations of meanings and the human language sentences that express them. Obviously, one cannot appeal to the properties of meaning representations to account for universal ways in which the surface sentences of languages diverge from such representations.

A radical alternative to the focus on the phylogenetic adaptation of humans to be better communicators or better conceptualizers is a focus on the linguistic adaptation of systems of communication to be replicable by human acquirers. This idea has been well expressed by Christiansen:

> What is often not appreciated is that the selective forces acting on language to fit humans is [*sic*] significantly stronger than the selective pressure on humans to be able to use language. In the case of the former, a language can *only* survive if it is learnable and processable by humans. On the other hand, adaptation towards language use is *one out of many* selective pressures working on humans – Thus, language is more likely to have adapted itself to its human hosts than the other way round. Languages that are hard for humans to learn simply die out, or, more likely, do not come into existence at all. Following Darwin, I propose to view natural language as a kind of beneficial parasite – i.e. a *nonobligate symbiant* – that confers some selective advantage onto its human hosts without whom it cannot survive.
>
> Christiansen 1994: 126

'Refocus' is the correct term to use here. Christiansen cannot deny that there are some special genetically specified characteristics in humans that enable them, and no other species, to act as hosts to complicated languages, so an element of innateness is not ruled out. Deacon (1997) has expressed a similar view to Christiansen's. The same general idea is now beginning to be explored by computational modellers, starting with Batali (1998) and continuing with Kirby (forthcoming). These researchers show how quite language-like systems can arise in populations of communicating agents starting, as our ancestors must have, from the total absence of any coordinated or structured system. Probably more will emerge from this line of research over the next few years.

DATES

'The timing of the origin of language is anyone's guess' (Richards 1987: 205). This assessment is near the mark, if not wholly right. The nature of the dating problem is to fit a series of vaguely and controversially hypothesized stages in the evolution of language around a handful of approximate (and also controversial) dates for key non-linguistic events in human evolution.

The three key dates usually mentioned are of two phylogenetic transitions and one cultural transition in *Homo sapiens*. The phylogenetic transitions are *habilis* to *erectus* around 1.7 m years ago and archaic *Homo sapiens* to anatomically modern *sapiens sapiens* (between 200,000 and 100,000 years ago). The cultural transition is the Upper Palaeolithic revolution in toolmaking (45,000–40,000 years ago), which I collapse here for convenience with the emergence of 'modern' art forms around the same time. The *erectus*-to-*sapiens* date is contested by multi-regional evolution theorists (see Wolpoff 1988), who claim that there was no relatively sudden speciation event, but rather a long (perhaps one million year) period of interbreeding between more modern and more conservative varieties in various parts of the Old World. The revolutionary character of the changes in tool making around 40,000 years ago is also disputed by some.

As far as 'stages' in linguistic evolution are concerned, the most specific suggestion is Bickerton's, of a simple two-stage progression from protolanguage to full human language. Protolanguage is described as concatenation of vocabulary items according to pragmatic pressures (e.g. put the 'word' for the most salient idea first), with no level of grammatical organization involving phrases or inflections or grammatical words such as determiners, auxiliaries or case-markers. It is like Tarzan-talk. Bickerton gives examples from pidgins, the efforts of trained apes, human children under two years of age and language-deprived adults.

Bickerton suggests that *Homo erectus* spoke protolanguages. It is tempting to align Bickerton's step from protolanguage to full human language with the emergence of anatomically modern humans between 200,000 and 100,000 years ago. If there is a view which is held by more scholars than any other, on however flimsy grounds, it is probably that fully modern language came on the scene with the appearance of anatomically modern humans. But this currently conventional wisdom needs to be subjected to careful criticism as more evidence and arguments appear.

This 'catastrophic' two-stage model is in contrast to continuous models. Continuity models do not immediately appeal to linguists familiar with the modular structure of languages. Linguists analyze languages, with some reason, into components such as lexicon, phonology, syntax and semantics, all organized along rather distinctively different principles, like the separate but interacting organs of the human body. It is hard to see a differentiation between phonology and syntax as a continuous process; there must have been some kind of phase change. To a linguist, a statement such as that simple versions of modern language were used a million years ago is unclear, because it does not specify the sense in which 'simple' is intended and seems to treat a language system as a kind of undifferentiated lump that you can simply get 'more of'.

The Bickertonian picture of over a million and a half years during which *Homo erectus* used protolanguages is easier to envisage as a continuum, with perhaps gradually expanding vocabularies, gradually faster speech and comprehension, and steady compression of (proto)language acquisition into the critical period before puberty. Such gradual changes can be (intuitively) reconciled with the increase in brain size over the period.

Say, following the currently popular view, that anatomically modern humans were also the first humans equipped with a fully modern language acquisition device (LAD). What would they have done with it? The LAD needs input, a language already spoken in the environment, or else it remains dormant. The first *Homo sapiens sapiens* would, according to the popular idea, have been born into a protolanguage-speaking environment. From here, it is a simple step, again following Bickerton's ideas, to full human language via processes essentially like those of creolization witnessed in modern times.

Another view (e.g. Krantz 1980) associates the emergence of fully modern languages with the sudden marked improvement in stone tool technology around 40,000 BP. It is argued that what explains this technological explosion was the ability to describe to others, in language, the more complicated procedures needed for making the new improved tools. The theory relies on an impression of what might be learnable by mere observation and what tasks require linguistic instruction. If one accepts this view of the later emergence of modern languages, one has to ask what anatomically modern humans were doing for the preceding 60,000 years. A possible answer is that the socio-cultural transition from protolanguages to modern languages took 60,000 years; but this seems unlikely in the light of modern evidence from creolization.

SUMMING UP

Individual human languages evolve perceptibly, by a process of cultural evolution, over a couple of generations. The human language faculty has taken millions of years to evolve to its present state. Being unique, the human language faculty is not susceptible to such convincing adaptationist explanations as, say, the mammalian eye; yet clearly language is adaptive. Humans clearly benefit from possession of complex language, but equally, languages, considered as organisms in themselves, thrive in the hospitable environment of human minds and communities. The early story of the evolution of the human capacity for language involves the settling into place of a range of social, psychological and physiological preadaptations. Once all preconditions for language in humans were in place, it is likely that languages blossomed rapidly, starting before *Homo sapiens sapiens*' exodus from Africa, but also perhaps not achieving the full complexity of modern languages until after the expansion out of Africa.

ACKNOWLEDGEMENTS

This research was partly supported by ESRC grant R000236551 'The Evolutionary Origins of Innate Linguistic Constraints' and by a Fellowship at the Collegium Budapest. I thank Simon Kirby and Bob Berwick for useful discussions on this topic.

REFERENCES

Aiello, L. (1998) 'The foundations of human language', in Jablonski, N. G. and Aiello, L. (eds), *The Origin and Diversification of Language*, Memoir 24 (California Academy of Sciences, Berkeley: University of California Press), pp. 21–34.

Aitchison, J. (1991) *Language Change: Progress or Decay?*, 2nd edn (Cambridge: Cambridge University Press).

Alleyne, M. C. (1980) *Comparative Afro-American* (Ann Arbor, Mich.: Karoma Publishers).

Alleyne, M. C. (1986) 'Substratum influences: guilty until proven innocent', in Muysken, P. and Smith, N. (eds), *Substrata Versus Universals in Creole Genesis* (Amsterdam: John Benjamins), pp. 301–15.

Arensburg, B., Tillier, A. M., Vandermeersch, B., Duday, H., Schepartz, L. A. and Rak, Y. (1989) 'A Middle Paleolithic human hyoid bone', *Nature* 338: 758–60.

Arensburg, B., Schepartz, L. A., Tillier, A. M., Vandermeersch, B. and Rak, Y. (1990) 'A reappraisal of the anatomical basis for speech in Middle Paleolithic hominids', *American Journal of Physical Anthropology* 83: 137–46.

Batali, J. (1998) 'Computational simulations of the emergence of grammar', in Hurford, J. R., Studdert-Kennedy, M. and Knight, C. (eds), *Approaches to the Evolution of Language: Social and Cognitive Bases* (Cambridge: Cambridge University Press), pp. 405–26.

Berwick, R. C. and Weinberg, A. S. (1984) *The Grammatical Basis of Linguistic Performance* (Cambridge, Mass: MIT Press).

Bickerton, D. (1981) *Roots of Language* (Ann Arbor, Mich.: Karoma Publishers).

Bickerton, D. (1990) *Language and Species* (Chicago: University of Chicago Press).

Bickerton, D. (1991) 'Language origins and evolutionary plausibility', *Language and Communication* 11(1): 37–9.

Bickerton, D. (1998) 'Catastrophic evolution: the case for a single step from protolanguage to full human language', in Hurford, J. R., Studdert-Kennedy, M. and Knight, C. (eds), *Approaches to the Evolution of Language: Social and Cognitive Bases* (Cambridge: Cambridge University Press), pp. 341–58.

Byrne, R. and Whiten, A. (1988) *Machiavellian Intelligence: Social Expertise and the Evolution of Intellect in Monkeys, Apes and Humans* (Oxford: Clarendon Press).

Calvin, W. (1983) 'A stone's throw and its launch window: timing precision and its implications for language and hominid brains', *Journal of Theoretical Biology* 104: 121–35.

Chomsky, N. (1959) 'Review of B. F. Skinner's *Verbal Behavior* (New York: Appleton-Century-Crofts, Inc., 1957)', *Language* 35(1): 26–58.

Chomsky, N. (1986) *Knowledge of Language: Its Nature, Origin and Use* (New York: Praeger).

Christiansen, M. H. (1994) 'Infinite languages, finite minds: connectionism, learning and linguistic structures' (PhD thesis, University of Edinburgh).

Darwin, C. (1872) *On the Origin of Species by Means of Natural Selection*, 6th edn (New York: Heritage Press), page reference to reprint edition, 1963. .

Dawkins, R. and Krebs, J. R. (1984) 'Animal signals: mind-reading and manipulation', in Krebs, J. R. and Davies, N. B. (eds), *Behavioural Ecology: an Evolutionary Approach*, 2nd edn (Oxford: Blackwell Scientific).

Deacon, T. (1997) *The Symbolic Species* (New York: W. W. Norton).

Deacon, T. (1992) 'Brain-language coevolution', in Hawkins, J. A. and Gell-Mann, M. (eds), *The Evolution of Human Languages* (Redwood City, Calif.: Addison-Wesley), pp. 49–83.

Donald, M. (1991) *Origins of the Modern Mind: Three Stages in the Evolution of Culture and Cognition* (Cambridge, Mass.: Harvard University Press).

Donald, M. (1998) 'Mimesis and the executive suite: missing links in language evolution', in Hurford, J. R., Studdert-Kennedy, M. and Knight, C. (eds), *Approaches to the Evolution of Language: Social and Cognitive Bases* (Cambridge: Cambridge University Press), pp. 44–67.

Duchlin, L. E. (1990) 'The evolution of articulate speech: comparative anatomy of the oral cavity in *Pan* and *Homo*', *Journal of Human Evolution* 19: 687–98.

Dunbar, R. I. M. (1993) 'Coevolution of neocortical size, group size and language in humans', *Behavioural and Brain Sciences* 16: 681–94.

Dunbar, R. I. M. (1996) *Grooming, Gossip and the Evolution of Language* (London: Faber & Faber).

Eccles, J. C. (1989) *Evolution of the Brain: Creation of the Self* (London: Routledge).

Fouts, R. (1991) 'Dirty bathwater, innateness neonates and the dating game', *Language and Communication* 11(1): 41–3.

Gould, S. J. (1987) 'The limits of adaptation: is language a spandrel of the human brain?' (unpublished paper delivered to the Center for Cognitive Science, MIT).

Gould, S. J. and Lewontin, R. C. (1979) 'The spandrels of San Marco and the Panglossian paradigm: a critique of the adaptationist programme', *Proceedings of the Royal Society of London* 205: 281–8.

Hamilton, W. D. (1964) 'The genetical evolution of social behaviour, I and II', *Journal of Theoretical Biology* 7: 1–16, 17–62.

Heyes, C. M. (in press) 'Theory of mind in nonhuman primates', *Behavioural and Brain Sciences*.

Hoenigswald, H. (1960) *Language Change and Linguistic Reconstruction* (Chicago: University of Chicago Press).

Krantz, G. (1980) 'Sapienization and speech', *Current Anthropology* 21: 773–92.

Kimura, D. (1979) 'Neuromotor mechanisms in the evolution of human communication', in Whitaker, H. and Whitaker, H. A. (eds), *Current Trends in Neurolinguistics* (New York: Academic Press).

Kirby, S. (forthcoming) 'Language evolution without natural selection: from vocabulary to syntax in a population of learners', unpublished paper. Department of Linguistics, University of Edinburgh).

Kirby, S. and Hurford, J. R. (1997) 'Learning, culture and evolution in the origin of linguistic constraints', in Husbands, P. and Harvey, I. (eds), *Fourth European Conference on Artificial Life* (Cambridge, Mass.: MIT Press), pp. 493–502.

Lashley, K. S. (1951) 'The problem of serial order in behavior', in Jeffress, L. A. (ed.), *Hixon Symposium on Cerebral Mechanisms in Behavior* (New York: John Wiley & Sons).

Lieberman, P. (1992) 'On the evolution of human language', in Hawkins, J. A. and Gell-Mann, M. (eds), *The Evolution of Human Languages* (Redwood City, Calif.: Addison-Wesley), pp. 21–47.

Lieberman, P. (1975) *On the Origins of Language: An Introduction to the Evolution of Human Speech* (New York: Macmillan).

Lieberman, P. (1984) *The Biology and Evolution of Language* (Cambridge, Mass.: Harvard University Press).

Lieberman, P. (1991) 'Preadaptation, natural selection and function', *Language and Communication* 11(1): 63–5.

Lightfoot, D. (1991) 'Subjacency and sex', *Language and Communication* 11(1): 67–9.

MacMahon, A. M. S. (1994) *Understanding Language Change* (Cambridge: Cambridge University Press).

Miglino, O., Nolfi, S. and Parisi, D. (1996) 'Discontinuity in evolution: how different levels of organization imply preadaptation', in Belew, R. K. and Mitchell, M. (eds), *Adaptive Individuals in Evolving Populations: Models and Algorithms* (Redwood City, Calif.: Addison-Wesley).

Newmeyer, F. (1991) 'Functional explanation in linguistics and the origins of language', *Language and Communication* 11(1): 3–28.

Richards, G. (1987) *Human Evolution: An Introduction for the Behavioural Sciences* (London: Routledge & Kegan Paul).

Senghas, A. (1997) 'Children's contribution to the birth of Nicaraguan sign language' (PhD dissertation, MIT).

Sperber, D. (1994) 'The modularity of thought and the epidemiology of representations', in Hirschfeld, L. A. and Gelman, S. A. (eds), *Mapping the Mind: Domain Specificity in Cognition and Culture* (Cambridge: Cambridge University Press).

Sperber, D. and Wilson, D. (1986) *Relevance: Communication and Cognition* (Oxford: Basil Blackwell).

Trivers, R. L. (1971) 'The evolution of reciprocal altruism', *Quarterly Review of Biology* 46: 35–7.

Wilkins, W. K. and Wakefield, J. (1995) 'Brain evolution and neurolinguistic preconditions', *Behavioral and Brain Sciences* 18(1): 161–226.

Wolpoff, M. H. (1988) 'Multiregional evolution: the fossil alternative to Eden', in Stringer, C. B. and Andrews, F. (eds), *The Origins and Dispersal of Modern Humans* (Cambridge: Cambridge University Press).

Worden, R. (1998) 'The evolution of language from social intelligence', in Hurford, J. R., Studdert-Kennedy, M. and Knight, C. (eds), *Approaches to the Evolution of Language: Social and Cognitive Bases* (Cambridge: Cambridge University Press), pp. 148–66.

Wynn, T. (1991) 'Tools, grammar and the archaeology of cognition', *Cambridge Archaeological Journal* 1: 191–206.

CHAPTER 10

CULTURE, HONESTY AND THE FREERIDER PROBLEM

ROBIN DUNBAR

INTRODUCTION

Social life is founded on cooperation: to live in large groups and gain the ecological and other advantages that they provide, organisms must be willing to forego at least some of their immediate desires in the interests of keeping the group together. This tension between the immediate returns that derive from satisfying one's selfish interests and the longer-term benefits (to self) that derive from the advantages of group-living invariably places the stability of large groups in jeopardy. In effect, unless at least some individuals are willing to give way to the interests of others, the pressures of self-interest are likely to cause large social groups to fragment.

The problem of maintaining group coherence and stability through time obviously increases (probably exponentially) with group size. The more individuals there are, each trying to maximize his or her genetic interests, the less likely it is that common purpose will prevail. Divergent interests will become harder to reconcile and the risks of exploitation by those willing to cheat on the implicit contracts that underpin sociality rise dramatically. Evidence from the fossil record and modern primates suggests that average group sizes rose progressively through time from around 60–80 (values not untypical of living chimpanzees) to around 150 in modern humans (Aiello and Dunbar 1993). The increase in group size seems to have been exponential, with a much more rapid rate of increase during the last half million years than during the preceding 3–4 million.

In this context, freeriders (those who take the benefits that derive from social contracts while allowing everyone else to pay the cost) become a particularly intrusive problem. Economists and other social scientists have done a considerable amount of work on the problem of freeriders (notably in the context of the Prisoner's Dilemma[1] game), and the problem has

---

1. Prisoner's Dilemma is the name given to a classic game theory problem that turns out to be very characteristic of many social contract situations. The name derives from the fact that the 'game' was conceived in terms of two prisoners arrested on suspicion of a major crime. The police independently offer each a deal: if the prisoner will turn state's evidence against his companion, he will be charged only with a minor offence, while his companion will go down for the full rap. If both refuse to tell

proved to be of some interest to evolutionary biologists (e.g. Rapoport and Chummah 1965; Axelrod 1984; Sigmund 1993; Binmore 1994). Much of this has pointed to the fact that even though defection is a stable strategy in one-off Prisoner's Dilemma, cooperation can be stable in repeated games (i.e. those cases where individuals meet repeatedly). However, for cooperation to be a stable strategy, players need to be able to remember each other's past choices and must be able to impose some kind of punishment for defection.

This important result has often been seen as vindicating cooperative social behaviour. However, the key issue here is that games between the same individual be repeated frequently. In very large groups where individuals only rarely meet, the players may often be reduced to what is, in effect, a one-off game. Once again, defection is the stable strategy. We are all familiar with the problem. We encounter it daily in the form of used car salesmen, those who insist on parking in 'no parking' zones and those who cheat the taxman. We all know that we would be better off if honesty and adherence to sensible social contracts prevailed. Indeed, in the long term, we undoubtedly would be: traffic would flow more freely and the tax burden on all of us would be reduced by some small fraction. The problem is that the temptation to cheat is overwhelming because the benefits are high (it takes me less time to buy what I want from the shop or I pay much less tax) while the costs are minimal (the chances of being caught are small, so that even if the punishment is moderate I still end up in net profit, on average). Because, like the used car salesman, I am unlikely ever to meet again those whom I inconvenience, there is little incentive to toe the social contract line. I take the benefit while others pay the cost.

These social contract problems are closely related to another type of problem that has been extensively studied by economists, namely the *common pool resource* (or CPR) problem (see, for example, Hardin 1968; Orstrom et al. 1994). Common pool resources are those non-renewable (or slowly renewing) resources that give rise to communal zero-sum games: if I use up more than my fair share of the resource, it denies the resource to you. Familiar everyday examples include common grazing land, fisheries, forest resources, fossil fuel reserves, etc., but almost any kind of natural resource can in principle become a CPR if it is effectively non-renewable within some reasonable timeframe. The problem with these kinds of resources is that excessive use reduces their reserves faster than they can be replenished. Rational behaviour would dictate that individuals abide by a

---

tales, they will be convicted of some lesser offence (though one attracting a more serious penalty than they would face if they turned state's evidence). The two alternative strategies are usually referred to as Cooperate (refuse to turn state's evidence) or Defect (turn state's evidence). Because the benefits of defection are so great (conviction on a minor misdemeanour), the stable solution is to defect (it yields the lowest cost to each prisoner), especially if the companion makes the mistake of cooperating.

social contract that limits the rate at which they are used. Once again, however, the problem is that it always pays individuals to cheat and over-use the resource: they benefit immediately and directly, while the cost is borne by the rest of the community. The fact that the ultimate cost (complete destruction of the resource) may not be incurred until the next generation merely exacerbates an already unstable situation.

In this chapter, I want to explore some of the mechanisms that appear to have evolved to allow humans to minimize the impact of the freerider problem sufficiently to allow them to live in the large social groups that characterize our lineage.

THE FREERIDER PROBLEM

The central point of the freerider problem has been well illustrated in a simulation study by Enquist and Leimar (1993). They used a standard ESS (evolutionarily stable strategy) approach to model the history of alterna-tive strategies in group-living situations where successful reproduction was based on the exchange of resources (with the costs to the donor being half the benefits to the recipient, on the grounds that an unusable surplus is worth less to the owner than to the recipient who will die without it). The model considered two strategies, a cooperative one and a freerider, and these were allowed to evolve naturally in a virtual population. Two import-ant findings emerged.

First, freeriders who take the benefit but do not repay the gift are likely to be successful in any population where the coalition time (the time re-quired to establish bona fides before an exchange of resources is made) is short. The reasons for this are not hard to appreciate. When coalition time is short, donors do not have much opportunity to assess the honesty of the individuals they meet and, when they do, the cost to the freerider is mini-mal because he loses only a small investment when he is denied co-operation. Extending the length of time for which a coalition has to exist before an exchange of resources can be made (or increasing the costs by demanding some other more costly investment) makes it much harder for freeriders to survive simply because it reduces the rate at which they can encounter and exploit naive members of the group.

The second point is that a freerider's ability to prosper is directly related to the size and dispersion of the population. This is a simple consequence of the fact that freeriders are better able to keep one step ahead of discovery when they are in a large pool of naive individuals whom they are unlikely to re-encounter once they have been exploited. In effect, the search time to find the next naive individual is low because the pool of potential inter-actees is large relative to the rate at which exchanges are made. This effect is exacerbated when the population is fragmented into dispersed groups because there is a higher chance that each new group encountered contains only naive individuals: the risk of encountering someone you have previously exploited is close to zero.

The latter result also relates directly to the fact that memory for the outcome of past encounters is an important feature of all reciprocal exchanges (Trivers 1971; Axelrod 1984). In classic Prisoner's Dilemma games, one-shot games in which players never meet again always have defect (or cheat) as the stable strategy. Cooperation becomes a more viable proposition in such situations if games are repeated, and in this context memory for the past behaviour of potential players is crucial to the ability of cooperators to outcompete cheats. In large populations, freeriders are less likely to encounter those whom they have previously exploited. This effect is exaggerated if the population is patchily distributed, since the lack of communication between groups makes it less likely that the members of a new group will be aware of the freerider's behaviour.

In the light of this, Enquist and Leimar (1993) added a refinement to their model by allowing group members to exchange information about others' behaviour (a behaviour they termed 'gossiping'). Figure 10.1 shows the consequences of different levels of information exchange on the freerider's ability to survive in the state space defined by the two key independent variables (search time and coalition time). The upper-right (hatched) quadrant (marked 'no freeriders') is the zone in which freeriding is driven rapidly to extinction whenever such a strategy appears as a new 'mutant'. In the L-shaped area on the left and the bottom of the graph, freeriders do well and can evolve to stability within the population, ultimately driving out cooperators. The dashed lines show how the freerider's success zone is constrained if individuals can exchange information about others' behaviour. In effect, this is equivalent to extending the players' memory for past behaviour to interactions that an individual player has not personally experienced. Moreover, the degree of pressure on freeriders increases with the quantity of information that can be exchanged. Note, however, that only a modest amount of information exchange (25 per cent of all the events that occur) seriously reduces the freerider's opportunities. Introducing information exchange removes the advantages that low search times provided for the freerider by effectively extending a cooperator's memory for previous exchanges (including those he did not himself witness).

STRATEGIES TO ENHANCE HONESTY

KIN SELECTION

Probably the single most powerful mechanism available for controlling exploitation by freeriders derives from kin selection. Favouring kin

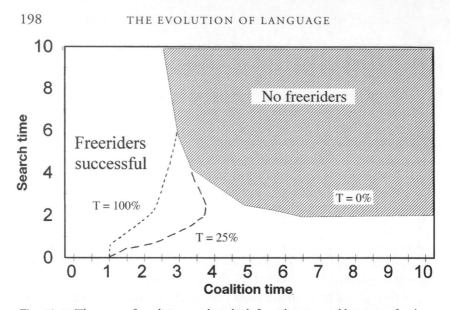

Fig. 10.1 *The range of conditions under which freeriding is a stable strategy for three different conditions of information exchange (*T*, where* T *is the percentage of information exchanged between individuals). Search time is the time taken by a freerider to find a new (naive) individual in the population; coalition time is the time investment that any individual has to make in a prospective partner before that partner will agree to collaborate. The area to the left of, and below, each line is that region in the state space where freeriding is a viable strategy (essentially, when either search or coalition times are very short). The hatched area shows the region where freeriding is not viable under any conditions (information transfer during gossiping is* T *= 0 per cent). The possibility of exchanging information about the behaviour of freeriders ('gossiping') reduces the area within which freeriding is a stable strategy. Note that the level of information exchange in this model can be interpreted either as the proportion of all information that is passed on by one individual to the next or as the accuracy of the information exchanged (or some combination of the two). (Redrawn from* Animal Behaviour, *vol. 45, no. 4, Enquist, M. and Leimar, O., 'The evolution of cooperation in mobile organisms', pp. 747–57, by permission of the publisher Academic Press.)*

counteracts the costs of freeriders not by making it difficult for freeriders to survive but by neutralizing the costs. In other words, concentrating one's social exchanges within the pool of one's relatives makes the fact of exploitation by freeriders of much less significance: any investment purloined by the freerider is repaid through the increased representation in the next generation of those genes that the freerider and his dupe hold in common. In effect, Hamilton's Rule[2] allows the evolution of freeriding within a population of relatives.

2. Hamilton's Rule is the principal result of Hamilton's (1964) seminal papers on kin selection and inclusive fitness. Hamilton showed that the likelihood that a gene for altruism would evolve to stability in a population depended simply on whether the number of extra reproductive opportunities gained

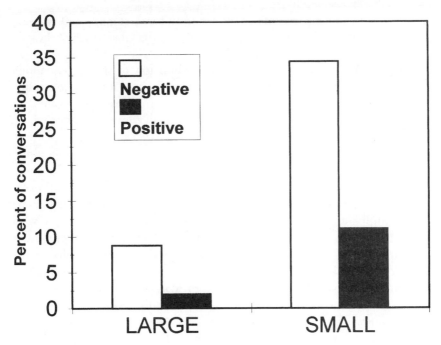

Fig. 10.2 *Effect of community size on the percentage of conversations and radio exchanges that contained references to the presence or absence of lobster concentrations within communities of Maine fishermen. (After Palmer 1991.)*

There are many examples of just this kind of tolerance of freeriding by relatives in human populations. One example might be meat-sharing among hunter-gatherers (Blurton-Jones 1984). Tolerating the begging or 'theft' of meat (and the subsequent elaboration of this into formal ritual) may be much less problematic if it is done by relatives than by unrelated individuals. A more clear-cut example, however, is that documented by Palmer (1991) in his study of lobster fishermen on the Maine coast of NE United States.

Palmer (1991) studied the exchange of information about the current status of local lobster grounds in two fishing communities. One was a small traditional fishing village whose inhabitants were descended from families that first settled there in the 1870s. The community contained the equivalent of twenty full-time lobstermen. The other community located nearby was a large busy tourist harbour with a significant seasonal influx of summer visitors. It contained some fifty full-time lobster fishermen and

by the recipient as a direct result of the altruist's behaviour (when devalued by the coefficient of relationship between them) was greater than the number of future reproductive opportunities lost by the altruist as a result of his action(s).

around twenty-five part-timers. Palmer monitored some 1,250 face-to-face conversations and radio exchanges between the lobstermen of the two communities.

Figure 10.2 shows that a far higher proportion of the conversations between fishermen in the small community contained information about the current presence or absence of lobster concentrations than was the case in the large community. Around 50 per cent of all conversations provided such information in the small community, compared to a mere 10 per cent in the large community. However, Palmer's observations also contained some unexpected results: Figure 10.3(a) shows that while the large community clearly favoured kin over non-kin when giving information on the actual whereabouts of lobster concentrations, those in the small community apparently favoured non-kin. (Kin were defined as people who were cousins or closer degrees of relatedness.) The fact that giving away information to non-kin was more often tolerated in the smaller community is itself an important result in the context of freeriders and I will return to it below. However, in the present context, these results obscure the fact that relatives are not necessarily equally available in the two communities. Figure 10.3(b) shows that, when we compare the observed frequencies of positive statements (those referring to the locations of lobsters) to what we would expect given the number of possible relatives in each community, we find that both communities favour relatives over non-relatives.

Note, nonetheless, the important fact that relatives are favoured disproportionately more in the large community. This suggests that people are much less willing to offer information to non-relatives in large communities where the anonymity and size of the community makes it much less likely that recipients will be able to reciprocate on a later occasion.

The importance of exchanges with kin highlights the problem of identifying relatives, especially in the kinds of large dispersed communities that are typical of most humans. One solution to this problem would obviously be badging – the use of culturally generated external signals of group membership. These might include things like particular styles of dress or ornamentation, the creation of elaborate hair designs, tattooing, etc. (see, for example, Irwin 1989). Badging allows individuals who belong

Fig. 10.3 (right) *Effect of community size on the percentage of conversations and radio exchanges among related and unrelated Maine fishermen that contained information on the presence of lobster concentrations in the locality. (a) Raw data. (b) Frequencies of exchanges relative to the mean number kin and non-kin in the community: the y-axis is the ratio of observed number of such exchanges to the number that would be expected given the number of kin vs non-kin in the population. Kin are defined as individuals whose degree of relationship is no less than cousins. (After Palmer 1991.)*

(a)

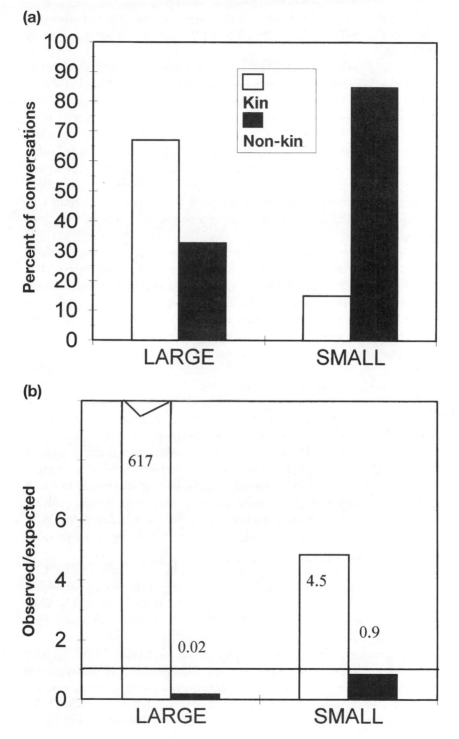

(b)

to the same community (and who thus share obligations and common reproductive and kinship interests) to be marked and thus more easily identified.

Most such external badges encounter a common problem, however: they are easy to fake. Recent work on the evolution of signalling has shown rather clearly that signals need to be costly to the signaller if they are to be reliable indicators of the signaller's status (Zahavi and Zahavi 1997). While elaborate hairstyles and tattooing that involve long periods under expert hands clearly do incur costs, these are unlikely to be costs of sufficient magnitude to discourage cheating. This is particularly so for signals that purport to be reliable indicators of group-membership and, more importantly, common kinship. Immigrants may simply be prepared to bear the cost of badging if this gives them access to the resources they need for reproduction.

One signal that lends itself to resolving this problem is language dialects (Irwin 1989). Dialects have two principal advantages in this respect: they can change rapidly over time and they can be learned fluently only during a limited time window during childhood (Nettle and Dunbar 1997). Pronunciation (and sometimes word use) are highly variable over relatively short periods of time, and as a result they can change relatively rapidly both over time within a population and across space. Because it is difficult to learn to speak another language without an accent later in life, sharing a dialect implies a geographically local common origin and may even identify an individual as belonging to a particular temporal cohort within a geographical region. Dialects thus offer all the advantages of visual signals while lacking the latter's susceptibility to cheating.

Nettle and Dunbar (1997) modelled the evolution of dialects in order to explore the role that they might play in controlling freeriders in a virtual population. The simulation involved a simple linear spatial model in which alternative strategies were allowed to compete until a stable state evolved. In the simulation, one hundred individuals were obliged to exchange 'gifts' (units of fitness) in order to reproduce, with the gifts being of higher value to the recipient than the donor (as in the Enquist–Leimar model). A generation was defined as a number of cycles in which individuals interacted in this way, and at the end of each generation the twenty wealthiest individuals in the population reproduced with a probability of 0.5, while the twenty poorest died with a probability of 0.5 (thereby maintaining a fixed population size).

The simulation began with a population of COOPERATORs who followed a standard *tit-for-tat* strategy. This founder population was seeded with CHEATs who accepted gifts from anyone, but never repaid the debt. Needless to say, CHEATs spread rapidly, driving COOPERATORs to extinction. To examine the effect of dialects as a means of kin-recognition, each individual was characterized by a dialect of six digits between 1 and 50. Dialects were allowed to change by one or more substitutions at the end of each generation. The population of *CHEATs* was then seeded with *POLYGLOTs* who operated on a *tit-for-tat* principle but were willing to accept gifts from any individual whose dialect was identical to theirs in five of the six numbers. In order to permit transfer of a gift, *POLYGLOTs* changed their dialect to match the giver's, but subsequently altered one of their six numbers randomly with a probability of $P = 0.01$ before moving on to interact with a new individual. In this case, *POLYGLOTs* drove *CHEATs* to extinction, typically in around twenty generations. This population was then seeded with *MIMICs* who acted as freeriders: they accepted gifts from anyone by changing their dialect to that of the bene-factor on first contact. Once again, this was a successful strategy.

At this point, dialects were allowed to evolve by random changes in the value of one position. *POLYGLOTs* were able to resist invasion by *MIMICs* providing memory span (the number of previous encounters with another individual that could be remembered) was more than five and the rate at which dialects changed was greater than around 30 per cent per generation (Figure 10.4). When the rate of dialect change was as low as 10 per cent per generation, *MIMICs* evolved to fixation (i.e. *POLY-GLOTs* went extinct) in about twenty generations. But when dialect change was as high as 50 per cent per generation, *MIMICs* were unable to gain a foothold, and would themselves be driven to extinction.

Although kin selection was not explicitly built into this model, it is not difficult to see that dialect will quickly become important as a badge of relatedness whenever dialect acquisition is based on learning from those individuals with whom you live at a critical early period of development (i.e. well prior to social independence).

The suggestion that dialects are badges of group membership would explain one of the more curious features of language acquisition, namely the fact that while we are capable of learning new languages throughout life, our ability to learn to speak a language as a 'native' seems to be restricted to a very brief period in early childhood. It is difficult to see why this should be so, since there is no intrinsic reason why dialect-acquisition should have to be limited to this period. After all, good mimics can pick up dialects later in life (albeit with considerable effort), so why can't we all do so?

A second point to notice is that dialects of this kind identify a larger community of kin than might normally be considered relevant. Palmer's (1991) study, for example, focused on a criterion of kinship drawn at the degree of relatedness equivalent to cousins. We are used to dialects being common to rather larger populations of individuals. However, two points need to be remembered here. First, like relatedness, dialects vary in their

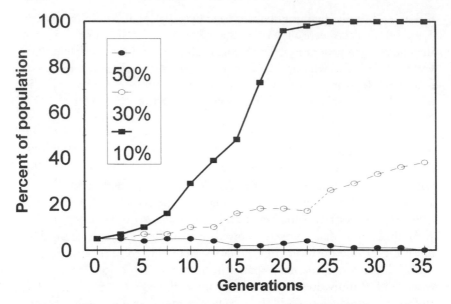

Fig. 10.4 *Effect of the rate of dialect change on the ability of* MIMICs *to invade a population of* POLYGLOTs *in a virtual world in which individuals have to exchange goods in order to reproduce, but can only do so when their dialects match (see text for details). The plotted values are the percentage of* MIMICs *in the population. Each population was initially seeded with five* MIMICs. *(Redrawn, with permission of the publisher, from Nettle and Dunbar 1997.)*

degree of similarity: cognate word forms diverge with geographic distance and frequency of interaction in exactly the same way as genetic similarity does (Cavalli-Sforza and Feldman 1981). Second, throughout most of our prehistory, we lived in small-scale communities that interacted rather rarely (judging by the experience of modern hunter-gatherers). This would have tended to reinforce dialect divergence even at the level of geographically adjacent communities. If the group size of 150 individuals predicted by our neocortex size is correct (as the empirical evidence would tend to suggest: Dunbar 1993), then the mean degree of relatedness in the group would have been in the order of second-cousins and most individuals would have had a focus of genetic interest within the group (see Hughes 1988). Thus dialects may have arisen in the context of small, socially incestuous groups with relatively high levels of biological kinship.

CUES OF HONESTY

An alternative mechanism that does seem to be important in the human context is direct cues of honesty. Although we may interact randomly with those individuals among whom we live, we do not necessarily extend these interactions into full-blooded relationships with all those individuals. We are highly selective in choosing the individuals we form long-term relationships with and, in particular, those we make long-term investment commitments to.

The obvious case of this is courtship. The costs of reproduction are so high in humans (thanks to the size of our brains: Aiello and Wheeler 1995) that reproduction requires a long-term commitment by both parties. However, it is always possible for either party to abandon the other, thereby leaving the deserted partner holding the baby (although, in humans and other mammals, there is an obvious asymmetry in how early in the process of reproduction the two sexes can successfully do this). In such a situation, the deserted partner can choose between ceasing to invest in the offspring (by engaging in abortion, infanticide or abandonment) and seeing that particular reproductive cycle through to conclusion in order not to waste the investment up to that point, even though doing so inevitably imposes a significant burden. Which option is preferred is likely to depend on the balance between past investment and future opportunities (Dawkins and Carlisle 1976).

The issue here is that the costs of desertion may be very considerable to the abandoned partner, thanks to the extended period of dependency in humans. Choosing a mate who is unlikely to desert may therefore be of paramount importance (although it should be remembered that this is likely to be tempered by considerations of investment value: a partner who can invest substantial quantities of resources or time into the current offspring before deserting may be preferable to a loyal mate who has little to offer). However, the optimal strategy will always be to try to ensure that a prospective mate is likely to remain loyal rather than deserting. Cues of honesty may therefore be very important in this context, and the process of courtship in humans can be seen as an extended process of negotiation and evaluation in which the respective mates assess each other on criteria that, at least in respect of females, include long-term commitment (Grammer 1989; Waynforth and Dunbar 1995).

On a more mundane day-to-day level, however, it is clear that we employ a number of mechanisms that are designed to detect and/or coerce those who cheat on socially agreed contracts. Cosmides (1989; Cosmides and Tooby 1992) has argued that humans have a hardwired 'cheat detection' module that is specifically designed to detect those who renege on social contracts. Her argument is based on empirical evidence that humans are very poor at solving logical reasoning tasks like the Wason Selection Task.[3] However, when the abstract Wason task is reformulated as

---

3. The Wason Selection Task (originally constructed by the psychologist Peter Wason) tests logical reasoning ability on a simple inferential task. The subject is presented with four cards bearing either a

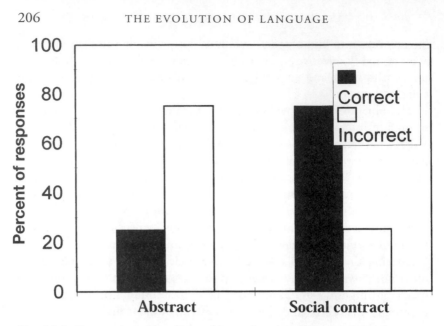

Fig. 10.5 *Frequencies with which subjects solve the abstract and social contract versions of the Wason Selection Task. (After Cosmides 1994.)*

a social contract task involving the detection of those who break some socially agreed rule, most people can solve the problem easily (Figure 10.5). Indeed, subjects may even draw subtle distinctions between those who cheat deliberately (culpable cheats) and those who infringe the contract by accident (Cosmides and Tooby 1992).

Cosmides's results do not require subjects to make any assessments of individuals other than on the basis of their past behaviour (whether or not they have broken the social rule). However, much of human behaviour is prospective: we make agreements with individuals in the expectation that those individuals will not renege on the contract in the future. In establishing prospective relationships of this kind, we appear to rely heavily on proximate cues of loyalty or honesty based mainly on facial expressions (as well as what we have might have heard about the individual concerned). Among the features we appear to rely on are shiftiness, the willingness to maintain eye contact, the warmth and naturalness of smiling, and so on. Direct face-to-face interaction thus seems especially important to us:

letter or a number (e.g. *A, 3, H* and *6*) and is told that a general rule asserts that there are always vowels on the reverse of cards which bear an even number on the face (in syllogistic logic terms, '*P* implies *Q*'). Which card or cards does the subject have to turn over to check that the rule is valid? Since the rule only states that even numbered cards have vowels on the obverse (and says nothing about any other possibilities), the correct cards to check are the *A* and the *3* (the *P* and *not-Q* options in the syllogistic equation). Approximately 75 per cent of subjects incorrectly choose either just the *A* card (the *P* option) or the *A* card and one of the other two (*P* and either *Q* or *not-P*).

we may even ask someone to 'look at me' when we want to discuss some especially sensitive matter. There are probably other cues that are important, particularly those associated with voice characteristics, that are used in the same way.

In addition, we use language itself to engage in social coercion. Verbal arguments ranging from pleading to threats all serve to persuade those with whom we live to behave in ways that suit our purposes (and sometimes without suiting theirs). In some cases, these may be formalized into cultural injunctions (commandments, legal rules, etc.). But essentially all these forms serve the same purpose. It is perhaps worth noting that language does not of itself persuade people to behave in a given way: it functions solely as a mode of communication. It works because it allows us to convey the message that retribution in the form of ostracism or physical violence will be the ultimate penalty for non-compliance. But its role is crucial in humans because it allows us to reach a wider circle of individuals more rapidly and more effectively than do any of the conventional mammalian (or primate) means of communication and information exchange.

Some experimental evidence for the importance of opportunities to interact and/or to impose social sanctions is provided by a series of experiments carried out by Orstrom et al. (1994). Their main concern was with common pool resources and the ways in which use of these is managed in traditional communities (and not being managed in modern polities). They ran a series of small groups in which individuals were allowed to invest or use a stock of capital in a common market. The subjects all sat at computer terminals, which were linked in such a way that they could see the net pattern of investment decisions (and thus the resulting payoffs to the group) but not which individuals were actually responsible for particular investment decisions. The optimal solution could easily be identified using standard game theory principles based on economic rational behaviour. However, the optimal solution required subjects to suppress any instinct to exploit others by capitalizing on short-term opportunities.

Orstrom et al. (1994) ran this experiment under several different conditions. In the baseline condition, subjects played the game in isolation without communicating with each other. In a second series, subjects were allowed to get together for a brief face-to-face discussion half way through the session, while in a third series they could meet for discussion as often as they wished. In a final series, subjects were allowed to have face-to-face discussions as often as they wished and were allowed to impose financial penalties on individuals who defaulted on the agreed group strategy. The identity of defaulters remained unknown to the group in all these cases though the fact of defaulting was evident from the on-screen information provided on investment decisions as the experiment proceeded. In the

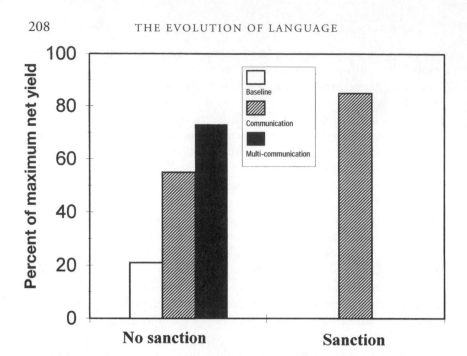

Fig. 10.6 *Group earnings (measured as the percentage of the maximum possible yield) achieved by subjects in a common pool resource game in which individuals invest to use a non-renewable resource in a computer-linked artificial world. In the baseline condition, subjects could not interact but could see from their computer screens how others were investing (but without knowing who was doing what). In the two 'communication' conditions, subjects were allowed to meet once or several times to discuss group strategy. In the sanction condition, the identity of contract-breakers was known and the group could (if it wished) levy financial penalties on defaulters. (*Source: Orstrom et al. (1994), Table 9.1.)

'sanction' condition, a communally agreed sanction could be imposed on the anonymous defaulter at the group's request during the experiment (in the form of a fine deducted from the defaulter's final payoff).

The results are shown in Figure 10.6. Increasing opportunity to discuss and harangue defectors (even when their actual identity was unknown) progressively increased the group's ability to approximate the maximum possible payoff. Adding the ability to sanction defectors improved the situation still further. It is clear that this worked by reducing individuals' willingness to defect from the implicitly or explicitly agreed common plan: the opportunity to communicate and to impose sanctions drastically reduced the frequencies of defection (Figure 10.7). Surprisingly, perhaps, verbal harangues and sanctions worked even when the defaulter's actual identity was not known, suggesting that we have a strong psychological predisposition to abide by group rules (see also Caporael et al. 1989).

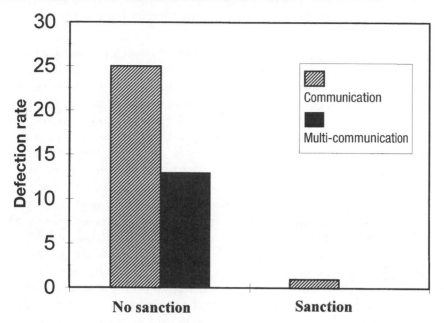

Fig. 10.7 *The rates with which players in the Orstrom et al. (1994) common pool resource simulation shown in Figure 10.6 defected from the communally agreed optimal investment strategy when different frequencies of face-to-face interaction and the imposition of sanctions were permitted.* (Source: *Orstrom et al. (1994), Table 9.1.)*

CONCLUSIONS

Humans appear to have evolved a number of mechanisms designed to control freeriding, largely because freeriding is such an intrusive problem in the large dispersed social groups that characterize our species. Indeed, it seems doubtful whether groups of the size that typify our species could be held together in the absence of such mechanisms. It seems likely therefore that two important features of language that must have emerged early in the course of its evolution were the ability to negotiate social contracts and the ability to exchange information on defaulters.

One point worth stressing in this context is that the freeriding problem emerges only *after* large groups have evolved. In other words, large groups cannot be seen as an answer to the freerider problem because the problem does not exist in small groups. This implies that increases in group size must have driven language evolution rather than the other way around because in the absence of large groups, languages (and, by extension, large brains) have no real function (see Dunbar 1993, 1997). It is perhaps equally clear that rule-governed social contracts cannot have been too far behind simply because these increase the efficiency with which individuals can work in groups.

We can see this as being analogous to the way we store and manage information in the cognitive domain: rather than storing information on the daily passage of events as they actually happened, the mammalian brain seems to work (at least according to the so-called 'mental models' hypothesis) by storing a handful of key points from which the narrative of events can later be reconstructed by interpolation (Johnson-Laird 1982). Rather than work out in detail the optimal behaviour for every situation, mammals (if not other vertebrates) use 'rules of thumb' that provide quick-and-dirty guidelines on what to do. Instant identification of the problem and its solution is required when faced with a real-world situation as it escalates rapidly out of hand because organisms that take too long to consider the significance of cues and/or the appropriate kinds of behavioural responses simply do not get a second chance. Neither volcanoes nor predators are noted for their willingness to offer thinking time to their victims. This short-circuiting of relatively slow and cumbersome cognitive processes enables us to operate in a rather complex world very efficiently by minimizing the storage capacity necessary to generate appropriate behaviour. We use our computing power only when we absolutely have to (see also Dickinson 1985). By analogy, cultural rules allow us to acquire guidelines on how to behave quickly and easily by inheriting them from other more experienced individuals. This way, we build on the collective experience, thus short-circuiting the laborious business of having to re-invent the wheel every generation (as most other animals are forced to do).

Cultural systems presumably act in much the same way by providing us with usable rules of thumb that have been developed by our predecessors as reasonable solutions to common everyday problems. (I use the term *culture* here to refer to the set of social rules that govern our behaviour in specific sociocultural contexts, but it can obviously also refer to that web of social knowledge that is used to define who we are and how we relate to other members of our species.) Exploiting the opportunity provided by the fact that language allows us to exchange information has enabled us to use a much larger database of experience and intellectual ability. This might account for one of culture's curious features, namely its apparent rigidity and resistance to change (at least when seen from the perspective of day-to-day life). A system that lacked resistance to change in the short term would lose the very advantages that culturally inherited rules provide us with (namely, that we do not have to waste time, energy and computing space working out the best way to behave). To be sure, an over-rigid rule system would be equally disadvantageous for a long-lived slowly reproducing organism because it would encounter all the same difficulties posed by genetically inherited features (i.e. a lack of flexibility and capacity for change in the face of a world whose states change on a timescale much shorter than our generation time). Hence perhaps the moderately slow pace of cultural change: changes in genetic form take on the order of 1,000 generations to bring to fruition, while cultural change seems able to produce the same effect in a single generation (see, for example, Voland et al. 1997), although if we put our minds to it we can effect such changes in a matter of days by learning at the level of the individual.

Thus, we can expect the evolution of socially agreed rules of behaviour to have been pretty much an inevitability once language and large groups had evolved. Precisely when this layer was added remains uncertain, although it must presumably lie between the appearance of language (in the social sense) at around 500,000 years ago (coincident with the appearance of *Homo sapiens*[4]) and the Upper Palaeolithic Revolution at around 40,000–50,000 years ago (the latest date for the appearance of 'modern' material culture that would be accepted by all archaeologists). However, we probably have to assume that culture predates the first archaeological evidence by some considerable time, perhaps doubling the true date for the Upper Palaeolithic Revolution. Art and artifacts of the quality that typify the Upper Palaeolithic cannot have been produced overnight, the more so if their production was associated with (or, more properly, followed on from) the development of sophisticated symbolic mentalization (Mithen, this volume). Watts (this volume), for example, has argued that the archaeological record does imply a much earlier beginning to the African Upper Palaeolithic Revolution (though others would argue about the interpretation of the empirical evidence: see Mithen, this volume). Beyond this, however, we probably cannot place the evolution of cultural systems at a particular point, although the temptation to associate it with the emergence of anatomically modern humans (and thus the 'Mitochondrial Eve') inevitably remains considerable.

REFERENCES

Aiello, L. C. and Dunbar, R. I. M. (1993) 'Neocortex size, group size and the evolution of language', *Current Anthropology* 34: 184–93.
Aiello, L. C. and Wheeler, P. (1995) 'The expensive tissue hypothesis', *Current Anthropology* 36: 199–211.

4. Aiello and Dunbar (1993) argued for a date around 250,000 years ago, but this was mainly because we were testing between two alternatives offered in the literature (a late date favoured by archaeologists at around 50,000 years ago and an early date favoured by palaeontologists at around the time of the appearance of anatomically modern humans, some 250,000 years ago). Our conclusion was simply that the combination of brain size and grooming time data favoured the earlier date over the later one. However, closer inspection of the data given in Fig. 3 of Aiello and Dunbar (1993) suggests that a point of origin nearer to the first appearance of archaic *Homo sapiens* would be more realistic.

Axelrod, R. (1984) *The Evolution of Cooperation* (Basic Books: New York).

Binmore, K. (1994) *Just Playing: Game Theory and the Social Contract* (Cambridge, Mass.: MIT Press).

Blurton-Jones, N. (1985) 'A selfish origin for human food-sharing: tolerated theft', *Ethology and Sociobiology* 5: 1–3.

Caporeal, L. R., Dawes, R. M., Orbell, J. M. and van de Kragt, A. J. C. (1989) 'Selfishness examined: cooperation in the absence of egoistic incentives', *Behavioural and Brain Sciences* 12: 683–739.

Cavalli-Sforza, L. L. and Feldman, M. W. (1981) *Cultural Transmission and Evolution: A Quantitative Approach* (Princeton, NJ: Princeton University Press).

Cosmides, L. (1989) 'The logic of social exchange: has natural selection shaped how humans reason? Studies with the Wason selection task', *Cognition* 31: 187–276.

Cosmides, L. and Tooby, J. (1992) 'Cognitive adaptations for social exchange', in Barkow, J. H., Cosmides, L. and Tooby, J. (eds), *The Adapted Mind* (Oxford: Oxford University Press), pp. 163–228.

Dawkins, R. and Carlisle, T. R. (1976) 'Parental investment, mate desertion and a fallacy', *Nature* (London) 262: 131–3.

Dickinson, A. (1985) 'Actions and habits: the development of behavioural autonomy', *Philosophical Transactions of the Royal Society of London* B 308: 67–78.

Dunbar, R. I. M. (1993) 'The co-evolution of neocortical size, group size and language in humans', *Behavioural and Brain Sciences* 16: 681–735.

Dunbar, R. I. M. (1997) *Grooming, Gossip and the Evolution of Language* (Cambridge, Mass.: Harvard University Press).

Enquist, M. and Leimar, O. (1993) 'The evolution of cooperation in mobile organisms', *Animal Behaviour* 45: 747–57.

Grammer, K. (1989) 'Human courtship behaviour: biological basis and cognitive processing', in Rasa, A., Vogel, C. and Voland, E. (eds), *Sociobiology of Sexual and Reproductive Strategies* (London: Chapman & Hall), pp. 147–69.

Hamilton, W. D. (1964) 'The genetical evolution of social behaviour. I, II', *Journal of Theoretical Biology* 7: 1–52.

Hardin, G. (1968) 'The tragedy of the commons', *Science* 162: 1243–8.

Hughes, A. (1988) *Evolution and Human Kinship* (Oxford: Oxford University Press).

Irwin, C. (1989) 'A study in the evolution of ethnocentrism', Reynolds, V., Falger, V. S. and Vine, I. (eds), *The Sociobiology of Ethnocentrism* (London: Chapman & Hall), pp. 131–56.

Johnson-Laird, P. (1982) *Mental Models* (Cambridge: Cambridge University Press).

Nettle, D. and Dunbar, R. I. M. (1997) 'Social markers and the evolution of reciprocal exchange', *Current Anthropology* 38: 93–9.

Orstrom, E., Gardiner, R. and Walker, J. (1994) *Rules, Games and Common-Pool Resources* (Ann Arbor: University of Michigan Press).

Palmer, C. T. (1991) 'Kin-selection, reciprocal altruism and information sharing among Maine lobstermen', *Ethology and Sociobiology* 12: 221–35.

Rapoport, A. and Chummah, A. M. (1965) *Prisoner's Dilemma* (Ann Arbor: University of Michigan Press).

Sigmund, K. (1993) *Games of Life* (Oxford: Oxford University Press).

Trivers, R. L. (1971) 'The evolution of reciprocal altruism', *Quarterly Review of Biology* 46: 35–57.

Voland, E., Dunbar, R. I. M., Engel, C. and Stephan, P. (1997) 'Population increase in sex-biased parental investment in humans: evidence from 18th- and 19th-century Germany', *Current Anthropology* 38: 129–35.

Waynforth, D. and Dunbar, R. I. M. (1995) 'Conditional mate choice strategies in humans: evidence from "Lonely Hearts" advertisements', *Behaviour* 132: 755–79.

Zahavi, A. and Zahavi, A. (1997) *The Handicap Principle: A Missing Piece of Darwin's Puzzle* (Oxford: Oxford University Press).

CHAPTER 11

LANGUAGE VARIATION AND THE EVOLUTION OF SOCIETIES

DANIEL NETTLE

The Old Testament relates the story of how, during the wars of Israel, the Gileadites defeated the Ephraimites and captured the fords of Jordan. The story goes on:

> When any Ephraimite who had escaped begged leave to cross, the men of Gilead asked him, 'Are you an Ephraimite?', and if he said, 'No', they would retort, 'Say shibboleth'. He would say 'Sibboleth', and because he could not pronounce the word properly, they seized him and killed him at the fords of the Jordan. At that time, forty-two thousand men of Ephraim lost their lives.
>
> Judges, 12: 4

In this incident, which is one of the first recorded contributions to sociolinguistics, dialect is used as an unfalsifiable indicator of group membership. The distinction between [s] and [ʃ] marks a social boundary which is, unfortunately, of literally vital importance. In this chapter, I consider the role that language plays in the creation and maintenance of social boundaries, and the adaptive importance that such boundaries may have had in the evolution of human societies. In the first section, I discuss a major problem relating to social evolution, namely that of the evolution of cooperation. In the second section, I discuss the origin and social significance of linguistic diversity. Putting these two themes together, I argue that our propensity to create distinct languages and dialects around the social groups which are important to us is a psychological adaptation to the problem of maintaining solidarity in large groups of cooperating individuals.

THE PROBLEM OF THE EVOLUTION OF SOCIETY

Between the societies of hunter-gatherers, which presumably resemble to some extent all early human societies, and the social groups of our nearest ape relatives, a huge change has occurred in the way knowledge is gathered and transmitted. Whereas apes and all other mammals construct their

214

models of the world using the information they can gather through their own senses and such innate knowledge as they have inherited, much human knowledge is acquired in verbal form from others. Apes and monkeys communicate, but as far as we know this only serves to draw attention to current intentions, dangers, activities and so on. They do not exchange information about that which is absent from their immediate cognitive environment. Language, on the other hand, is a dedicated system for transmitting propositions on any conceivable subject, whether it exists in the present, beyond the present, or nowhere at all. Thus human beings can build up a store of collectively held knowledge, which permits cultural and technological evolution to progress at a far faster rate than could be achieved by genetic transmission of information or by individual learning. Durkheim clearly understood that this *socialization* of knowledge was the foundation of human society:

> The great difference between animal societies and human societies is that in the former, the individual creature is governed exclusively from *within itself*, by the instincts ... On the other hand human societies present a new phenomenon of a special nature, which consists in the fact that ways of acting are imposed, or at least suggested *from outside* the individual and are added on to his own nature.
>
> Durkheim 1982: 248

Society is possible because human beings cooperate:

> Collective representations are the result of an immense cooperation, which stretches out not only into space but into time as well; to make them, a multitude of minds have associated, united, and combined their ideas and sentiments; for them, long generations have accumulated their experience and their knowledge.
>
> Durkheim 1976: 16

Of course, cooperation is not limited to language. The generosity and cooperativeness of people in 'primitive' societies is the classic evidence of man's social nature. It is not simply that people in such societies exchange that which they have a surplus of in direct return for other things which would be more useful to them. That would be easy enough to explain from the point of view of immediate self-interest. On the contrary, human exchange is typically displaced and indirect. Gifts or help are given to friends with no specific requirements about repayment apart from a general moral obligation to help out if the situation demands it in the future (Weissner 1977; Mauss 1966). Furthermore, information and ideas are exchanged with no element of book-keeping nor possibility of verification of their worth. Without wanting to adopt a romanticized view of 'primitive communism', we can nonetheless agree with Sahlins (1972) that cooperation within hunter-gatherer social groups is *generalized*. And indeed, even in our own post-industrial societies, individuals are surprisingly willing to behave cooperatively, even to strangers, in the absence of any immediate reward to themselves (Caporael et al. 1989).

For Durkheim, the emergence of society was a new phase of natural history, whose explanation was to be sought in the principles of 'general biology' (Durkheim 1984: 3). His comments were remarkably prescient. The biologists Maynard Smith and Szathmàry (1995) have recently argued that during evolution there have been a limited number of revolutionary transitions in the way information is organized and transmitted from generation to generation. The evolution of language and culture, and the increase in complexity in economic life which goes with it, constitute one of these transitions. At each transition, a problem arises: even if the evolution of the larger unit (the cultural group in this case) will be beneficial to the entities at the lower level (individuals), its emergence will almost certainly be disrupted by selection for 'individualists' at the lower level. Let us examine what this means in the case of the evolution of society.

It would be easy to suppose that the evolution of language and culture was unproblematic, as it seems so beneficial to all. Pinker and Bloom appear to take this view in their seminal paper on the subject:

> [There is] an obvious advantage to being able to acquire ... information second-hand: by tapping in to the vast reservoir of knowledge accumulated by other individuals, one can avoid having to duplicate the possibly time-consuming and dangerous trial-and-error process that won that knowledge.
>
> Pinker and Bloom 1990: 712

However, for a strategy to evolve, it must not just increase the fitness of the organisms involved. It must also be *evolutionarily stable*. By this, it is meant that there must be no alternative strategy which gives competitors a higher fitness. In the case of social exchange, there are such strategies. Individuals who deceive others in order to further their own interests, or 'freeload', enjoying the benefits of society without paying the costs, will, under most circumstances, have higher fitness than those abiding by the social contract. There is no escape from this impasse; the greater the benefits of a social contract, the greater will be the fitness of a freeloader who takes the benefit without paying the cost. It is of no import that freeloaders will drive the cooperators whom they prey on extinct and be left with no livelihood. Evolution is blind and individualistic, and so cooperation is driven out. The empirical proof of this rather unsettling contention is simply the rarity of sustained cooperation in the social groups of other animals. When we examine the great apes, animals presumably close to our hominid ancestors in intelligence and lifestyle, we find a collection of individualists intent on manipulating and deceiving each other (Byrne and Whiten 1988).

It seems, therefore, that the origin of society does require special explanation. As in other great evolutionary transitions, some condition must have obtained which suppressed or negated disruptive selection.

The existing literature on the evolution of language has scarcely discussed this question, focusing instead on the kind of cognitive and articulatory mechanisms required for human language (e.g. Lieberman 1984; Pinker and Bloom 1990). To this extent it is extraordinarily naive from an evolutionary point of view. I doubt that mechanistic considerations were ever a constraint on the evolution of language, or that they explain why we have it and apes do not. On the contrary, if there is a selective pressure for something, natural selection will exapt whatever materials are available to achieve it. Similarly, models of language use (Sperber and Wilson 1987) have started from the assumption of a group of people cooperating to transmit information to each other. Thus they have assumed precisely that which is most important and problematic: the social structure which makes language possible (Bourdieu 1977).

A considerable literature has grown up on the problem of how cooperation between individuals may evolve (Axelrod 1984; Axelrod and Dion 1988). There are two situations where this is known to be possible. Firstly, where animals are related, they have an intrinsic interest in each other's survival, and will behave altruistically towards each other. This explains perhaps the greatest rival to human language in the animal kingdom, the code which bees use to signal the whereabouts of honey (Von Frisch 1967). As the honey is beyond their perceptual horizon, the code used is both displaced and arbitrary in the same way that human language is. However, the bees of a hive are so highly related that this system of cooperation could virtually be seen as the transmission of information from one part of an organism to another. This explanation will not extend to contemporary human groups. Even in the simplest societies, the transmission of information and material goes far beyond close kin (Weissner 1977).

The second way in which cooperation may evolve is through reciprocity. This seems a more promising source for the evolution of society; our idea of a social contract involves an ultimate benefit to all parties. In fitness terms, it will pay an individual to help another as long as there is a high probability of them meeting again in the future for the other to reciprocate (Axelrod 1984). In sessile organisms, such continuity is assured, and several examples of cooperation can be found. However, in mobile organisms, the establishment of cooperation is much more difficult, as freeloaders can simply move from group to group exploiting them and leaving before their debt is called in (Enquist and Leimar 1993). Such freeloaders quickly drive cooperators extinct. In highly mobile animals such as hominids, this must have been a major constraint on the evolution of cooperation. It is, however, dependent on population density. If the population is very sparse and the benefits of cooperation are high, freeloaders cannot destroy cooperation, as they cannot find new victims at a fast enough rate to survive. The earliest human societies could have consisted of small, kin-based bands so widely dispersed as to make free-loading impossible, and within which individuals were so dependent on each other, presumably for ecological reasons, to preclude forsaking the group and striking out alone. If this were the case, then a crisis in co-operation would have occurred as population density increased and freeloading became a viable option.

This, then, is the problem of the evolution of society: that of explaining how such generalized and extensive coordination, cooperation and trust could have evolved and persisted in a Darwinian world of individuals. Social theory has come up against this fundamental problem repeatedly. Hobbes concluded that only the rise of the state, with its ability to dis-cipline and punish, could end a state of perpetual war of man against man. Marcel Mauss, in his famous analysis of the sociology of exchange, con-cluded that the gift, with its obligatory reciprocity, enforced alliances in stateless societies the way the state did elsewhere. However, the problem of enforcing the social contract still arose:

> In primitive or archaic types of society, what is the principle whereby the gift received has to be repaid? What force is there in the thing given which compels the recipient to make a return?
>
> Mauss 1966: 1

Mauss' answer is opaque: the obligation to repay inheres in the spirit of the gift itself.

Durkheim's writings on the subject are more enlightening, and once again prescient from a modern evolutionary point of view. Durkheim demolished the argument from political economy that cooperation existed because particular individuals formed social contracts with one another, for, as he points out, contracts are worthless if either party turns out to be a freeloader: 'The contract is not sufficient by itself, but is only possible because of the regulation of contracts, which is social in origin' (1984: 152). A background of solidarity and mutual trust is required to underpin the social order: 'The members are united by ties which extend deeper and far beyond the short moments during which exchange is made' (1984: 226). In the case of primitive societies, solidarity stems from 'similarity', the consciousness of belonging to the same social or ethnic group. This surely contains a correct insight: people do feel morally obliged to those with whom they share identity. For Durkheim, shared identity was gen-erated primarily by common ritual activity. In this chapter, however, I will argue that a shared language or dialect can function in a similar way. I now turn, then, to languages and dialects, and how they evolve.

THE PROBLEM OF THE EVOLUTION OF LANGUAGES

Anyone wanting to explain the evolution of language would have to explain why we have not just language, but many different languages. Linguistic boundaries tend to be social ones. In stateless societies, the largest social groupings – tribes or nations – are demarcated by a language or at least a dialect boundary. If language were a cultural invention, like money or writing, it would be perfectly natural to find that its form differed locally throughout the world in this way. However, the capacity for language is certainly innate (Pinker and Bloom 1990), and today's languages probably stem from a single ancestor. This raises two questions: why there should be a locus for culturally transmitted variation at all, and why this should have led to the formation of ethnolinguistic boundaries.

Pinker and Bloom (1990) have addressed the first question. They point out that language is not wholly innate, but leaves parts to be acquired from the environment; they explain this fact in several ways. Firstly, to represent a complete language, (including all the words) genetically might consume excessive genotypic space. Secondly, as the language faculty must be expected to change by genetic drift, an individual with an innate language might fall out of kilter with his peers. It would thus be advantageous to have a code with developmental flexibility to home in on that spoken in the group. Thirdly, as Hinton and Nowlan (1987) find, once most of a trait is determined genetically, selective pressure to represent the rest in the genotype declines, because learning can be relied on to fill it in.

These factors may well have been relevant in the evolution of our flexible linguistic abilities. They do not of themselves explain why almost every important human social formation has its own speech form. That also requires an explanation of how diversification in language occurs. The standard account (for example, of Pinker 1994: Chapter 8) is as follows: small variations occur and are fixed in language owing to the variable nature of linguistic performance and acquisition, and so, where subpopulations become isolated from each other, their languages gradually drift apart until they are mutually unintelligible.

Though a process of variation, drift and mutual isolation is responsible for some change in language, it is not a full picture of the facts as we understand them. This is because the account relies on the assumption that groups whose languages diverge are physically or economically isolated from each other. We know ethnographically that this is often simply not true. The tribes of hunter-gatherers, so long regarded as pristine communities, have actually always been involved in economic relations with neighbouring peoples, despite the linguistic differences (Bird-David 1986; Solway and Lee 1990). Study after study has found that pre-industrial societies were not isolated from each other, but formed, in Eric Wolf's phrase, a 'vast and interconnected manifold', whose internal divisions were always shifting as economic interests waxed and waned (Wolf 1982; see, for example, Hays 1993 on New Guinea; Abu-Lughod 1989 on Europe and Asia; Hoffman 1984 on Asia; Terrell, Hunt and Gosden 1997 on the Pacific). In seems that ethnolinguistic boundaries can evolve and persist despite the flow of goods or even personnel across them (Barth 1969).

The lack of isolation of many language communities is more obvious if we examine our own society. Class and regional differences in dialect persist, as do minority languages such as Welsh. It cannot be argued that Welsh speakers or speakers of non-standard dialects have no access to standard English: they are bombarded with it constantly. Black English dialects in Philadelphia are diverging from standard English despite four to eight hours of exposure per day through school and television (Labov, cited in Chambers 1995). What determines whether a group will remain linguistically homogeneous is thus not just whether they have access to the same norms, but whether they choose to follow them. There is no necessary correspondence between linguistic boundaries and geographical or physical boundaries. On the contrary, it is the way language is deployed which creates the social boundaries (Mülhaüsler and Taylor 1982; Giles 1979).

In general terms, we believe that languages change because individuals preferentially identify with certain others and seek to sound like them (LePage 1968), and that members of social groups seek to create and actively maintain linguistic norms which make them distinct from out-group members. As we have seen, dialect boundaries constitute important social boundaries. Labov has shown that when a dialect group is threatened by an influx of outsiders, its members actually increase their usage of the linguistic variables which make their speech distinctive, increased contact thereby leading to linguistic *divergence* (Labov 1972). Similarly, Bourhis and Giles (1977) have shown that when Welsh speakers who are conscious of their Welsh identity are challenged by an aggressive English experimenter, they will broaden their accent, making themselves less intelligible, or even switch spontaneously into Welsh. This phenomenon has been replicated elsewhere (Bourhis et al. 1977). However, subjects who do not value their Welsh identity will not diverge. When interaction is positive and cooperative, subjects will quite automatically converge their speech styles (Giles and Smith 1979).

As well as sending social signals, people are skilled at decoding them. We are astoundingly and unconsciously adept at placing an accent in a class, ethnic or social category (Labov 1966). In fact, a single socially charged dialectal variable produced in forty seconds of continuous speech is sufficient to unleash a stereotyped social evaluation (Chambers 1995).

This is a remarkable ability given how poor we are in general at explaining and making conscious judgements about our own speech (Labov 1966; Trudgill 1983).

It seems, then, that far from using language simply to communicate information in an optimally efficient way, people use it to create and maintain social identity and social boundaries. This even enters into the way we think about language. People have strong and often irrational feelings that their highly valued dialect corresponds either to a Platonic ideal of what is correct or to a pure example of how language should be, as opposed to the corrupt and debased speech of their neighbours (Pinker 1994: Chapter 12; Thomas 1991). This is not just a Western tendency; see, for example, Woodburn (1986) on the Hadza.

Surveying these facts, the author of a recent review of sociolinguistics concluded:

> The fact that linguistic variability is universal and ubiquitous suggests strongly that it is fulfilling some essential human need ... The underlying cause of sociolinguistic differences ... is the human instinct to establish and maintain social identity.
> Chambers 1995: 208, 250

While I do not necessarily subscribe to the claim of innateness implied by his use of the word 'instinct', I agree with Chambers that the use of language to maintain social identity is an integral and fundamental part of human social and linguistic behaviour. My purpose here is to address its function and origin. I will do this by relating language variation to the problem outlined in the first section of this chapter: that of the evolution of cooperation.

The problem of maintaining generalized reciprocity in a large group of mobile individuals is that of boundedness: a mechanism must be found to prevent insiders from defecting and outsiders from interloping. Creating a distinctive language would seem to be a way of doing this. Freeloaders from outside would find it much more difficult to enter the group, as their speech would immediately reveal their origins. This has the important effect of raising the upper limit on the size of cooperating groups beyond the number of individuals one knows personally (cf. Dunbar 1993). The crucial corollary of the fact that language variation excludes outsiders is that it constrains insiders to remain within the group. Enquist and Leimar (1993) have shown that the real difficulty in forming reciprocal relationships with other mobile organisms is that the other may simply terminate the coalition and leave before the debt is paid back. However, by developing a distinctive in-group language and making it socially obligatory to learn it and use it, one makes it much more difficult for would-be defectors to leave as they would have to learn a different dialect or language wherever else they went. This effectively increases the cost to them of defecting, and could well make the difference between cooperation surviving and it breaking down.

It is important to be clear that I have not slipped into a group selectionist argument here. Under a very wide range of circumstances, it is fitness-enhancing for individuals to live in cooperating social groups – but only as long as the cooperators are not exploited by cheaters. It can thus be fitness-enhancing for individuals to take anti-cheating countermeasures, and so no appeal to group selection in any form is necessary. Now I am not suggesting that any one individual can create a separate language or dialect, but that is not necessary to my argument. Neither need we sloppily attribute agency to the social group as occurs in too much bad anthropology and say that 'the group' creates a separate language to protect 'itself'. All I am suggesting is that the individual behavioural strategy which may be summed up as 'sound like those you wish to cooperate with, and cooperate with those that sound like you' is likely to be evolutionarily stable over a much wider range of circumstances than a 'cooperate with anyone' strategy. Computer simulations seem to support this claim (Nettle and Dunbar 1997).

This, I propose, is the adaptive significance of sociolinguistic variation (Labov 1972; Chambers 1995). It serves to maintain the unity of groups within which generalized reciprocity is the norm. This is more of an interpretative statement than a scientific hypothesis, but it does yield certain predictions, which we may test against real data. Firstly, people should strive to create distinctive linguistic norms around the social groups which they value. We have already seen that this is the case. Secondly, linguistic boundaries should coincide with the boundaries of systems of reciprocity. Thirdly, people should generally be more prepared to cooperate with or behave altruistically towards those who share the same dialect as themselves. We will now examine these last two predictions in the light of some ethnographic and psychological data.

THE LANGUAGE OF COOPERATION

It seems to be the case in hunter-gatherer societies that reciprocity is more intense within the linguistic group than outside it. The !Kung San, for example, form a system of sharing and exchange consisting of 'a community of others who will give assistance of any kind as they can, and place no demands upon the amount or timing of return except that in a reversed situation of have and have not, a return will be made' (Wiessner 1977: 98). However, this community only extends up to the ethnolinguistic boundary: 'People, even San, of a different language group … are foreign people and to be regarded with suspicion' (p. xix). Among the Naiken and other hunter-gatherer societies, reciprocity within the group is generalized, while in transactions with out-group members, it is balanced, meaning that full and specific returns are sought for all goods and services (Bird-Davis 1986: 23–5). Within tribes, generosity and largesse are prized, whereas in dealings with outsiders, commercially motivated activities such as haggling and deceit are not considered wrong (Sahlins 1972). The morality of exchange is thus relative to the social identities of the participants.

We might ask if users of the right social dialect are more successful at obtaining cooperation in our own society. In fact there is evidence that this is so. People attest a greater feeling of solidarity for strangers using their own dialect than for others (Giles and Powesland 1975), and are more likely to collaborate with their research (Giles, Baker and Fielding 1975) or help out in a simulated time of need (Feldman 1968; Gaertner and Bickman 1971; Harris and Bardin 1972). This effect – the solidarity which can be invoked by the use of the right speech variety – has been used to explain why low-prestige non-standard dialects persist (Bouchard-Ryan 1979), and why socially mobile individuals switch back to their native dialects in certain types of interaction (Blom and Gumperz 1972). Indeed, the cooperative norm which is maintained inside ethnolinguistic groups may well explain many of Caporael et al.'s (1989) findings. They found that subjects were much more cooperative toward strangers, even at cost to themselves, than a Darwinian world-view appears to predict. However, it must be borne in mind that the people the subjects were cooperating with were already identifiable as members of the same language group, which makes the likelihood of future interaction with them or their associates much higher. As we have seen, the closer the stranger's speech is to that of the subject, the more likely he is to obtain cooperation.

It seems, then, that there is empirical evidence to support all three of the predictions made above about the function of linguistic variation. The account proposed of the evolution of both cooperation and linguistic diversity seems at least plausible, and computer simulation suggests that it makes sense in evolutionary terms (Nettle and Dunbar 1997). Our ability to use language for social evaluation and the construction of social identity could thus be an integral part of our cultural solution to the problems of living in very large social groups. I say cultural solution, because it is unclear whether the mechanisms of language variation and social identity I have discussed are genetically specified. It is equally possible that they are instead a coupling of our generally astute social intelligence to our equally developed linguistic abilities as part of a culturally inherited, socially learned behavioural package.

CONCLUSION:
THE EVOLUTION OF BABEL

I have argued that the creation of distinct languages and dialects is a way of maintaining solidarity in cooperating groups. This is not meant to imply that cooperative relationships do not occur between members of different ethnolinguistic groups, which they clearly do. It is simply that we seem to be adapted to use and decode speech as a social marker, and indeed speech gives us a great deal of honest social information. Nor do I mean to legitimate xenophobia. Social identity is always being renegotiated and redefined, and can be used inclusively as well as exclusively. Furthermore, we should try and understand the social asymmetries, inequities and prejudices that persist in societies ostensibly based on universalism and the rule of law (cf. Lang 1992).

The social marking hypothesis I have described gives us some picture of how linguistic boundaries might have played a role in the development of human societies. In the very earliest societies, population densities (and indeed total population size) were low and degrees of relatedness in local bands would have been relatively high. Freeloading, then, may not have been a viable strategy. Perhaps language itself evolved under these rather special conditions and was initially relatively uniform. As population size and density increased, the opportunity for interlopers and freeloaders to move from group to group would have arisen, and only then would the creation of linguistic diversity be selected for.

This could shed some light on an archaeological puzzle. Archaeologists have often argued that the first clear evidence for language in the material record comes with the Upper Palaeolithic in Europe and Western Asia at around 50,000–45,000 BP, where local variation, rapid cultural change and symbolism become evident. On the other hand, many anthropologists would want to put the origin of language much further back, given that anatomical modernity had long been in place and that the rapid encephalization of our ancestors took place very much earlier, in the Late Middle Pleistocene (Aiello and Dunbar 1993; Foley and Lahr 1997). Now it may be that what we are picking up in the Upper Palaeolithic is not the origin of language itself but the beginning of its use to create social boundaries. Language might have already existed in a relatively uniform, slow changing state for many millennia, but with increases in population size and new social problems, groups might have begun to close their boundaries and deploy language differences actively to define them. Such a scenario correlates very well with the observed changes in material culture, which involve more local diversity and a great increase in the rate of local evolution. It also makes sense of the fact that there is no anatomical change in humanity associated with the Upper Palaeolithic transition, and that equivalent transitions in other regions (such as the Late Stone Age in Africa) come at different times. Rather than a biological change associated with the onset of linguistic abilities, the Upper Palaeolithic seems more like a demographically induced change in social organization and the use of language and culture. Indeed, Gilman (1984) has specifically argued that the Upper Palaeolithic industries are a product of behavioural responses to the problems of maintaining 'corporate solidarity' which was becoming more problematic in the face of increased population density. If my argument and my speculative conclusions are correct, then that was the time when human language became what it universally is today: not just language, but the language *of someone*.

ACKNOWLEDGEMENTS

I am especially grateful to Robin Dunbar for discussion of these matters, as well as to Leslie Aiello, Deborah Clarke, Rob Foley, Chris Knight, Camilla Power and Merrilyn Onisko for their advice and comments. The usual disclaimers apply.

REFERENCES

Abu-Lughod, J. L. (1989) *Before European Hegemony: The World System A.D. 1250–1350* (New York: Oxford University Press).

Aiello, L. C. and Dunbar, R. I. M. (1993) 'Neocortex size, group size and the evolution of language', *Current Anthropology* 34: 184–93.

Axelrod, R. (1984) *The Evolution of Cooperation* (New York: Basic Books).

Axelrod, R. and Dion, D. (1988) 'The further evolution of cooperation', *Science* 242: 1385–90.

Barth, F. (1969) *Ethnic Groups and Boundaries* (London: Allen & Unwin).

Bird-David, N. H. (1986) 'Hunter-gatherers and other people – a re-examination', in Ingold, T., Riches, D. and Woodburn, J. (eds), *Hunters and Gatherers, Volume 1* (Oxford: Berg), pp. 17–30.

Blom, J. P. and Gumperz, J. J. (1972) 'Social meaning in linguistic structures: code switching in Norway', in Gumperz, J. J. and Hymes, D. (eds), *Directions in Sociolinguistics: The Ethnography of Communication* (New York: Holt Rinehart & Winston), pp. 407–35.

Bouchard-Ryan, E. (1979) 'Why do low-prestige language varieties persist?', in Giles, H. and St Clair, R. N. (eds), *Language and Social Psychology* (Oxford: Basil Blackwell), pp. 147–57.

Bourdieu, P. (1977) 'The economics of linguistic exchange', *Social Science Information* 6: 645–68.

Bourhis, R. Y. and Giles, H. (1977) 'The language of intergroup distinctiveness', in Giles (ed.), *Language, Ethnicity and Intergroup Relations* (London: Academic Press), pp. 119–34.

Bourhis, R.Y., Giles, H., Leyens, J. P. and Tajfel, H. (1977) 'Psycholinguistic distinctiveness: language divergence in Belgium', in Giles, H. and St Clair, R. N. (eds), *Language and Social Psychology* (Oxford: Basil Blackwell).

Byrne, R. and Whiten, A. (1988) *Machiavellian Intelligence: Social Expertise and the Evolution of Intellect in Monkeys, Apes, and Humans* (Oxford: Clarendon Press).

Caporael, L. R., Dawes, R. M., Orbell, J. M. and van de Kragt, A. J. C. (1989) 'Selfishness examined: cooperation in absence of egoistic incentives', *Behavioural and Brain Sciences* 12: 683–739.

Chambers, J. K. (1995) *Sociolinguistic Theory* (Oxford: Basil Blackwell).

Dunbar, R. I. M. (1993) 'Co-evolution of neocortex size, group size and language in humans', *Behavioural and Brain Sciences* 16: 681–734.

Durkheim, E. (1976) *The Elementary Forms of the Religious Life* (London: Allen & Unwin).

Durkheim, E. (1982) *The Rules of the Sociological Method* (London: Macmillan).

Durkheim, E. (1984) *The Division of Labour in Society* (London: Macmillan).

Enquist, M. and Leimar, O. (1993) 'The evolution of cooperation in mobile organisms', *Animal Behaviour* 45: 747–57.

Feldman, R. E. (1968) 'Responses to compatriots and foreigners who seek assistance', *Journal of Personality and Social Psychology* 10: 202–14.

Foley, R. A. and Lahr, M. M. (1997) 'Mode 3 technologies and the evolution of modern humans', *Cambridge Archaeological Journal* 7: 3–36.

Gaertner, S. L. and Bickman, L. (1971) 'Effects of race on the elicitation of helping behaviour: the wrong number technique', *Journal of Personality and Social Psychology* 20: 218–22.

Giles, H. (1979) 'Ethnicity markers in speech', in Scherer, K. R. and Giles, H. (eds), *Social Markers in Speech* (Cambridge: Cambridge University Press), pp. 251–90.

Giles, H. and Powesland, P. F. (1975) *Speech Style and Social Evaluation*, European Monographs in Social Psychology No. 7 (London: Academic Press).

Giles, H. and Smith, P. (1979) 'Accommodation theory: optimal levels of convergence', in Giles, H. and St Clair, R. N. (eds), *Language and Social Psychology* (Oxford: Basil Blackwell), pp. 45–65.

Giles, H., Baker, S. and Fielding, G. (1975) 'Communication length as a behavioural index of accent prejudice', *International Journal of the Sociology of Language* 6: 73–83.

Gilman, A. (1984) 'Explaining the Upper Paleolithic revolution', in Spriggs, M. (ed.), *Marxist Perspectives in Archaeology* (Cambridge: Cambridge University Press), pp. 115–26.

Harris, M. B. and Bardin, H. (1972) 'The language of altruism: the effects of language, dress and ethnic group', *Journal of Social Psychology* 97: 37–41.

Hays, T. E. (1993) '"The New Guinea Highlands": region, culture area, or fuzzy set?' *Current Anthropology* 34: 141–64.

Hinton, G. E. and Nowlan, S. J. (1987) 'How learning can guide evolution', *Complex Systems* 1: 495–502.

Hoffman, C. L. (1984) 'Punan foragers in the trading networks of Southeast

Asia', in Schrire, C. (ed.), *Past and Present in Hunter-Gatherer Studies* (Orlando, Fla.: Academic Press), pp. 123–49.

Labov, W. (1966) *The Social Stratification of English in New York City* (Washington, DC: Center for Applied Linguistics).

Labov, W. (1972) *Sociolinguistic Patterns* (Philadelphia: University of Pennsylvania Press).

Lang, K. (1992) 'Language and economists' theories of discrimination', *International Journal of the Sociology of Language* 103: 165–83.

Lieberman, P. (1984) *The Biology and Evolution of Language* (Cambridge, Mass.: Harvard University Press).

LePage, R. B. (1968) 'Problems of description in multilingual communities', *Transactions of the Philological Society* 1968: 189–212.

Mauss, M. (1966) *The Gift: Forms and Functions of Exchange in Archaic Societies* (London: Cohen & West).

Maynard Smith, J. and Szathmàry, E. (1995) *The Major Transitions in Evolution* (Oxford: W. H. Freeman).

Mülhaüsler, P. and Taylor, T. (1982) 'What do social markers mark?' *Journal of Literary Semantics* 11: 125–32.

Nettle, D. and Dunbar, R. I. M. (1997) 'Social markers and the evolution of reciprocal exchange', *Current Anthropology* 38: 93–9.

Pinker, S. (1994) *The Language Instinct* (Harmondsworth: Penguin).

Pinker, S. and Bloom, P. (1990) 'Natural language and natural selection', *Behavioural and Brain Sciences* 13: 707–84.

Sahlins, M. (1972) *Stone Age Economics* (Chicago: Aldine).

Solway, J. S. and Lee, R. B. (1990) 'Foragers, genuine or spurious? Situating the Kalahari San in history', *Current Anthropology* 31: 109–46.

Sperber, D. and Wilson, D. (1987) *Relevance: Communication and Cognition* (Oxford: Basil Blackwell).

Terrell, J. E., Hunt, T. L. and Gosden, C. (1997) 'The dimensions of social life in the Pacific: human diversity and the myth of the primitive isolate', *Current Anthropology* 38: 155–96.

Thomas, G. (1991) *Linguistic Purism* (London: Longmans).

Trudgill, P. (1983) *On Dialect: Social and Geographic Factors* (Oxford: Basil Blackwell).

Von Frisch, K. (1967) *The Dance Language and Orientation of Bees* (Cambridge, Mass.: Harvard University Press).

Weissner, P. (1977) *Hxaro: A Regional System of Reciprocity for Reducing Risk among the !Kung San* (PhD dissertation: University of Michigan).

Wolf, E. (1982) *Europe and the People without History* (Berkeley: University of California Press).

Woodburn, J. (1986) 'African hunter-gatherer social organisation: is it best understood as a product of encapsulation?' in Ingold, T., Riches, D. and Woodburn, J. (eds), *Hunters and Gatherers, Volume 1* (Oxford: Berg), pp. 31–64.

CHAPTER 12

SEX AND LANGUAGE
AS PRETEND-PLAY

CHRIS KNIGHT

Lie and alternative, inherent in language ... pose problems to any society whose structure is founded on language, which is to say all human societies. I have therefore argued that if there are to be words at all it is necessary to establish *The Word*, and that The Word is established by the invariance of liturgy.

Rappaport 1979: 210–11

Language can be studied independently, or as an aspect of human sociality. Theoretical linguistics could not exist as a discipline were it not for the relative autonomy of language as a system. Ultimately, however, this system functions within a wider domain of signals which include cosmetics, dress, art, ritual and much else whose study takes us beyond linguistics.

A Darwinian theory of the origins of language must therefore address two issues. Firstly, it must explain the relative autonomy of language. Secondly, it must elucidate the evolutionary relationship between speech and a wider biological, social and symbolic domain of signals and displays.

Primates negotiate socially through displays of dominance, submission, appeasement, threat, sexual arousal and so forth. Each vocal signal forms part of a more complex visual-auditory display which includes posture and facial expression. A chimpanzee may express fear, for example, by a 'pant-scream' accompanied by a 'grin'. Presentation of the rump accompanied by a 'pant-grunt' signals 'respect'. Very different is the intimidatory 'roaring pant-hoot' of an aroused chimpanzee male. Consisting of a series of low-pitched calls, this is always accompanied by a charging display (Goodall 1986: 114–45, 360).

The point about calls of this kind is that they have not been decoupled as low-cost conventional tokens from the wider system of energetically demanding display. In the human case, such decoupling has evidently occurred, giving rise to a tokenistic, digitally organized system – speech – operating on a level quite independent of bodily display (Burling 1993).

At some point in the evolutionary past, the ancestors of modern humans must have had a repertoire of primate-style gestures and displays. Signals of this kind live on as the human species' own gesture-call

228

system – a 'universal language' of smiles, frowns and other 'hard to fake' emotional expressions including laughter, crying and so forth (Burling 1993; Ekman 1982). However, while important on the level of personal relationships, in the human case this system no longer carries the main burden of expressing and constituting sociopolitical structure at the global level. Rather, in the case of human hunter-gatherers and other pre-state societies, this function of exciting, mobilizing and giving expression to collective structural relationships has been taken over by ritual. In all traditional cultures, humans invest enormous amounts of energy in the ritual domain. Unlike speech, ritual signals are not confined to a single channel; neither are they necessarily effective in communicating complex trains of thought. Like animal gesture/calls, human ritual displays are characteristically loud, multimedia, emotionally infectious and heavily redundant (Rappaport 1979: 173–246).

Despite evidence of evolutionary continuity, human ritual signals differ from their animal counterparts in two ways. Firstly, structure-generating ritual performances are staged not by individuals acting independently but by whole coalitions, whose members dance, drum, sing or otherwise rhythmically coordinate in asserting group identity and a boundary against outsiders (see, for example, Cohen 1985; Harrison 1993). In the human case, moreover, the cognitive outcome is an internal domain of communal pretend-play or 'counter-reality'. Human ritual performance, when successful, generates a whole new cognitive domain – a virtual world discernible on another representational level from the currently perceptible or 'real' one (Durkheim 1912; Gellner 1992: 36–7; Turner 1967).

In speech, pressure for communicative speed and efficiency selects heavily against costly display in favour of tokenistic signalling. In ritual performance, reverse pressures apply, driving signallers to prolong, to repeat and to incur heavy costs. Ritual signals cannot be replaced by tokens without loss of effect. In trance-inducing rhythmic drumming, for example, nothing short of the direct physical and emotional impact of hands repeatedly hitting drumskins will do. Percussionists are not supposed to drum tokenistically. Or take the example of wailing or other public expressions of grief at a funeral. It is the wrenching, costly body-signals which matter, especially when these appear irrepressible. Where mourners remain dispassionate, resorting simply to tokens, there may be little point in staging the ritual at all. In ritual, to lose the display, replacing it by a conventional token, is simply to lose the signal.

Intrinsic credibility or 'indexicality' (Pierce 1940) is, then, the hallmark of ritual signals. Paradoxically, however, such signals are deployed within ritual precisely to displace the individual's reality-based cognition, substituting a collectively defined 'other-world' (cf. Chase, this volume). A funeral occurs when a loved one has died. It is precisely that disturbing social absence which provokes counter-measures, the deceased's continued 'presence' being constructed by emotionally convincing display. If the illusory realm generated by ritual fails to eclipse 'this world', then something is wrong. This is why we feel irritated by someone munching food or otherwise distracting attention during a visit to the theatre. Like a stage-show or television soap-opera, ritual must successfully interfere with the processes of ordinary perception/cognition (Bloch 1985), enabling participants to cut adrift from their own personal reality into an alternative, communal one. At the theatre, reality fades as the auditorium lights are dimmed. A hush descends and the curtain slowly rises, revealing a well-lit stage. We are wafted into another world.

Ancient Greek theatre evolved from ritual. Pre-state societies may not have theatre in the modern sense, but everywhere, performances are staged in giving tangible form to myth (Fontenrose 1959; Warner 1959). Cross culturally, ritual time tends to begin around dusk, when shadows lurk and the hold of reality fails. Trance-inducing dance, fasting and/or hallucinogens may enhance the effect. The whole point of all this is to make people see 'beyond' perceptible reality into the other-worldly domain – that of morally authoritative intangibles (cf. Turner 1967: 93–111). The gods and spirits, normally invisible, must be experienced at least periodically as more real than reality itself.

THE RELATIONSHIP BETWEEN SPEECH AND RITUAL

Primate gesture/calls, then, are holistic, both audible and visible signals being embedded in a unitary system of display. By contrast, in the human case, 'ritual' constitutes a gestural system differentiated from vocal speech, the two having evolved along divergent trajectories (see Table 12.1).

To these contrasts we can add another, arrived at by inference on the basis of Darwinian signal-evolution theory (Dawkins and Krebs 1984; Zahavi 1987, 1993; see discussion in Knight et al. 1995). According to this body of theory, where we find high-cost, repetitive, multimedia displays, we may infer a function in terms of social manipulation, conflict and exploitation. Resistance on the part of receivers sets up selection pressures acting on signal design. Signallers who encounter 'sales resistance', like modern commercial advertisers, are driven to respond by prolonging and repeating signals, increasing amplitude and resorting to costly multimedia displays. Peacocks provide examples of this, as do caribou bulls bellowing at one another during the rutting season. Zahavi (1987) has shown how the discernible costs of such displays enhance their credibility

Table 12.1 *Signals: speech versus ritual*

Speech	Ritual
Cheap signals	Costly signals
Interpersonal	Group-on-group
Two-way communication	One-way signals
Low amplitude	High amplitude
Dispassionate	Emotive
Vocal-auditory	Multi-media
Digital	Analog
Discrete-combinatorial	Holistic
Productivity/creativity	Repetition/redundancy
Stress on novelty	Stress on conservatism
Conventionally coded	Iconic and indexical
Focus on underlying intentions	Focus on body-boundaries and surfaces

by tapping and hence testing the very reservoirs of quality that signallers are attempting to advertise. High-cost signalling of this kind may be regarded as representing a victory on the part of sceptical receivers spurring signallers to ever greater competitive effort.

By contrast, where we find low-cost, quiet and efficient signals, a cooperative audience can be inferred. If signallers can afford to cut their emission costs, it can only be because listeners are investing corresponding effort in receiving, decoding and acting on signals. This in turn means that signallers and receivers must have shared interests. For such 'conspiratorial whispering' (Dawkins and Krebs 1984) to evolve, signallers must be imparting useful information to receivers. Logically, the ultimate cost-cutting strategy would be to resort to purely tokenistic, wholly conventional signals which can be processed categorically at speed – relieving listeners of the need to evaluate gradations in physical performance. According to Zahavi (1993), however, animal 'conspiracies' are never sufficiently cooperative. Internal conflict and scepticism precludes ultimate reliance on tokenistic 'paper money'. Nowhere in the living world do we find purely conventional signalling – with the one puzzling exception of human speech.

This discussion allows us to establish one more contrast – this time functional – between speech and ritual. On the basis of Darwinian signal evolution theory, it can be inferred that speech emerged in a cooperative context while ritual did not. For speech to have evolved, 'conspiratorial whispering' in the human case must have been anomalously trusting. By contrast, ritual – with its costly, inefficient features of redundancy and display – can only have emerged out of conflict, manipulation and exploitation.

FORM AND FUNCTION OF
RITUAL SIGNALS

Speech is utterly different from ritual. Yet there remains a connection. Opposition is itself a relationship, and it is clear that speech could have no force or function were it not for its paradoxical connection with ritual.

The inscription on a banknote – 'I promise to pay the bearer on demand' – inspires trust only thanks to a system of state printing controls, counterfeit detection and law enforcement including court proceedings and punishment for fraudulent abuse. We are able to use banknotes, then, thanks only to a system of communal action quite external to the paper used to print them. Hunter-gatherer societies are stateless. They lack courts, prisons, money or specialist law-enforcement agencies (Engels 1972 [1884]). However, they do perform rituals. My argument is that costly ritual is the pre-state system of communal action which backs up the otherwise valueless tokens central to speech.

Words resemble banknotes in that they are intrinsically worthless, requiring an external system of controls if they are to be usable at all (Knight 1998). Like commercial transactions, 'speech acts', as Austin (1978) has shown, are social transactions dependent on communal validation for their force. The implicit or explicit contracts by which speakers bind themselves are morally authoritative intangibles. But how is it that such intangibles are *representable*? What, for example, is a promise? Can such a thing be seen, heard, tasted, kicked or by any means perceived? Could a group of chimpanzees trade in entities of this kind?

To deal in social contracts is to agree to enter a virtual world, not unlike that of a board game such as Monopoly. Just as Monopoly money cannot be used without a display of commitment on the part of players, so 'promising' presupposes a certain background of commitments and formal expectations. Suppose I preface my propositional utterance with an oath – 'I swear to tell the truth, the whole truth and nothing but the truth'. For this to count, I must signal by my clothes, my evident situation or in other ways that I am someone of appropriate moral status – the right person to utter such words in this place and at this time. Only then will my oath be accepted as valid (Austin 1978). In short, a promise exists only in the context of commitment to a kind of game. Like an oath, its successful enactment is best thought of as a hard-to-fake, communally verifiable display of commitment or obligation. Only a speaker who can deliver on the hard-to-fake components of his signal can deploy the cheap tokens – 'words' – through which collusion in the verbal transaction is secured (cf. Austin 1978; Bourdieu 1992).

A human cultural system may be immeasurably more complex than any game of pretend-play. But just as a game is constructed out of pretend-play tokens and rules, so human symbolic culture in general is composed entirely of entities constructed via a kind of play.

It is such play which allows the Jalé of Papua New Guinea to restrict themselves to a lexicon featuring just two basic colour terms – roughly 'dark' and 'light'. In other cultures, playing by other rules which demand a further term, 'red' is predictably the next one to emerge (Berlin and Kay 1969). It need hardly be stressed that such minimal discriminations operate on a level quite independent of personal colour perception: all humans, in all cultures, discriminate perceptually between an immense variety of different colours. To take another well-known example, among the Nuer, named categories of time are those defined by shared ritual experiences specific to the culture, such as 'the time of milking the cattle', 'when the calves come home' and so forth (Evans-Pritchard 1940: 100–8). Here again, it is the ritual structure which defines the categories – this time temporal – which are available to be named.

Within a ceremonial house among the Kabyle in North Africa, the dry, light area of floor-space counts as 'the place of honour' while the darker, moister area is 'the place of the tomb' (Bourdieu 1990). No one in the dwelling who remained unaware of this distinction could speak or act within the house in an appropriate way. An Australian Aboriginal landscape is in a comparable way 'totemic' – structured by morally authoritative intangibles. Here, the red stains in a rock mark a mythical being's bloody death; there, a misshapen boulder is all that remains of a Dreamtime ancestor; in this pool dwells the fearsome 'Rainbow Snake' (Barnard, this volume; Mountford 1978; Strehlow 1947).

Such examples show how every linguistic term for a discriminable 'thing' in symbolic culture is tokenistic of some *game-defined* entity, in principle no different from the pretend-play components of a Monopoly game. Words do not map to external, perceptible realities – only to things established as 'real' through the playing out of the local game. This is why I would argue, contrary to Chase (this volume), that symbolic reference and symbolic culture are logically inseparable and so must have evolved together.

On the one hand, then, there is the perceptual level of representation. Life is made up of realities such as a chimpanzee might spontaneously perceive – realities such as the hardness or taste of a Monopoly board, or the clothing or body-odour of one of the players. But on the other hand, participants in game-like domains must negotiate their way through a virtual world – a world of contractual intangibles which 'exist' only because it is agreed to act collectively 'as if' they did. Ritual is this collective acting out. It is not an optional add-on with respect to the rest of symbolic culture. It is the actual playing of the game – life conducted 'as if' the gods or other morally authoritative intangibles were real (cf. Chase, this volume).

In entering into the spirit of a game, each player must override physical reality, which now becomes external to the game's own illusory domain. Suppose, for example, one player of Monopoly is larger or more muscular than another. This is irrelevant: it does not permit the stronger partner to take advantage. To play properly, the players must set aside the dispositions applicable in ordinary life in favour of the quite different rules internal to the game. Each player must undergo a kind of conversion experience, analogous to an initiation rite, after which nothing remains what it seemed. Portions of worthless cardboard now count as 'streets', small bits of wood are 'houses', bits of paper are 'banknotes'. Such eclipsing of reality transports participants into a shared domain of acted-out fantasy which constitutes the game.

In pre-state societies, 'rites of passage' (Van Gennep 1960 [1909]) are designed to bring about in each individual precisely that 'conversion experience' necessary for the local game to appear playable. Only once the gods, spirits and comparable intangibles seem experientially real are individuals in a position to function within the symbolic domain. There are good reasons why initiation rites tend to be painful, manipulative, coercive and generally 'unfair'. The reason is the same as that which makes all ritual unfair. Ritual, like warfare, cannot afford to assume that there are any rules.

It may seem paradoxical to reflect that while game-like behaviour must by definition be 'fair', ritual signals cannot be. The explanation is that if behaviour is to be judged as fair, a set of rules for making such evaluations must already exist. But what if no one wants to play by the rules? Imagine a festive family gathering spurning Monopoly in favour of socializing, eating or watching television. To get them to play, it will clearly be useless to offer Monopoly banknotes as bribes. All other tokenistic appeals will equally fail. The only solution is to step outside such pretend-play, intervening in reality itself. Loudly halt the conversation, take the food off the table, switch off the television. The convenor must 'cheat' in order to get people to play, switching off their involvement in perceptible reality, amplifying the attractions of pretend-play, overstepping all rules in securing compliance with rule.

This is the task of ritual. Like civil war, its function is to assert physical mastery by a particular coalition dictating the terrain on which future games are to be played. It is therefore no surprise to find that ritual signals differ from words in presupposing no prior adherence or commitment. Ritual, like violence, impacts on its human victims directly, seeking out vulnerable spots in the targeted biological and psychological material. Coercive intimidation, hallucination, dance, rhythm, seduction and emotional manipulation all have their place. In much of Aboriginal Australia, boys were initiated into rule-governed adulthood by having their genitals attacked in practices ranging from circumcision to the excruciating ordeal of subincision (Montagu 1974). If part of the definition of 'fairness' is two-way negotiation on the basis of agreed rule, then this was clearly unfair. But all ritual signals have to work like this. To secure commitment to the world of 'rules' and other such communal make-believe, the habits and dispositions of ordinary life must first be coercively defeated (Bloch 1985). We can put this another way by saying that no one would be 'taken in' by ritual signals with their improbable 'other-worldly' messages if such signals did not hit below the belt, using what by rational or logical standards would seem unfair methods of persuasion.

EVOLUTION OF COLLECTIVE DECEPTION: THE 'WARFARE' MODEL

Young primates may engage in play – such as play-fighting – which prepares them for adult life (Bruner et al. 1976). But they do not engage in communal pretend-play – play in which all agree to act out an imaginary scenario. Even if they were capable of this, it seems doubtful whether they would have a motive. Why invest energy in colluding with someone else's illusory world when the real one is so much more engaging?

Of course, primates do not engage only with reality. Primate 'tactical deception' has been closely studied, in part because it arguably prefigures human 'symbolic' usage. In the primate case, however, reality-defying signalling is not cooperative. It is always 'Machiavellian', individualistic and competitive. Suppose a baboon falsely signals by its posture that it has seen a threatening leopard, seeking by this deceptive signal to gain a selfish advantage (cf. Byrne and Whiten 1985). Can we speak of the fictional leopard as 'symbolic'? Clearly not. The signaller's selfishness means that conspecifics will have no reason to collude with the fiction. The imaginary 'leopard' will therefore not be taken up by others and sustained. Once the fiction is exposed, all interest in it will disappear. On this basis, 'memic' evolution of fictions (Dawkins 1976) will simply never get off the ground.

Collectively sustained deception, by contrast, is the essence of the game-playing known as 'symbolic culture'. How close do chimpanzees get to this in the wild? When a group of common chimps raids into a neighbouring territory, the leaders may insist on silence from the whole band, enforcing this through reprimands (Goodall 1986: 490–1). Although the group is now physically present in the invaded neighbourhood, we might say that its members are 'pretending' not to be. However, this still falls short of symbolism. Silence provides no fictional signal which can be collectively elaborated or sustained. To generate symbolism, communal pretend-play would have to go a step further – from cooperative non-signalling to active reality-defying display.

Coalitions strong enough to constrain their members' behaviour do not form in a vacuum. They need an external threat capable of generating internal cohesion on the necessary scale. It has been suggested that evolving *Homo* recurrently engaged in group-on-group contests equalling or exceeding ingroup/outgroup conflict between neighbouring bands of common chimpanzees; ingroup 'moral' codes may have emerged in such contexts (Alexander 1989). This theory would lead us to suppose that something akin to 'war' drove the evolutionary emergence of human morality and symbolic culture.

It must be conceded that 'primitive warfare' provides a plausible context for the emergence of collective deception. Success in warfare depends not merely on direct physical violence but also on psychological factors such as surprise, intimidatory display, rumour and the advance dissemination of fear. Turning to the evolution of *Homo,* it is not difficult to picture early prefigurations of such group-on-group psychological tactics, and to understand how they may have led some way down the road towards symbolism.

Aggressive displays by coalitions of pre-modern humans would have had internal as well as external functions, coming under correspondingly contrasting selection pressures. Within an aggressive coalition, while preparing to fight, individuals can afford to communicate their intentions internally by means of cryptic 'nods' and 'winks'. In other words, *short-hand, abbreviated versions* of the behavioural routines involved in coalitionary defence or war preparations may suffice in such contexts. However, given the risks of reliance on cheap signals (Zahavi 1987, 1993), even such internal tokenism will remain ultimately dependent on the shared obligation to resort at least periodically to genuine fighting. Only each individual's sustained display of genuine commitment to fight the enemy – clearly, a costly signal – will generate the internal trust necessary for low-cost ingroup tokens to work.

Here, then, we have a possible solution to our basic question: How did 'speech' become decoupled so decisively from 'ritual'? The 'primitive warfare' model (Alexander 1989) suggests an answer: this decoupling was a consequence of group-on-group conflict, which – to the extent that firm ingroup/outgroup boundaries became established – drove ingroup signalling down one evolutionary trajectory and external signalling along a radically divergent one, the two systems nonetheless remaining mutually interdependent.

Aggressive displays are iconic and indexical (Peirce 1940): just as smoke means fire, so a body of men performing a war dance means war. When I see and hear the signs of an approaching army, I am persuaded to flee neither by symbolic metaphor, nor by assent to any code, but directly in proportion as the drums, pennants and weaponry seem to *demonstrate* the threat posed by that force. The signals, then, work only by claiming a verifiable fit with the currently perceptible world. Suppose I deduce that the displays are mere bluff, exaggerated out of all proportion to the violence which can really be mounted. Then the signals have failed in their purpose.

This is a weakness in the theory that symbolism arose out of group-on-group conflict or 'warfare'. It would seem that the model cannot get beyond indexicality – signals which remain ultimately reality-bound. What, then, of the 'counter-reality' which constitutes human cultural symbolism? In this, signals can be seen, perceptually, to bear no relationship to reality. Yet far from nullifying the message, recognition of such patent pretend-play prompts a search for meaning 'on another level'. In observing the pretend-play, we ask: What is the signaller *intending* us to understand (cf. Grice 1969)?

In this context, the kinds of conflict intrinsic to 'warfare' may be simply too unremitting to generate symbolic culture. No army can afford to see through the enemy's bluff, discern the signalling intention – and then collude with that intention. Yet cooperation of this kind is precisely what symbolic communication entails. Every signal, viewed in terms of its own intrinsic properties, is wholly unconvincing. This being so, we seek to discern what the signaller is *attempting* to convey (Grice 1969). The difference between ritual display and the use of symbolic tokens is that the former does not assume prior collusion – ritual faces the task of *securing* cooperation from the target, whether by fair means or foul. Cooperation in *symbolic* performance, whether ritual or verbal, by contrast does assume prior collusion. Even should the audience 'see' on a perceptual level that everything is pure pretence, they must still suspend disbelief. It is difficult to see how 'warfare' could bring this about.

In addition to this difficulty, the 'warfare' model fails to capture the essence of hunter-gatherer ritual as a means of demarcating ingroup/outgroup boundaries. In warfare, each army or aggressive coalition wins on some occasions, loses on others. By contrast, human hunter-gatherers invest enormous amounts of energy in elaborate ritual performances *which are not expected to fail.* Investment in performances such as initiation rites in normal times far outweighs investment in violence aimed at territorial neighbours. In fact, Australian Aboriginal ritual structures appear designed precisely to transcend simple ingroup/outgroup territorial conflict, setting up 'chains of connection' – structures of ritually defined interdependence – stretching across the landscape. In north-east Arnhem Land, Australia, a major initiation ceremony such as the *Djungguan* gathered together clans normally dispersed over a wide area, often speaking mutually incomprehensible dialects (Warner 1957). A simple 'territorial warfare' model would not predict any of this.

THE EVOLUTION OF INITIATION RITES

Ritual is not quite the same thing as war, although it may be valid to conceptualize it as 'war by other means'. A crucial difference is that warfare relies overwhelmingly on physical violence. Ritual by no means excludes violence, but performers reduce the costs of actual fighting by resorting in the first instance to display. Ritual display, moreover, is not necessarily or exclusively aggressive or intimidatory – it may equally be seductive (cf. Miller, Power this volume). Hence while military strategies can be discussed without reference to sexual strategies, this is not possible in the case of ritual action. When dancers prepare for a collective ritual display, *all* the signalling potentialities of the human body are in principle there to be drawn upon. Hunter-gatherer ritual performances in fact establish ingroup/outgroup boundaries recurrently coinciding with those between exogamous kin-groups. The aim is less to kill than to impress the enemy and in consequence to secure the best possible deal in marital exchanges with the outgroup – using not only threats but gifts and all available techniques of manipulation, exploitation and seduction (Knight 1991).

For Darwinians, a deeply rooted and pervasive form of intraspecific 'warfare' is the inevitability of conflict between the sexes (Dawkins 1976; Trivers 1972; Hill and Kaplan 1988). A model of human ritual as originating in 'warfare' pitting all females against all males would clearly be unrealistic. However, females are related to males not only as mates/spouses. They are also mothers/sisters/kin. If the concept of sexual conflict is integrated with that of coalitionary kin-bonding, we may construct a model of sexual 'warfare' which has promising potential to account for the emergence of symbolic culture in forms consistent with data from the hunter-gatherer ethnographic record.

Suppose males in alliance with sisters and other kin conduct 'warfare' against outgroup males, seeking to exploit their muscle-power by offering marital access only in return for provisioning. This is not an unreasonable idea: hunter-gatherer 'brideservice' embodies precisely this principle. A young man seeking a bride first has to prove himself as a hunter. When he has made a kill, he may stand a chance of sexual acceptance. He takes the meat to the kin of his chosen bride. They may inspect the meat and, if satisfied, allow the young man to stay a night. If he wants future sex, he will have to bring more meat. Should he prove unlucky, lazy or incompetent, he may be told to stay away. To avoid unwanted liaisons, many hunter-gatherers remain distrustful of sons-in-law for years, preventing them from asserting permanent marital rights in their brides. Even after a child has been born, the young man will usually be expected to make substantial regular contributions of meat to both the bride and her kin (Collier and Rosaldo 1981; see discussion in Knight 1991: 122–53).

Success in this strategy presupposes women's ability to mobilize male kin where necessary against uncooperative mates or spouses. Where this condition is met, the relationship between wife's kin and in-marrying bridegroom may be emphatically hierarchical and one-sided. Among many hunter-gatherers, a male will not even be considered as a potential son-in-law before he has undergone initiation, the function of which is to teach him what ritual obligation means. There must be no answering back. Victory to the 'wife-givers' is predetermined long in advance (Knight 1991: 122–53). If this is 'war', then, it is peculiar in that the same side invariably wins. This may seem less puzzling, however, when we remember that for the 'defeated' side, there is much consolation. The 'exploited' outgroup males are in fact being allowed access to the group's fertile females. The reproductive fitness of these males will be enhanced if they obtain hunted meat not in order to eat it themselves but as a form of currency which can be traded for sexual access, with the benefits accruing to their offspring (cf. Hill and Kaplan 1988). On Darwinian grounds, we would not expect these males to resist such 'exploitative' arrangements beyond a certain point.

In all this, loud ritual signals are securing coalitionary dominance in order to maintain a system of economic 'exploitation'. The immediate beneficiaries are coalitionary alliances of mothers and their offspring, who would otherwise be unable to secure comparable meat-supplies (cf. Key and Aiello, this volume). Note, however, that the strategy is one in which males as mates are being exploited not by females acting alone but by mixed-sex kin-based coalitions. Ingroup males, no less than females, are engaging in the necessary economic 'exploitation' of outgroup males who in turn – as brothers in relation to their own kinswomen – help sisters/mothers 'exploit' *their* in-marrying spouses and sons-in-law.

In evolutionary perspective, the emergence of such coalitionary strategies may be seen as female-driven (Power and Aiello 1997). Evolving human females, heavily burdened with increasingly encephalized, slow-developing offspring, would have been under pressure to secure investment from wherever this could be obtained. Support in rearing offspring could potentially be enlisted from (a) local kin-related females, (b) kin-related males and (c) male sexual partners. I have argued (Knight 1991; Knight et al. 1995) that the optimal strategy was to draw on support from all three, securing coalitionary backing from (a) and (b) in the task of economically exploiting (c). Females enhanced their fitness, if this model is accepted, by combining sexual allure with coalitionary organizing skills aimed at maximizing 'brideservice' exploitation of spouses.

To make this model testable, we may explore its internal logic, drawing out theoretical predictions which can then be checked against the findings of hunter-gatherer ethnographers, archaeologists, rock-art specialists and others with relevant test-data.

A major problem would have been posed by menstrual bleeding. When she menstruates, a female signals her imminent fertility. For reasons quite independent of 'culture', this amounts to a 'danger' signal to all other females in the vicinity (Power, this volume). The problem for pregnant and lactating mothers is that they cannot display such blood. The all-too-evident distinction set up between the menstruant and other local females tells philanderer males whom to bond with and whom to temporarily abandon. Left to themselves, males under such circumstances may compete for access only to cycling (hence fertilizable) females. Success may then go to those dominant males best at abandoning any pregnant or breast-feeding partner in favour of a newly menstruating female – best at driving off the competition, bonding with the menstruant and mate-guarding her until impregnation has been achieved. Subdominant males may then find themselves threatened with loss of their sexual partners at the very moment when these are imminently fertile. As males compete for access to visibly menstruating females, non-cycling females will lose out, abandoned by their distracted mates.

In real life, however, every male strategy for asserting monopoly control over female reproductive value is likely to be met by a female counter-strategy (Gowaty 1997). Again quite independently of 'culture', a mother should simply *not allow* her menstruating daughter to be coopted and privatized under male sexual dominance. Defending against this possibility, she should bond tightly with the especially valuable female at precisely such a time. Sisters, brothers and other close relatives should equally feel threatened, bond with her and resist on her behalf.

As Power (this volume) has pointed out, the obvious additional counter-strategy for females threatened temporarily by their inability to menstruate is to cheat. Thanks to the intrinsic nature of the signal, which offers shareable blood, cheating is a possibility. What can prevent pregnant and breast-feeding mothers from painting up anyway with surrogate 'menstrual' blood? In this context, any red pigment – a daughter's menstrual blood, blood from an animal, red berry juice, red ochre – may serve the purpose. Dominant males may in theory still draw a dividing line between genuinely and artificially menstruating females. But this can be countered if local females physically bond with any menstruant, preventing active discrimination between them.

The outcome will be a situation in which, whenever a woman menstruates, the signal sparks a contest. On the one hand, this is a contest for dominance between sexually motivated males. But on the other hand, contesting this whole dynamic are the menstruant's kin, who have no interest in allowing the outcome to be decided by naked sexual conflict between outgroup males. Their interest lies in retaining control over the menstruant, preventing any outgroup male from successfully privatizing her. That way, they can ensure that additional mating effort expended by outgroup males accrues to themselves as a coalition. If all equally 'paint up', constructing the menstruant as inseparable from themselves, then every outgroup male can be fed the illusion that his current partner is imminently fertilizable. In this way, success in turning the menstrual signal from a threat into a communal asset can in principle be achieved. The whole strategy may be conceptualized as a form of female 'cheating'. Subverting the 'natural' game of male philandering and inter-female sexual competition, females backed by male kin establish monopolistic control over their own sexual availability, thereby introducing a new game.

An advantage of this 'sham menstruation' model (Power and Aiello 1997; Power, this volume) is that it is archaeologically testable (Watts, this volume). It also parsimoniously accounts for the evolutionary emergence of initiation ritual (Van Gennep 1960 [1909]) as the key institutional mechanism for generating and perpetuating the uniquely human domain of counter-reality or 'symbolism'.

The term 'counter-reality' is here used to mean reality inverted or turned upside-down. We may now see how a strategy of menstrually-linked sexual and political *counterdominance* (cf. Erdal and Whiten 1994) would by its internal logic have produced such an effect. Chimpanzees who display the 'female' sexual posture of submission to males as a 'token of respect' (Goodall 1986: 129, 360) are not turning the world upside-down. By contrast, anatomically modern human females who *resisted* philanderer males, establishing such resistance as an evolutionarily stable strategy, may well have started a social revolution while constructing a symbolic domain at the same time.

Non-human primate females signal 'no' very simply, by displaying sexual lack of arousal or interest. An anoestrous female chimp has no problem in keeping males at bay. Her body itself sends a clear message, and males are unlikely to be interested. Human females, however, have developed continuous sexual receptivity, and the biological human male is liable to 'read' the corresponding signals as indicating 'possible yes'. This confronts women with a rather special challenge. If they are to signal an unmistakable 'no', this cannot be 'left to nature'; deliberate measures may have to be taken.

Signalling 'yes' involves an indexical display of individual sexual identity, fertility, readiness, reproductive value and so forth. A moment's thought will clarify why signalling 'no' in the human case would have generated the opposite – communal 'counter-reality'. The key point is that for a coalition of human females to signal 'no' must logically be to *reverse* the normal body-language displays indicating 'yes'. To see what this entails, let us take the case of a female chimpanzee in oestrus. In a competitive display, she signals with her rump that she is definitely a chimpanzee (and no other species), definitely female (rather than male) and that she is in her fertile state. We might gloss this as an advertisement conveying three messages: '*right species, right sex, right time*'. From this we may deduce the signals logically indicative of sexual 'no' or defiance. The alluring display in the human female case should be reversed, so as to read '*wrong species, wrong sex, wrong time*'. The female coalition, whenever one of its members is menstruating, should not only blur the distinction between themselves and the menstruant, indicating by artifical cosmetics 'we are all menstruating' (cf. Power, Watts this volume). They should also dance or otherwise signal in body-language 'we are animals' and 'we are males'. Reality, on this basis, will be countered on all fronts.

ORIGINS OF THE SYMBOLIC DOMAIN

The value of this model is that it accounts for the whole pretend-play game – the game of symbolic cultural production and reproduction – which must be established if speech as a subsystem is to work. This game involves sex, kinship and also economics; its premise is that 'rules' operate across the board.

A reality-defying representation is now being staged in direct pursuit of a fitness-enhancing kin-coalitionary strategy of exploiting the pro-visioning energies of outgroup males. Attempts by such males to fight over, harass or privatize an imminently fertile daughter/sister are resisted. A young woman's first menstruation now triggers a performance – a public display of her fertility, marriageability and equally her current inviolability and inseparability from her kin-group. Protecting her may mean forming around her a solid wall of resistance. Signalling 'no' to outgroup males involves staging a kind of 'theatre of the absurd' – females posturing as 'male', humans pretending to be 'animals'.

The outcome is a simple form of 'initiation ritual', triggered by the onset of menstrual bleeding, involving coercive monopoly control over the menstruant, constructing 'blood' (real or surrogate) as the ultimate taboo-signal, generating a communal domain of 'counter-reality' – and ensuring that the central reality-defying representation is well respected and defended. Members of the ingroup embrace the paradoxical, 'totemic' representation ('wrong species' etc.) as an expression of their own group identity/inviolability (cf. Durkheim 1912). We would expect outgroup males to perceive the display as deceptive – those supposed 'males' are clearly only females, those alleged 'animals' really human beings. However, since the 'deceptive exploiters' include these males' own spouses and offspring, the victims will have good reasons to accept the underlying message. For them, the point to grasp is that *some things are sacred*. In the final analysis, 'No' means 'No'. The pretend-play displays which signal this are literally false. Yet they are 'true' on another level – as metaphorical fictions through which communal resistance is expressed. 'Symbolic culture' is now enabling cooperation between camps which might otherwise have been constructed as 'enemies'; such cooperation may be fitness-enhancing, yet in being secured via coercion it is also in a sense 'unnatural' (cf. Chase, this volume).

We have now modelled an 'initial situation' capturing the essence of human magico-religious ritual and belief (cf. Knight 1991, 1997; Knight et al. 1995). On the one hand, there is currently perceptible reality. On the other, ritual performers are insisting on the secondary status of this reality. 'Counter-reality' – a domain in which the sexes merge, 'sacred' blood flows and humans metamorphose into animals – is being vigorously asserted, and for moral reasons accorded higher status. Among the Khoisan, menstrual onset triggers a performance known as the 'Eland Bull Dance' (Figure 12.1), in which the girl herself is constructed as the 'Bull' (Power and Watts 1997; Watts, this volume). Core myths of this kind are not idle fantasies; they have moral, 'sacred' status (cf. Durkheim 1912; Fontenrose 1959). Anyone who expresses doubt is clearly not entering into the spirit of the game.

Now that the basic principle of symbolism is established, new possibilities for linguistic evolution are opened up. To maintain group cohesion and communal identity in opposition to the outgroup, full performative display – 'ritual' – continues to be required, the corresponding costly signals of coalitionary commitment serving internally to authenticate a novel system of low-cost tokenistic communication between conspirators (Knight 1998). Speech can be conceptualized as communal pretend-play, which – along one evolutionary trajectory – becomes adapted for specialised ingroup use to the exclusion of outsiders (cf. Nettle, this volume). The very high levels of ingroup trust now established mean that within each ritually defined coalition, discriminable portions of communally standardized pretend-play can be reduced to vocal tokens – 'words'. Instead of meeting resistance, use of such tokens in fictional elaboration finds social support, placing conspirators under pressure to externalize complex trains of thought via extended signal sequences. Mental processes, for the first time, can be rendered transparent via a repertoire of low-cost tokenistic substitutes for shared, acted-out representations. Darwinian selection pressures, in this novel situation, favour those most fluent in handling such tokens, each speaker recursively embedding fictions whose mutual relationships remain represented in the mind as bodily gestures (cf.

Fig. 12.1 'Wrong sex/wrong species/wrong time': *Southern San rock painting, Fulton's Rock, Drackensberg Mountains, Natal, South Africa (redrawn after Lewis-Williams 1981: Fig. 10). The image depicts a young woman undergoing her first menstruation ceremony – the 'Eland Bull Dance'. The young woman is shown enrobed within the circular outline of her special menstrual hut. In ritual construction, she is both gender-reversed and species-reversed. She herself is the 'Eland Bull'; around her dance 'eland cows' playfully engaged in 'copulation' with her. Note the 'eland tails' of the female dancers and the barred penises (indicating ritual sexual abstinence) of the males.*

Johnson 1987). Exapting neurophysiological capacities evolved at an earlier stage for handling a system of calls still heavily embedded in mimetic gesture (Armstrong et al. 1994; Donald 1991), syntactical speech now rapidly evolves.

If this model is accepted, the first 'word' in human language betokened not a physical thing, but a morally authoritative intangible. We can put this another way by saying that the founding speech-act must have been *contractually* effective (cf. Deacon 1997; Rappaport 1979: 173–221). It invoked the most general of all pretend-play representations, at the apex of the ritually constructed taxonomy. If the earliest language-users had been religious in the contemporary sense, that 'ultimate' reality would have been 'God'. While among southern African hunter-gatherers, *wrong sex/wrong species/wrong time* yields 'Eland Bull' (Power and Watts 1997), in Aboriginal Australia, the same paradoxical negativity yields 'Rainbow Snake' (Knight 1983, 1988, 1991: 88–121). At the deepest level, believers strive for certainty via ritual and liturgical invariance (Rappaport 1979). For this reason, certain core features of the founding signal resist change. To this day in Christian belief and iconography, Divinity is paradoxically both human male and sacrificial lamb, his blood ensuring rebirth by washing sin away. In the beginning was 'The Word' – the performative convening of the human symbolic domain.

REFERENCES

Alexander, R. D. (1989) 'Evolution of the human psyche', in Mellars, P. and Stringer, C. (eds), *The Human Revolution. Behavioural and Biological Perspectives in the Origins of Modern Humans* (Edinburgh: Edinburgh University Press), pp. 455–513.

Armstrong, D. F., Stokoe, W. C. and Wilcox, S. E. (1994) 'Signs of the origin of syntax', *Current Anthropology* 35: 349–68.

Austin, J. L. (1978) *How to Do Things with Words* (Oxford: Oxford University Press).

Berlin, B. and Kay, P. (1969) *Basic Color Terms: Their Universality and Evolution* (Berkeley: University of California Press).

Bloch, M. (1985) 'From cognition to ideology', in Fardon, R. (ed.), *Power and Knowledge: Anthropological and Sociological Approaches* (Edinburgh: Scottish Academic Press), pp. 21–48.

Bourdieu, P. (1990 [1970]) 'The Kabyle house or the world reversed', in *The Logic of Practice* (Oxford: Polity Press).

Bourdieu, P. (1992) *Language and Symbolic Power* (Cambridge: Polity Press).

Bruner, J. S., Jolly, A. and Sylva, K. (eds) (1976) *Play: Its Role in Development and Evolution* (New York: Basic Books).

Burling, R. (1993) 'Primate calls, human language, and nonverbal communication', *Current Anthropology* 34: 25–53.

Byrne, R. and Whiten, A. (1985) 'Tactical deception of familiar individuals in baboons', *Animal Behaviour* 33: 669–73.

Cohen, A. P. (1985) *The Symbolic Construction of Community* (London: Tavistock).

Collier, J. F. and Rosaldo M. Z. (1981) 'Politics and gender in simple societies', in Ortner, S. B. and Whitehead, H. (eds), *Sexual Meanings. The Cultural Construction of Gender and Sexuality* (Cambridge: University Press), pp. 275–329.

Dawkins, R. (1976) *The Selfish Gene* (Oxford: Oxford University Press).

Dawkins, R. and Krebs, J. R. (1984) 'Animal signals: mind-reading and manipulation', in Krebs, J. R. and Davies, N. B. (eds), *Behavioural Ecology. An Evolutionary Approach* (Oxford: Blackwell Scientific), pp. 380–402.

Deacon, T. (1997). *The Symbolic Species. The Co-evolution of Language and the Human Brain* (London: Penguin Books).

Donald, M. (1991) *Origins of the Modern Mind. Three Stages in the Evolution of Culture and Cognition* (Cambridge, Mass.: Harvard University Press).

Durkheim, E. (1912) *Les Formes élémentaires de la vie religieuse* (Paris: Alcan).

Ekman, P. (1982). *Emotion in the Human Face.* Second Edition (Cambridge, England: Cambridge University Press).

Engels, F. (1972 [1884]) *The Origin of the Family, Private Property and the State* (New York: Pathfinder Press).

Erdal, D. and Whiten, A. (1994) 'On human egalitarianism: an evolutionary product of Machiavellian status escalation?' *Current Anthropology* 35(2): 175–83.

Evans-Pritchard, E. E. (1940) *The Nuer* (Oxford: Clarendon Press).

Fontenrose, J. (1959) *Python. A Study of Delphic Myth and its Origins* (Berkeley: University of California Press).

Gellner, E. (1992) *Reason and Culture* (Oxford: Blackwell).

Goodall, J. (1986) *The Chimpanzees of Gombe. Patterns of Behavior* (Cambridge, Mass. and London: Belknap Press of Harvard University Press).

Gowaty, P. A., (1997) 'Sexual dialectics, sexual selection, and variation in mating behavior', in Gowaty, P. A. (ed.), *Feminism and Evolutionary Biology: Boundaries, Intersections, and Frontiers* (New York: Chapman & Hall), pp. 351–84.

Grice, H. (1969) 'Utterer's meanings and intentions', *Philosophical Review* 78: 147–77.

Harrison, S. (1993) *The Mask of War. Violence, Ritual and the Self in Melanesia,* (Manchester and New York: Manchester University Press).

Hill, K. and Kaplan, H. (1988) 'Tradeoffs in male and female reproductive strategies among the Ache, I and II', in Betzig, L. L., Bogerhoff Mulder, M. and Turke, P. (eds), *Human Reproductive Behaviour* (Cambridge: Cambridge University Press), pp. 227–305.

Johnson, M. (1987) *The Body in the Mind. The Bodily Basis of Meaning, Imagination, and Reason* (Chicago and London: University of Chicago Press).

Knight, C. D. (1983) 'Lévi-Strauss and the Dragon: *Mythologiques* reconsidered in the light of an Australian Aboriginal myth', *Man* (n.s.) 18: 21–50.

Knight, C. D. (1988) 'Menstrual synchrony and the Australian rainbow snake', in Buckley, T. and Gottlieb, A. (eds), *Blood Magic. The Anthropology of Menstruation* (Berkeley and Los Angeles: University of California Press), pp. 232–55.

Knight, C. D. (1991) *Blood Relations. Menstruation and the Origins of Culture* (New Haven, Conn. and London: Yale University Press).

Knight, C. D. (1997) 'The wives of the sun and moon', *Journal of the Royal Anthropological Institute* (n.s.) 3: 133–53.

Knight, C. D. (1998) 'Ritual/speech coevolution: a solution to the problem of deception', in Hurford, J. R., Studdert-Kennedy, M. and Knight, C. (eds),

Approaches to the Evolution of Language: Social and Cognitive Bases (Cambridge: Cambridge University Press), pp. 68–91.

Knight, C. D., Power, C. and Watts, I. (1995) 'The human symbolic revolution: a Darwinian account', *Cambridge Archaeological Journal* 5(1): 75–114.

Lewis-Williams, J. D. (1981) *Believing and Seeing. Symbolic Meanings in Southern San Rock Paintings* (London: Academic Press).

Montagu, M. F. A. (1974) *Coming into Being Among the Australian Aborigines. The Procreative Beliefs of the Australian Aborigines* (London and Boston, Mass.: Routledge & Kegan Paul).

Mountford, C. P. (1978) 'The rainbow-serpent myths of Australia', in Buchler, I. R. and Maddock, K. (eds), *The Rainbow Serpent* (The Hague: Mouton), pp. 23–97.

Peirce, C. S. (1940) 'Logic as semiotic: the theory of signs', in Buchler, J. (ed.), *The Philosophical Writings of Peirce* (New York: Dover, 1955 edn), pp. 98–119.

Power, C. and Aiello, L. C. (1997) 'Female proto-symbolic strategies', in Hager, L. D. (ed.), *Women in Human Evolution* (London and New York: Routledge), pp. 153–71.

Power, C. and Watts, I. (1997) 'The woman with the zebra's penis. Gender, mutability and performance', *Journal of the Royal Anthropological Insitute* (n.s.) 3: 537–60.

Rappaport, R. (1979) *Ecology, Meaning and Religion* (Berkeley, Calif.: North Atlantic Books).

Strehlow, T. G. H. (1947) *Aranda Traditions* (Melbourne: Melbourne University Press).

Trivers, R. L. (1972) 'Parental investment and sexual selection', in Campbell, B. (ed.), *Sexual Selection and the Descent of Man 1871–1971* (Chicago: Aldine), pp. 136–79.

Turner, V. (1967) *The Forest of Symbols. Aspects of Ndembu Ritual* (Ithaca, NY and London: Cornell University Press).

Van Gennep, A. (1960 [1909]) *The Rites of Passage* (London: Routledge & Kegan Paul).

Warner, W. L. (1957) *A Black Civilization* (New York: Harper).

Zahavi, A. (1987) 'The theory of signal selection and some of its implications', in Delfino, U. P. (ed.), *International Symposium of Biological Evolution* (Bari: Adriatic Editrice), pp. 305–27.

Zahavi, A. (1993) 'The fallacy of conventional signalling', *Philosophical Transactions of the Royal Society of London* B 340: 227–30.

FURTHER READING

GENERAL

Boyd, R. and Richerson, P. (1985) *Culture and the Evolutionary Process* (Chicago: University of Chicago Press).

Boyer, P. (1994) *The Naturalness of Religious Ideas* (Berkeley: University of California Press).

Dennett, D. (1961) *Darwin's Dangerous Idea* (London: Allen Lane).

Durham, W. H. (1991) *Coevolution: Genes, Culture and Human Diversity* (Stanford, Calif.: Stanford University Press).

Runciman, W. G. (1998) *The Social Animal* (London: HarperCollins).

Wright, R. (1994) *The Moral Animal* (New York: Abacus).

ARCHAEOLOGY AND PALAEOANTHROPOLOGY

Hager, L. (ed.) (1997) *Women in Human Evolution* (London and New York: Routledge).

Knight, C. D. (1991) *Blood Relations: Menstruation and the Origins of Culture* (New Haven, Conn.: Yale University Press).

Mellars, P. (1996) *The Neanderthal Legacy: An Archaeological Perspective from Western Europe* (Princeton, NJ: Princeton University Press).

Mithen, S. J. (1996) *The Prehistory of the Mind: A Search for the Origins of Art, Science and Religion* (London: Orion).

Steele, J. and Shennan, S. (eds) (1996) *The Archaeology of Human Ancestry: Power, Sex and Tradition* (London and New York: Routledge).

Stringer, C. and Gamble, C. (1993) *In Search of the Neanderthals* (London: Thames & Hudson).

Stringer, C. and McKie, R. (1996) *African Exodus: The Origins of Modern Humanity* (London: Random House).

EVOLUTIONARY BIOLOGY

Andersson, M. B. (1994) *Sexual Selection* (Princeton, NJ: Princeton University Press).

Axelrod, R. (1984) *The Evolution of Cooperation* (New York: Basic Books).

Dawkins, R. (1976) *The Selfish Gene* (Oxford: Oxford University Press).

Goldsmith, T. H. (1991) *The Biological Roots of Human Nature: Forging Links Between Evolution and Behaviour* (Oxford: Oxford University Press).

Harrison, G. A. (ed.) (1993) *Human Adaptation* (Oxford: Oxford University Press).

Maxwell, M. (ed.) (1991) *The Sociobiological Imagination* (New York: State University of New York Press).

Ridley, M. (1993) *The Red Queen: Sex and the Evolution of Human Nature* (London: Viking).

Ridley, M. (1996) *The Origins of Virtue* (London: Viking).

Runciman, W. G., Maynard Smith, J. and Dunbar, R. I. M. (eds) (1996) *Evolution of Social Behaviour Patterns in Primates and Man* (Oxford: Oxford University Press).

Waal, F. de (1996) *Good Natured: The Origins of Right and Wrong in Humans and Other Animals* (Cambridge, Mass.: Harvard University Press).

LANGUAGE AND COMMUNICATION

Bickerton, D. (1991) *Language and Species* (Chicago and London: University of Chicago Press).

Bickerton, D. (1996) *Language and Human Behaviour* (London: UCL press).

Bourdieu, P. (1989) *Language and Symbolic Power* (Cambridge: Polity Press).

Deacon, T. (1997) *The Symbolic Species* (London: Penguin).

Dunbar, R. I. M. (1996) *Grooming, Gossip and the Evolution of Language* (London: Faber & Faber; Cambridge, Mass.: Harvard University Press).

Hauser, M. D. (1996) *The Evolution of Communication* (London and Cambridge: MIT Press).

Hurford, J. R., Studdert-Kennedy, M. and Knight, C. D. (eds) (1998) *Approaches to the Evolution of Language: Social and Cognitive Bases* (Cambridge: Cambridge University Press).

Lieberman, P. (1991) *Uniquely Human: The Evolution of Speech, Thought, and Selfless Behavior* (Cambridge, Mass.: Harvard University Press).

Pinker, S. (1993) *The Language Instinct* (New York: Morrow).

Zahavi, A. and Zahavi, A. (1997) *The Handicap Principle* (Oxford: Oxford University Press).

EVOLUTIONARY PSYCHOLOGY

Barkow, J. H., Cosmides, L. and Tooby, J. (1992) *The Adapted Mind: Evolutionary Psychology and the Generation of Culture* (Oxford: Oxford University Press).

Byrne, R. W. and Whiten, A. (1988) *Machiavellian Intelligence: Social Expertise and the Evolution of Intellect in Monkeys, Apes, and Humans* (Oxford: Clarendon).

Cheney, D. L. and Seyfarth, R. M. (1990) *How Monkeys See the World* (Chicago: University of Chicago Press).

Crawford, C. and Krebs, D. (eds) (1998) *The Handbook of Evolutionary Psychology: Ideas, Issues, and Applications* (London: Lawrence Erlbaum).

Pinker, S. (1998) *How the Mind Works* (London: W. W. Norton).

Plotkin, H. (1998) *Evolution in Mind* (New York: Harvard University Press).

Shore, B. (1996) *Culture in Mind* (Oxford: Oxford University Press).

Whiten, A. and Byrne, R. W. (1997) *Machiavellian Intelligence II: Extensions and Evaluations* (Cambridge: Cambridge University Press).

SOCIAL ANTHROPOLOGY

Barnard, A. (1992) *Hunters and Herders of Southern Africa: A Comparative Ethnography of the Khoisan Peoples* (Cambridge: Cambridge University Press).

Hiatt, L. R. (1996) *Arguments about Aborigines: Australia and the Evolution of Social Anthropology* (Cambridge: Cambridge University Press).

Hughes, A. (1988) *Evolution and Human Kinship* (Oxford: Oxford University Press).

Ingold, T., Riches, D. and Woodburn, J. (eds) (1988) *Hunters and Gatherers Volume 1: History, Evolution and Social Change* (Oxford, New York and Hamburg: Berg).

Ingold, T., Riches, D. and Woodburn, J. (eds) (1988) *Hunters and Gatherers Volume 2: Property, Power and Ideology* (Oxford and New York: Berg).

Kuper, A. (1988) *The Invention of Primitive Society: Transformations of an Illusion* (London: Routledge).

Lévi-Strauss, C. (1969 [1949]) *The Elementary Structures of Kinship*, revised edn, trans. Bell, J. H., von Sturmer, J. R. and Needham, R. (Boston, Mass.: Beacon Press).

Maddock, K. (1973) *The Australian Aborigines: A Portrait of their Society* (London: Allen Lane, Penguin Press).

AUTHOR INDEX

SUBJECT INDEX